THE NEW POPULISM
The Politics of Empowerment

THE NEW POPULISM

THE POLITICS OF EMPOWERMENT

Edited by Harry C. Boyte and Frank Riessman

TEMPLE UNIVERSITY PRESS   *Philadelphia*

Temple University Press, Philadelphia 19122

Copyright © 1986 by Temple University, except Ch. 12, which is © C. Spretnak.

Published 1986

Printed in the United States of America

The paper used in this publication meets the minimum requirements
of American National Standard for Information Sciences—
Permanence of Paper for Printed Library Materials, ANSI Z39.48-1984

Library of Congress Cataloging-in-Publication Data

The New populism.

  Bibliography:
  Includes index.
   1. Populism—United States—History—20th century—
Addresses, essays, lectures. 2. United States—Politics
and government—1981-   —Addresses, essays, lectures.
I. Boyte, Harry Chatten, 1945-   II. Riessman,
Frank.
E876.N48 1986   973.927   86-1873
ISBN 0-87722-429-3 (alk. paper)

CONTENTS

Contents

Six
POPULISM AND EQUALITY

Seven
THE POLITICS OF POPULISM

Contents

ACKNOWLEDGMENTS

Conversations over the course of this book project with a number of people have been very helpful in clarifying themes and ideas. We want to especially thank Sara Evans, Tom DeWar, Michael Ansara, S. M. Miller, Heather Booth, Manning Marable, Alan Isaacman, Mary Dietz, Elizabeth Minnich, Adrienne Asch, John Richard, Alice Palmer, and Steve Max for extensive discussions about the meaning and nature of populism and its reappearance.

We would also like to thank Janet Boyte Ferguson for her proofreading and Geraldine Harrison for her contribution in putting together this volume.

Social Policy magazine and its staff have played a major role in the development of this book.

INTRODUCTION

Harry C. Boyte

BEYOND POLITICS AS USUAL

Most simply, populism calls for the return of power to ordinary people. Richard Darman, deputy secretary of the treasury for Ronald Reagan, made the point to conservatives when he argued that populism "is anti-elitist, opposed to excessive concentrations of power, oriented toward fairness and toward a degree of levelling." On the Democratic side, Tom Harkin, freshman senator from Iowa who helped found the Populist Caucus, similarly described populism as based on the conviction that "freedom and democratic institutions rest on the widest possible dissemination of wealth and power—and we've come to the point where too few people have too much and the rest of us have too little."[1]

Populism is a different sort of language and political vision. Both its key ideas—"returning power" and "people"—call to mind traditions, values, and themes unlike politics as usual.

3

Traditional conservatives focus on individual acquisition and the marvels of big business. Populism, however, expresses strong skepticism about concentrated economic power. Though it speaks a language of self-interest, it also suggests values much wider in range than those embodied in material goods. Populism grows from the life of actual communities that seek to control the forces that threaten to overwhelm them.

In fact, Ronald Reagan has achieved much of his success through populist-sounding appeals. During the fight for the 1980 Republican nomination, Washington *Post* polls found that "in sharp contrast to other Republicans, Reagan does substantially better with rank-and-file Republicans who seem skeptical about big business." Instead of posing as the candidate of big business—those he called "the country club set"—Ronald Reagan called himself the candidate of the blue-collar worker and the small businessman. Most to the point, Reagan rhetorically championed those hometown institutions and commitments that seemed increasingly at risk. Reagan's theme has commonly been the need for what he calls "a shift of power away from Washington." More thoughtful conservatives like George Will have observed that this has been the key to his appeal. "Mondale's notion of community," wrote Will after the 1984 election, "was [that] the people would be prodded by the central government into a 'national' community . . . Reagan's message [in contrast] has been more complex than the 'rugged individualism' of simple-minded conservatism." Instead, in the elections of both 1980 and 1984, Reagan spoke "the language of the small republic renaissance." He called for "an end to giantism" and for "a return to the human scale . . . that human beings can understand and cope with; the scale of the local fraternal lodge, the church organization, the block club, the farm bureau."[2]

But does Reagan represent the authentic legacy of populism? And why is it that progressives—supposedly the champions of the underdog, the outsiders, the discontented, and the powerless—seem to have ceded such language to the right wing in recent years? Such questions suggest the need to step back from immediate political debates of the moment and examine the challenge an emerging populism poses to the conventional left and right.

The modern left wing took shape in the period from 1770 to 1840, when critics began to describe the ravages of capitalism and the trend toward the creation of classes in modern society. John Stuart Mill and Karl Marx both used an initial typology of classes that included landlords,

4

capitalists, and laborers. For Marx, this division was increasingly super-seded by the simple categories of bourgeoisie and proletariat.[3]

For a century and a half the left's descriptions of the pain and suffering caused by the ravages of capitalist industrialization have had great appeal and analytic power. They have spoken to people's experiences of material suffering in the modern world and, more subtly, to the sense of homelessness and displacement that comes from what Marx called the "obliteration" of people's histories, identities, communal roots, and family ties by an economy that seeks to measure every relationship in terms of profit or loss, dollars and cents. But phrased as a theory of social change, the left's approach has proven more and more disastrous. The left in the modern world has been able to name the problems, or at least many of them. But its solutions have been trapped by the very terms of the system that it challenges.

Though the left has seen the destruction of rooted, communal identities and traditions as tragic, in a way it has always held that such destruction is a necessary part of "progress," leading toward political emancipation. For Marx, there had to be a "radical rupture" with what had gone before. For Engels, "the driving of workers from hearth and home" that accompanied urbanization and industrialization was "the very first condition of their intellectual emancipation." In his view, "modern, large-scale industry . . . has turned the worker, formerly chained to the land, into a completely propertyless proletarian, liberated from all traditional fetters, a free outlaw." With varying degrees of sophistication and nuance, such a view of communal and traditional institutions as bulwarks of the status quo has retained a compelling hold over the left ever since. Douglas Kellner summarized the usual argument: "[dominant] ideology is transmitted through an ideological apparatus consisting of the family, school, church, media, workplace and social group."[4]

Thus the left has held that the erosion of the fabric of communal life is the necessary precondition of progressive action. Collective solidarity is forged by "masses"—those whose ties to communal roots of place, religion, ethnicity, and so forth have been sundered. Indeed, the typologies that left-wing theorists have developed to describe various social movements are built around such a process. Thus, E. J. Hobsbawm contrasts "primitive" protests grounded in communal ties and "modern secular" movements like the trade unions and socialist parties that supposedly have severed such connections. Similarly, the Tillys separate "reactive" communally based movements from "proactive" modern movements. Ralph Miliband argues that "the Marxist notion of a 'most radical rupture' with traditional ideas signifies a break with all forms of tradition and must expect to encounter the latter not as friend but as foe."[5]

Such perspectives are essentially strategic arguments for how change comes about. They are also associated with a vision of the good society, reflected in a range of socialist ideologies. "Socialism" is a word that first appeared in the writings of Robert Owen as a militantly secular alternative to any religiously based visions of the future. It came to mean, most formally, the "socialization of the means of production" accomplished by government action. The concept of "socialization" itself entails a basic theory of social transformation that retains its attraction for modern intellectuals who have long since developed doubts about the simple nationalization of industry. Though more rooted communitarian socialist perspectives periodically emerged, from William Morris's in the nineteenth century to Martin Buber's in the twentieth, the socialist vision of the "new man" (and, more recently, the "new woman") has customarily rested upon the conviction that the future community that replaces the atomization of capitalism will be a new association of men and women. People's motivations under socialism would be kinder and more generous than the dog-eat-dog morality of capitalist institutions today. But their ties to the past and to continuous, traditional communal relations would be sundered, in ways that resemble modern, contractual relationships formed in large-scale institutions like corporations and government bureaucracies. Thus, even the most democratic and humane expressions of socialist policy, like the social democratic programs of Europe, envision the state as taking on more and more functions previously performed by communal and voluntary associations. And they display in practice a marked hostility toward independent voluntary groups.[6]

American liberals speak a different vocabulary than their European socialist counterparts. But they have nonetheless shared an essentially contractual understanding of social progress. The Lockean heritage that increasingly dominated political discourse through the nineteenth century saw freedom as a process of individual detachment from older, communal ties. America, in the words of Louis Hartz, "begins and ends" in this sort of liberalism: "The master assumption of American political thought has been atomistic social freedom."

Throughout the twentieth century, mainstream progressive approaches have echoed the views of Herbert Coly, longtime editor of New Republic, who argued that "the great community" of the state would replace local and voluntary community settings as the arena of citizenship. In the modern world, Coly proposed, citizens no longer had to "assemble after the manner of a New England town meeting," since new forms of mass communications and large-scale organization meant "the active citizenship of the country meets every morning and evening and discusses the affairs of the nation with the newspaper as an impersonal interlocuter." Through various public agencies and electoral reforms—regulatory commissions, civil service, nonpartisan local elections, direct election of senators, and women's suffrage and protection of minority rights—citizens would be able to develop "a loyal realization of a comprehensive democratic social ideal." The democratic social ideal, in turn, would gradually tame and replace the ravages of unbridled free-market capitalism.

In fact, as Michael Harrington has pointed out, behind such a theory of government has been an "invisible social democratic movement" with important similarities to European social democratic and labor parties— labor unions and other national reform groups that looked to the expanding welfare state as the engine of progress. From the mainstream liberal viewpoint, voluntary associations, ethnic identities, ties to church, synagogue, or other local institutions were seen as hindrances to cosmopolitan awareness. Garry Wills put it clearly when he wrote that "the smaller the locale, the stricter the code; and this code . . . has always been at odds with the social openness, the chances for initiative, praised by liberals." [7]

Yet in the 1960s and 1970s the images of our destiny as radically new and uprooted began to unravel at many points. In part, challenges to the notion of freedom as deracination came from broad movements like civil rights and those of women, Hispanics, and others. The popularity of the television series "Roots" was in itself an expression of widespread public sympathy with the black quest for a rediscovery of historical and cultural identities. This search for roots gained power, as well, from the massive economic and cultural dislocations of the 1970s and 1980s, which have seen the loss of many millions of manufacturing jobs, family farms, and small businesses. In recent years the search for rootedness is also visible in the rise of general ethnic group consciousness; in the public reception given works like Michael Novak's *The Rise of the Unmeltable Ethnics*; in the popularity of movies like *The Deer Hunter, Local Hero, Places in the Heart*, and in books like *And Ladies of the Club* and *Lake Wobegon Days*. It has been apparent in the religious revival. It is embodied in the growing neighborhood movement that swept through America's cities in the last decade, in farmers' protests, citizen efforts, and a new generation of what the New York *Times* calls "rock and roll musicians burning with fervent grassroots populism."[8]

Such developments are raw material for populist insurgency and language. Millions of Americans have simultaneously sought to rediscover hometown, historical, and spiritual roots and to defend them against forces threatening their ways of life. This dynamic produces populism, as people begin to see the solution as a return of power to ordinary citizens.

Populism is a language of inheritance. It grows from a sense of aggrieved "peoplehood," as distinct from personhood. It emerges from the conviction that an elite has dishonored an historically, culturally, or geographically constituted people, its memories, origins, common territory, ways of life. Thus there is a certain class feeling in populism—the belief that common people are mistreated by the powerful. But the very vagueness of these ideas leads to a volatility in politics, and points in different directions than concepts like the left wing's notions of class or modern liberals' ideas of interest groups.

The idea of social class is historically specific, the product of modern industrialization. The notion of people, on the other hand, dates back to antiquity and has been used by movements and groups with widely varying aims and compositions. Class can be analyzed with graphs and charts and research questionnaires. But the idea of a people is associated often with place. It is understood symbolically rather than abstractly and quantitatively, through stories, legends, oral traditions, folk remedies, foods, rituals, music, ways of speaking, and remembering. A people has a moment of origin and birth, tales of evolution, spaces that it has filled in and become attached to. These themes, in sum, are all those elements that traditional left-wing theory has held must be ruptured, as part of the process of creating the new man. Thus, as Gianna Pomata's essay points out, Stalinism, a stark and brutal expression of Marxist themes, saw the destruction of even the memory of populism as essential.

Consciousness of being part of a group as enormously complex and variegated as "the American people" coexists necessarily with a myriad of separate identities as "peoples." This was a point about black Americans made, for instance, by W. E. B. Du Bois throughout his career. For those groups like white, Anglo-Saxon Protestants, who have always had relatively greater power in the culture, much is taken for granted about what being a member of "the American people" means. But these ideas can seem far from settled—or even sometimes as oppressive, foreign, and alienating—from other points of view. From the perspective of those like women, or in different terms, the disabled, whose roles traditionally have been relatively invisible in public life and idiom, the formal and overt history of every people has certain deep ambiguities and questions. For anyone, moreover, social mobility, fragmentation of work life and the home, the mass culture, consumer society, and a variety of other forces have made any simple statement of continuity across time and space impossible.

Finally, the new populism that emerges today grows in a specific context that has made ideas such as grassroots democracy, local control, and power to the people seem impossible to many Americans. Alan Brinkley's study of 1930s movements like those of Father Coughlin and Huey Long, *Voices of Protest*, found that they used a populist vocabulary much like that of the Populists in the 1880s and 1890s. But the differences were more important than the surface similarities. The farmers' cooperatives that formed the base of the first populist movement "encouraged an active process of community-institution-building," Brinkley points out. "From them emerged marketing cooperatives, community cotton gins and flour mills, cooperative stores and credit unions." Put together, such institutions constituted "an alternative to the emerging centralized corporate economy." But in the 1930s there was little active community building, and forms of participation that did occur had little of the open, participatory democratic spirit of the first movement. "What was most conspicuously absent" from the thirties, concludes Brinkley, "was a genuine belief in possibilities." Enormous concentrations of economic power, mass communications, the growth of bureaucracy, urbanization, and the consumer culture had dramatically reshaped American society and made belief in "government by the people" far more difficult to sustain.[9]

All these dynamics help explain, in turn, populist-sounding rhetoric from the right wing today. Much of neoconservative thought has taken shape in what seems to be, superficially, a populist reaction to progressive distancing from communal settings. In theoretical terms neoconservatism has its roots in the 1950s, when social critics like Robert Nisbet argued that totalitarianism required the destruction of every sort of independent communal and voluntary association. Even the most innocent, like musical clubs, were outlawed by the Nazis, for instance, because they were organized "for purposes, however innocent, that did not reflect those of the central government." Current theorists like Peter Berger and Richard Neuhaus have drawn on this tradition to advance the concept of "mediating structures," communal groups that they believe make up bulwarks against the dangers of modern life and the all-encompassing state. "The best defenses against the threat," says Berger, "are those institutions, however weakened, which still give a measure of stability to private life. These are, precisely, the mediating institutions, notably those of family, church, voluntary association, neighborhood and subculture." Progressives' failing is that they see mediating institutions as barriers to progress. Thinking on the left, conservatives charge, "is abstract, universalistic, addicted to what Burke called 'geometry' in social policy. . . . The great concern is for the individual ('the rights of man') and for a just public order, but anything 'in between' is viewed as irrelevant, or even an obstacle, to the rational ordering of society." [10]

Thus conservatives have charged the left with the pattern it often reflects—a distancing from rooted, communal ties. Their effectiveness has been all too apparent in recent political history, not only in the United States but throughout much of the industrialized world as well. Most figures on the right, however, despite their populist-sounding appeals, in fact have been simply critical and reactive, despairing about any possibilities of significant democratic change in large institutions. They have warned of the dangers of the "great state" and have rhetorically defended communal values and settings. But from the conservative viewpoint, the expansive, democratic spirit of the first Populist movement is simply incomprehensible. Instead of the foundation of democratic action, community becomes a refuge from the world.

For conservatives today, like the left, the fabric of community life is seen as a bulwark of order and the status quo. Indeed, the very rationale for smaller scale settings is precisely what they see as their function in providing order, stability, and resistance to change. "Without mediating structures," writes Berger, "the political order [is unsettled] by being deprived of the moral foundation on which it rests." In short, such settings are seen in defensive and, above all, static terms. Protest politics from the right is an attempt to salvage what remnants of tradition and identity can be saved, in a world whose fundamental centers of power seem immutable. But such a solely defensive perspective undermines the very community institutions conservatives profess to champion. Every community is left on its own. The corrosive impact of unbridled capitalism and of the

10

marketplace on values of family, religious faith, neighborhood, and the like is ignored.

As Sheldon Wolin points out, authentic populism today is the culture of democracy because it is the practice of sustaining and cultivating community institutions in hard times, in the face of a dominant culture driven by contractual models of human relationships. But "populism" from the right, in treating community merely as a residual category, as a source of refuge and solace, simultaneously strips the person of every communal and historical tie when it articulates an economic philosophy. Acquisitive individualism becomes the measure of success in the public world. No model of collective action is imaginable through which people can regain control over massive economic dislocations, from plant closings to hazardous waste dumps or acid rain, nor does any notion appear of how different communities might join together to pursue a common good. Despite President Reagan's eloquent invocation of "families, communities, workplaces and voluntary groups" as the true source of "the invincible American spirit," he has defined such values in entirely private terms, not as sources of citizenship or democratic vision. In his first inaugural address, he defined the American people as "a special interest group." In subsequent years the administration has proven strikingly hostile to independent grassroots citizen initiatives.[11]

So the question posed by the new populism is, ultimately: is it possible? Or, at least, is populism possible in any sense that resembles the democratic, inclusive, and transformative spirit of the Populists one hundred years ago? It is a question that raises complex and central issues — but ones that the authors represented here go about addressing in fresh and imaginative ways. This collection is full of the disagreement, debate, and sense of excitement that seem appropriate to an authentic populism. It takes on the character of a charged conversation. It ranges widely but focuses on the most substantive problems of politics and culture in our time.

Partly, answering the question, What does a "progressive" or "democratic" populism mean? requires a retrieval of memories and traditions that have been all but forgotten. Lawrence Goodwyn has pioneered in such historical recovery in the United States, and he sketches parallels between Populists a hundred years ago and populists today. Manning Marable's article advances the process with a fascinating story about the election of his great-grandfather Morris, a former slave, to sheriff in a northern Alabama community with support of black and white farmers

11

alike. It was the sort of local alliance that once gave populism a remarkable cultural daring, even in the Deep South of the 1890s. The Populist Party was seen as a threat to the white supremacist racial order, and, interestingly, often to the system of gender roles as well, since women could participate fully as members and officers in every level of the Alliance cooperatives. Robert Bellah makes the point that such retrieval is not only about historical events: it concerns a remembering of older languages of commitment and citizenship that have been gravely weakened today. As Gianna Pomata makes powerfully clear, Europe, as well as the United States, suffers from the radical amnesia about the past that makes difficult even the imagining of serious alternatives to "politics as usual."

In an important essay, Sheldon Wolin argues that populism is a fundamentally different sort of political language than the contractual understanding of politics that has shaped discussion from Thomas Hobbes to Ronald Reagan today. Populism is the "language of inheritance," of birthright, that re-members those unique, human relationships at the heart of any decent vision of politics and society. Similarly, Joe Holland, Charlene Spretnak, and Mary Dietz reflect, in different ways, on the fashion in which modern ways of thinking detach us from our roots and our understandings of interconnection with each other, with the natural world, and with those who preceded us and those who will come after. A democratic populism also requires asking new sorts of questions about whom "the people" includes, what is the nature of community, of politics, of public life. Adrienne Asch, Elizabeth Minnich, and, in different terms, Cornel West all pose these sorts of challenges. But populism has no text in which to look for answers. Indeed, in both form and substance it is an evolving dialogue. Gar Alperovitz, Michael Ansara, S. M. Miller, Colin Greer, and others argue different directions for its development.

Though it has yet to achieve the successes of the right, a progressive and democratic populism has begun to emerge that reawakens generous and hopeful instincts among the people. Progressive populism today takes often lively political form. It finds spokesmen and women that include figures as diverse as Tom Harkin, Jesse Jackson, Jim Hightower, Barbara Mikulski, and Raymond Flynn, whose style is chronicled by Robert Coles.

But basically a progressive populism differs from the right wing in ways that have to do with much more than electoral politics. Populist rhetoric from the right names people's experiences of powerlessness, helplessness, and victimization. But, ultimately, it suggests no solution. Right-wing populism speaks to people simply as victims. It offers scapegoats, promises great leaders, holds out vicarious victories, and invokes nostalgic images of "the way things used to be"—accompanied by efforts to impose rigid moral prescriptions on private behavior. Right-wing populism conveys, most basically, a sense of hopelessness about the prospects for real democratic self-government. It sees government as simply the enemy, not the instrument of citizens joining together for the common good. It breeds fear, suspicion and a sense of unbridgeable difference. And it privatizes all those common bonds whose sustenance and enhancement were once the central populist objective.

The first populists talked about "the cooperative commonwealth" in their newspapers. They sang about it around campfires. They detailed its programs in their vast lecture circuits. They had in mind the insight that we are bound together. As the magazine *Commonwealth* put it in 1893, "What has made this land of ours a source of wealth is a social element vast and precious. . . . We owe all that we value to the Community in whose life we live and move and have our being." The populist vision of the commonwealth was much like Tom Harkin's today, that living resources like the land "are not inherited from our ancestors, but borrowed from our children." [12]

For the first populists, the commonwealth was neither abstract nor sentimental. It grew from practical experiences in the first populist movement's cooperatives, called Alliances. Through the Alliances, ordinary men and women gained some power and came to believe that they might actually be able to save their farms and rural communities. They remembered the insight of Thomas Jefferson, that free government depends upon the free and voluntary association of ordinary citizens, joining together to fight concentrated power and privilege. In the 1980s, one hundred years later, the foundations for an authentic populism are similarly to be found in citizen initiatives.

Voluntary citizen initiatives, from the community organization to the farm cooperative, from a self-help group like MADD (Mothers Against Drunk Driving) to the nuclear freeze, teach a new hope that the large-scale institutions of modern society might in fact be made more responsive and more democratic. And they educate ordinary people for authentic citizenship, inculcating the values and skills of an authentic public life where empowerment of the people means more than rhetorical posturing. It is a hope that can have contagious effect, far beyond those immediately involved. The stories of these efforts at actual empowerment are at the heart

13

of populism. Studs Terkel has long chronicled them, and he does so here. Julian Rappaport and Frank Riessman address the themes of empowerment from other directions, discussing personal self-help and change and their relation to broader civic action. Mike Miller argues the importance of citizen groups as the foundation of populism. Finally, leaders and organizers like Cora Tucker and Ernesto Cortes reawaken the populist tradition in American communities, and give it new meanings.

Notes

1. On public reactions to the term "populist," see for instance "A Liberal by Any Other Name May Get More Votes," New York Times, Nov. 24, 1985; Richard Darman, "Historic Tax Reform: The Populist Correction," speech to the Institute for Research on the Economics of Taxation, Washington, D.C., April 15, 1985; Tom Harkin, interview with Harry C. Boyte, April 30, 1985, Washington, D.C.

2. Hedrick Smith, "Reagan's Populist Coalition," New York Times, March 6, 1980; Reagan quoted from William A. Schambra, The Quest for Community and the Quest for a New Public Philosophy (Washington, D.C.: American Enterprise Institute, 1983), pp. 32–33; George Will, "The Real Campaign of 1984," Newsweek, Sept. 2, 1985.

3. On the history of the concepts of class see, for instance, Raymond Williams, Keywords: A Vocabulary of Culture and Society (New York: Oxford University Press, 1976), pp. 51–59.

4. Karl Marx, Eighteenth Brumaire of Louis Bonaparte (New York: International Publishers, 1963); Friedrich Engels, The Housing Question (Moscow: Progress Publishers, 1970), p. 29; Douglas Kellner, "Ideology, Marxism and Advanced Capitalism," Socialist Review 42 (1978).

5. E. J. Hobsbawm, Primitive Rebels: Studies in Archaic Forms of Social Movement in the 19th and 20th Centuries (New York: W. W. Norton, 1959); Charles and Louis Tilly, The Rebellious Century (Cambridge: Harvard University Press, 1975); Ralph Miliband, Marxism and Politics (Oxford: Oxford University Press, 1977), p. 44.

6. On the history of the word "socialism," see Williams, Keywords, pp. 238–43; on conventional socialist programs in Europe, see for instance, Michael Harrington, Socialism (New York: Bantam, 1972), and The Twilight of Capitalism (New York: Simon & Schuster, 1976).

7. Louis Hartz, The Liberal Tradition in America (New York: Harcourt, Brace, 1955), p. 62; Herbert Croly, The Promise of American Life (New York: Macmillan, 1909), pp. 453, 139; Garry Wills, Nixon Agonistes: The Crisis of the Self-Made Man (New York: New American Library, 1969), p. 463.

8. On sources of the new populism, see for instance, Boyte, Booth, and Max, Citizen Action and the New American Populism (Philadelphia: Temple University Press, 1986); New York Times, Jan. 5, 1986.

9. Alan Brinkley, *Voices of Protest* (New York: Knopf, 1982), p. 166.

10. Robert A. Nisbet, "The Total Community," in Marvin E. Olsen, ed., *Power in Societies* (New York: Macmillan, 1970), p. 423; William Schambra, *The Quest for Community and the Quest for a New Public Philosophy* (Washington, D.C.: American Enterprise Institute, 1983), describes Nisbet's central role in modern conservative thought; Peter Berger, *Facing Up to Modernity* (New York: Basic, 1977), p. 134; Peter Berger and Richard Neuhaus, *To Empower People: The Role of Mediating Structures in Public Policy* (Washington, D.C.: American Enterprise Institute, 1977); *Election Campaigns and Elections*, Winter, 1985, 23.

11. Berger, *Facing Up*, p. 135; Reagan quoted from New York *Times*, Aug. 20, 1985; on the behavior of the administration toward citizen initiatives, see Boyte, Booth, and Max, *Citizen Action*.

12. Joseph Wood, *Commonwealth*, Jan. 1893.

One

HISTORICAL AND INTERNATIONAL PERSPECTIVE

One
Lawrence Goodwyn

POPULISM AND POWERLESSNESS

An awesome irony hangs over twentieth-century politics. Signs of progress are abundant; increasing productivity around the world has generated an unprecedented swirl of material comforts. While these products, from bread and rice to computers and video tape recorders are almost obscenely maldistributed among the people of the planet, the steady upward trajectory of production is a global fact that all forecasters can rely upon. The familiar litany that expresses the idea of progress—the understanding that, though difficulties persist, "progress" is being made —remains intact.

Yet for increasing numbers of people, this thought no longer has the consoling power that helped sustain social morale during earlier stages of the industrial revolution. Increasing centralization of production has led to increasing concentration of political and military power everywhere, giving rise to elaborate structures of social control that seem to have a momentum and logic beyond the reach of people imbued with the idea of rational choice. The imminent possibility of nuclear apocalypse fortifies and dramatizes these popular intuitions about uncontrollable forces, yet the unease of which I speak has a sweep that goes beyond the arms race. At the heart of much of modern politics is an emerging cultural discovery, one that is at once simple and profoundly sobering: millions of people, including many that social scientists are fond of describing as members of elite groups, have been overtaken by a sense of their own powerlessness. The central social irony of the twentieth century is grounded in the discovery that though industrial productivity has increased, the corresponding liberation of human energy that was always presumed to be an inherent by-product of technological innovation has proven to be maddeningly elusive. In terms of their ability to participate effectively in politics, people increasingly feel trapped, not liberated.

This circumstance is far more pervasive than we have yet given ourselves permission, as a society, to acknowledge. Within the confines of the idea of progress, thoughts about proliferating powerlessness are in themselves culturally inadmissible. In a democracy that works reasonably well, people *must* be getting more powerful, not less so, if the progressive mystique is to retain its inherited relevance. The logical dynamic is such that one must ignore specific evidence in order to retain the underlying progressive assumption and thus hang on to the sense of well-being that goes with it.

A pivotal distinction becomes relevant here and needs to be spelled out as plainly as possible in both cultural and political terms. On one level—a level not associated with political action—popular powerlessness is simply accepted, as a parlor aside or as a barroom wisdom. In the vernacular, the knowledge that "you can't fight city hall" is a centerpiece of conventional political understanding in America. Similarly, in matters of economics, "the rich get richer," and as the saying goes, "and the poor get poorer." In a meritocracy, "what counts is not what you know, but who you know." In public discourse, politicians are understood to be in somebody's "hip pocket." They "don't tell the straight story." On a more polysyllabic level, they are "inherently hypocritical." In the popular wisdom about politicians, the point that is stressed is that "you can't trust them, not any of them." The closer one gets to power, in geographical terms, the greater the popular skepticism. City hall is no cup of tea, but the state capitals are worse and Washington is awash in lobbying and boodle. Under the circumstances, a politician's most effective appeal is to

disassociate from politics and campaign against all "insiders" everywhere and "Washington" in particular. Citizens can be persuaded to take a chance on such candidates, but the results over the years have not been very satisfying, for the appealing candidates become, in office, politicians who promptly sound and act in depressingly familiar ways. The result is to fortify once again the popular interpretation: "all politicians are alike."

It is important, I think, to sort through the sundry cultural and psychological implications of this familiar interplay between the governors and the governed. The street-corner understanding that "they ought to clean the whole crowd out" has all the appearances of an active political formulation, a sign of operative ethical health in the society as a whole. But in fact, the historical record of the twentieth century is quite clear that this popular political stance is inherently passive rather than incipiently operative or active. Popular skepticism serves the purpose of providing average citizens with a way of disassociating from the dynamics that routinely frustrate and victimize them. It is as if there are millions of American voices quietly asserting that "No one is fooling us; we *know* our pockets are being picked." The message is psychologically crucial to popular self-respect and thus to civic morale itself. But it is also necessary to emphasize that this message is quite passive, politically. Popular skepticism materializes in a terminology of resignation. It is the language of good citizens who feel trapped and powerless.

How can the idea of progress be sustained under such circumstances? Cannot one entertain the supposition that popular identification with this long-standing cultural assumption has now become fundamentally imperiled? Not at all. Even the most casual inspection of the day-to-day events of American life shatter any such speculation. The mystique of progress is at the very heart of modern American life and is routinely employed to explain and rationalize any number of acts that otherwise do not seem to make sense. Are forests cut down to make room for parking lots? People do not like it, but are powerless in the face of predictable justification. Progress. Are plants closed and jobs exported to sweatshops in Hong Kong or the Philippines? Workers do not like it, but are told that a modern and progressive company has no other choice. Friends of workers do not like it either, but are told "that is the way the world works."

In this way Americans discover that a heavy chunk of coercion lies concealed in the velvet glove of progress. It is helpful to observe that this surprising development is almost invariably seen as a specific discontinuity

21

rather than evidence that points to a general cultural malady. A specific corporation is perceived to be ruthlessly coercive; a specific construction project is revealed to be transparently costly and inappropriate. Popular skepticism can easily find expression in such conclusions; indeed, one can gain a temporary sense of social relevance and political purposefulness by opposing some of the more visible examples of progress-run-amuck.

But workers who desperately band together to try to buy a runaway plant soon encounter other progressive structures and customs—banking practices and prevailing interest rates and such—that make autonomous action hazardous if not impossible. Workers cannot save their standards of living through the costly, interest-laden payouts organic to plant purchases. Rather, they have to cut their own wages ruthlessly to pay the crushing overhead. And even that often cannot save a runaway plant. The result most often is simply another body of evidence indicating "you can't fight city hall."

The result of these structural dynamics is a political and cultural circumstance so discordant, and so culturally unsanctioned, that it is rarely commented upon by political pundits or academic social scientists. The American population as a whole possesses a profoundly divided consciousness. The fact is the political centerpiece of our time, the central irony of modern American culture. It lies like a concealed bombshell beneath the idea of progress that blankets the surface of public life.

It is essential to specify the components of this divided consciousness and to arrange them in relationship to one another so as to make visible the extraordinary political and psychological tension concealed therein. On the one hand, Americans experience their day-to-day lives under the imperatives shaped by the structures of power that have materialized in modern industrial society. These structures are—as they have always been in human history—hierarchical and, as such, play a causative role in shaping the social relations of the whole society. Roles are learned and people experience their lives playing them, well or poorly, in a thousand variations on the themes of deference and authority. However complex and frustrating these social relations prove to be in daily life, they are perceived to take place in a larger society that, as we have seen, is understood to be "progressive." But (and here we have the unsanctioned disjunction) as "progress" impinges directly upon the places where people work, or the neighborhoods in which they live, they do not believe it. That is to say, they do not believe the specific justification offered for a change in work rules, for a plant closing, for the redlining of a neighborhood, or whatever hierarchical practice is about to be visited upon them. In short, their acceptance of progress is general and their disbelief is specific. The faith is public, the skepticism is private. Increasingly, as industrialization has proceeded, Americans live and experience this contrapuntal reality.

Given the enormous cultural investment in the idea of progress, the faith is taken for granted; the skepticism is the component that is so difficult to express. It is politically crucial to spell out this distinction clearly. Americans are fully aware that their skepticism will be understood as deviant. It can be privately held but it cannot be publicly expressed, except within one's own safe circle, be it the family, a workplace washroom, or a shared neighborhood environment. These latter social spaces, tiny as they are, are the only real public forums Americans have been able to create for themselves within the cramped quarters of a highly industrialized society.

All of which brings us out of the realm of social analysis into the broader arena of national political life. The starting point is the fact that America does not abound in 1986 in institutional places where democratic politics can authentically take place. Such democratic places have to be created by the people themselves; they have to create the social spaces and then fill them with appropriate institutional forums through which democratic ideas can be conceived, debated, formulated, and eventually expressed. Unfortunately, the creation of these self-generated forums is a political task that is not popularly understood to be a central component of democratic politics. Yet, this kind of elemental political activity is *the* starting point. It is central. But it is not understood to be either. We are, in short, bogged down at the premise.

Such an assertion sounds unbelievable, of course. How can this be? it is fair to ask. Did we not create, long ago, a democratic constitution? Have we not finally, after conquering certain racial and gender barriers, attained universal suffrage? Premises? Do they not abound? Are we being asked to believe that the Founding Fathers did not exist? That we have no democratic heritage? That the rendering of American history has been some sort of elaborately erroneous act of conspiracy by many generations of historians? Democratic premises? Of course we have them!

Not really. Not in ways that have clear and operative meaning in contemporary American life. The triumph of the Founding Fathers was that they carved out their own space—in a hall in Philadelphia that had no notable previous record as a fountainhead of democratic creativity. They generated their own space, and they filled it with purpose—by talking seriously to one another for an extended period of time. Out of this activity came a new institutional form, the tripartite system of governance known as the Constitution of the United States. The Founders made their private hopes public ones. Subsequent to this process in 1787, Americans have not since organized a comparable self-generated social space for autonomous democratic activity. But—to anticipate the obvious response —why should they have? Is not one constitution adequate? Yes, of course it is. The issue, however, does not turn on this specific result—a highly serviceable organic political document—but rather on the self-generated means by which it came into being. It is the *democratic space* that is the issue. The ideas imbedded in the Constitution came into being and subsequently obtained public visibility because the space in which to have those collective ideas was created, purposefully, by aspiring democratic theorists who wanted to give public life to their most deeply held private aspirations. Without the hall in Philadelphia, without the will to fill the hall with ideas freely exchanged, there would have been no Constitution. Though we applaud the result, and even misdescribe the result as a premise, the real premise was the will to create the space.

Americans need to confront the fact that we have no such remotely comparable space in contemporary life. No institutional space. No authentically democratic space. Where is the political party rooted in and responsive to voluntary associations of citizens? Stripped of all television punditry, the two major parties are not spacious palaces of democracy but rather comparatively small backrooms where contending elites negotiate among themselves, beyond the purview or the knowledge of the citizenry as a whole. In our private sophistication, we know that the two major parties are not homes where Americans discuss their most deeply held hopes and fears; rather, they are places we visit on election day in the fragile hope that the vague statements we have heard from contending politicians have some sort of tangible meaning. In this deepest political sense, the nation's political institutions are remote from the American people. They are institutions that are "out there" in the larger society, somewhere away from daily life. They are on television where, thanks to refinements attributable to modern marketing techniques, they are both highly visible and opaque. Physically, the nation's politicians are in our homes; it is their meaning that is a planet away.

24

It is not a purely American malfunction. The remoteness of twentieth-century governments from their surrounding populations is a worldwide phenomenon traceable to a common source: the "march of industrial progress" has universally generated centralized structures of power. One of the shared similarities of these governments—socialist, capitalist, or military—is the functional distance they have traveled from the private aspirations of their citizens.

Can the private and public lives of Americans be reconnected through their own conscious political efforts? Can the unwanted presence of divided consciousness be transcended? Can the political parties be made into something more than a place to visit once every two to four years? Is a democratic politics possible in America in the late twentieth century?

This volume of essays is dedicated to the possibility that such a democratic renewal is possible. Indeed, lurking in our heritage—in concrete historical ways that are not common to many other industrial nations—is an historical legacy that can most usefully be drawn upon, in the spirit of a new democratic flowering.

That legacy, as the title of this book indicates, is populism. Indeed, the populist heritage offers some crucial elements of guidance and, once we get our premises straight, these elements are rather easily grasped.

First, some essential points of commonality that connect the Populists of the late nineteenth century with Americans in our own time. They, like us, had a number of grievances attributable to the growth of industrialization and the centralization of economic and political power that accompanied this growth. They felt that ordinary American citizens like themselves had no effective input into political decision making in Washington or in their states. They felt the Republican Party was a rather undisguised expression of the political preferences of American corporations and that the Democratic Party had become a slightly less transparent but equally effective vehicle of the same corporations.

As historians are fond of recalling, Populists called their rivals "the two old parties" who were responsive to "concentrated capital." They dubbed their own party, in conscious contrast, the "People's Party." Scholars record the surprisingly strong showing of the new party in its maiden campaign in 1892, the subsequent decline of its internal cohesion after 1896, and its rapid eclipse soon after. The historical verdict: the People's Party was creative, it was earnest, it was vividly democratic in many ways, its time was brief, and many of the party's proposed reforms ultimately came into being in later generations. Historians tend to give the

Populists a grade of "C" in longevity and staying power and an "A-" or so in popular vitality and creative platform writing.

But, however they are appraised, the activities of the Populists from 1892 to 1986 have far less relevance to modern Americans than their earlier—and far less studied—experience from 1884 to 1892. From activities in those years came the most telling Populist legacies, the ones that animate many of the suggestions in the essays that follow in this volume. In that span of eight earlier years, the democrats of populism were not known as "Populists" (a term they coined later), but rather as "Alliance-men." It was in their own self-generated institution, the National Farmers Alliance and Industrial Union, that the future Populists generated the political ideas, the internal social relations among themselves, and the vision for a more democratic America that subsequently informed the political platform of the People's Party. It is the creativity of these years, the Alliance years, that speaks with special clarity to the divided consciousness of modern Americans.

If the original Populists were permitted to see modern "political activists" in action, they would conclude that twentieth-century people have spent too much time arguing among themselves in tiny groups gathered around remote kitchen tables. The Populists would feel that modern activists have not spent enough time thinking about ways of getting out of the kitchen and connecting with the larger society. And, they would say, "you must create nearby institutional spaces in the vicinity" (what we urban people would now call "neighborhoods"). Give the space a name (theirs was called a "sub-alliance") and encourage people to band together to create a real political agenda. Do not worry whether the agenda has immediate prospects for instant acceptance: just be sure it is real—that is, that it reflects what people really want. Based on their own experience, the Populists would not fear that people, once encouraged to be really candid with one another, would promptly want the moon and ask for too much. On the contrary, they knew that the buffeting people take from normal politics is such they are inclined to be rather resigned and to expect very little. Indeed, it is a Populist wisdom that people have to be encouraged to give voice to real hopes, rather than the narrower hopes they have been persuaded to believe are the only ones obtainable.

But perhaps the most significant institution of the Populists—one that they came to learn from their own organizing experience in democratic movement building—is that once people agree to work together for an agreed-upon goal, the experience of working toward that objective has the effect of raising their sights by transforming their understanding of how power actually works in America.

Originally, the reformers recruited people to their Alliance by asking them to join their Alliance cooperative. These cooperatives came to be quite elaborate and to have intricate but widely understood goals that turned on commercial, agricultural, and financial realities at work at the time. Alliancemen did not feel ordinary Americans needed to be especially "aware" or have a "high political consciousness" in order to be recruitable. They knew that people would join a cooperative, even a relatively simple cooperative with modest goals, because elements in the idea sounded reasonable. It was what happened after they joined that gave the movement its vitality.

Self-generated popular goals—even modest goals—are not viewed with favor by the functionaries of established political institutions. It was the original Populist discovery. Mayors, and the local business elites who had elected mayors, had an instinctive response, one that Populists soon came to understand as predictable and universal: "We haven't heard of this proposal." "Where did you get this idea?" Unstated, but implicit, was a more elemental accusation: "Who do you people think you are anyway?"

Such responses had enormous educational impact on the rank-and-file members of the Alliance. One of the political realities of the late nineteenth century, one generation after the Civil War, imparted a special poignancy to this discovery. In the North and West most officeholders outside the largest cities were Republicans, esteemed representatives of the "party of the Union." In the South most officeholders were Democrats, properly sanctioned representatives of the "party of the Lost Cause." As a result of the political emotions dating from the Civil War, officeholders in both parties had powerful sectional credentials in their own region. It therefore constituted a special kind of cultural shock for southern farmers to learn that "their" Democrats held most nonbusiness connected southerners in contempt; and the discovery of the same kind of contempt, visited upon nonbusiness elements in the North and West by Republican politicians, had a similar educational impact on Alliancemen in those regions. Though their cooperatives were organized originally around economic objectives, the shared experience that members gained from observing the opponents of their cooperatives was profoundly "political." It

27

was not the Alliance platform that taught the membership the realities of American politics; it was the experience they encountered in collective assertion that proved so educational.

By the time the Alliance had grown to two million members, largely concentrated in twenty states in the South and West, the participants had learned a number of rather elemental lessons in democratic conduct. Popular movements, organized without permission, so to speak, of self-appointed cultural authorities, possessed an autonomy that alarmed traditional elites habituated to ruling through narrow formulas of governance. The business press (Alliancemen quickly discovered that even a "free" press is a business press) was mobilized to wage cultural war on the movement. Alliance proposals—though considered by modern economists and political scientists to be eminently reasonable and level-headed—were denounced as "anarchistic." The characterization carried more clout in the late nineteenth century than the appelation "socialistic," although that term, too, was occasionally applied. Given the prominence and prestige of major party political leaders and of editors of metropolitan dailies across the land, such denunciations were not to be dismissed out of hand, however irrelevant they were to the observable facts. The Alliance countered with its own internal mechanisms of democratic communication. First in time and most important in impact was the Alliance lecturing system, numbering one lecturer per sub-alliance—over 40,000 in all by 1892. Later came the Reform Press Association, which banded together some 1,000 newspapers, largely rural, across the western granary and the southern cotton belt. By these self-generated institutional means, Alliance members insulated themselves against outside demagogy. In this area, the Populist admonition to twentieth-century activists would take the form of a maxim: democratic movements, operating in hierarchically organized societies, need internal mechanisms of communication to protect the movement against hierarchical cultural attacks.

The other great legacy of the Populist years comes in the form of a negative caution. After Alliancemen formed the People's Party in 1892, the new institution attempted to recruit by conventional political methods —rallies, speaking tours, the creation of a vigorous Populist press, and the like. The rallies were massively attended, the papers carefully read. But the People's Party turned out to be politically strong only in those areas where the Alliance had previously been organizationally strong. The cooperative experience, not conventional political proselityzing, had educated the movement's rank and file. For every American recruited to

Populism after 1892, there were twenty recruited to the Alliance before 1892. A democratic sequence thus came into view: the movement recruited, and the movement's experience educated and politicized the membership. Americans joined the Alliance with their conventional political assumptions, including some profound political illusions about how power worked in America, all fully intact. It was their experience in the movement that changed rank-and-file Alliancemen into authentic democratic advocates or, as the nation knew them, Populists.

Populists learned a great truth: cultures are hard to change. But they also learned that if one wishes to try, one builds a movement that is sufficiently real in its appeal to the populace that their subsequent experience in the movement alters their inherited political assumptions.

The final Populist legacy is not something original Alliance organizers learned, but rather something they brought with them in the first place. In the very earliest days, when the Alliance was confined to a handful of rural counties in the Southwest, the original organizers gave themselves permission not to be resigned in the presence of the elaborate layers of economic, political, and cultural hierarchy that loomed over American life. They set out to fulfill some large hopes: to gather the bulk of the population in a collective popular effort to "regain control of American politics and return the government to the American people." To this end, —one generation after a bitter civil war—they recruited Republicans in the North and Democrats in the South and invited adherents of both parties to leave their ancestral political homes in order to create a democratic political alternative. In an era of rigid racial segregation and palpable cultural and experiential divisions between town and country, they gave themselves permission to envision a North-South, urban-rural, black-white, farmer-labor "coalition of the plain people."

It is proper to add, with benefit of hindsight, that they made some tactical errors and that their strategic vision, as comparatively sophisticated and demonstrably ambitious as it was, was not unfailingly prescient. But they also possessed a certain ingredient in their organizing style, one that grew out of this democratic sense of self, that helped overcome any theoretical or tactical shortcoming they may have had: the Alliance organizers did not condescend to the people they tried to recruit. Rather, they did something disarmingly bold: they listened to them, they responded, and they jointly worked out a democratic agenda for the nation to consider.

Two

Gianna Pomata

A COMMON HERITAGE:
THE HISTORICAL MEMORY
OF POPULISM
IN EUROPE AND
THE UNITED STATES

In the summer of 1874, in Czarist Russia, thousands of young men and women—students, nurses, doctors, university teachers—left their homes in the cities for the villages in the countryside, in order to "go to the people."

Although prepared by decades of ideological and organizational ferment, the "go to the people" movement was largely spontaneous. "Even the contemporaries who tried in their memoirs to minimize its chaotic nature admit that there was no central direction. In fact, there was no organization of any kind to control it. . . . The majority of the students set out individually or in small groups of friends."[1] In a symbolic act of renunciation, they dismissed their usual clothes to dress in peasant garments. What they wanted was to learn about the life and misery of the peasants and share it. Their dominant idea was that the intellectuals owed a "debt" to the people and should, in accordance with this duty, sacrifice their lives to them. As a participant said, "it was not a political movement; it rather resembled a religious movement. . . . People not only thought to attain a distinct practical object, but also to satisfy an inward sentiment of duty, an aspiration towards their own moral perfection."[2] It is not surprising that a religious aura surrounded them: "every man who is close to the people has been sent by God." Like the early Christians, they also believed in a religion of equality; their mission was to tell the people how "all men are equal; all men are born naked; all men are born equally small and weak."[3] For many of them the "mad summer" of 1874 constituted the end of any normal life. From the villages they were sent to prison, from prison to exile. The survivors were going to be the "cadres" of the future revolutionary parties in Russia, or, scattered abroad, the propagators of populist ideas in the rest of Europe. "All their lives were stamped by the renunciation they made in the summer of 1874."[4]

The "go to the people" movement, the springtime of Russian Populism, can be seen as paradigmatic of populist movements in European history, in the last century as well as in the more recent past. Its history evokes striking parallels, for instance, for the people who—like me—have participated in the students' movements in Europe in the 1960s and 1970s, in Milan, Paris, or Berlin. I can remember the move from the lecture rooms into the "open air" of hundreds of places of cultural and political activity—"counter-schools" for working-class children, grassroots trade unionism, groups of neighborhood action, women's consciousness-raising groups. I remember that a general motivation, beyond divided ideological allegiances, was the need to find a more authentic culture and the belief that this culture was to be found among the "people," in the heritage of memory, experience, and struggle of the working classes.

The need to establish a bridge between the educated elite and the culture of the people is a strand of thought that runs, intermittently but tenaciously, through the last two centuries of European experience. Its roots lie in the Romantic movement of the end of the eighteenth and the beginning of the nineteenth century. Romanticism expressed a radical change in the attitude of European intellectuals to popular culture. Suddenly, folktales and folk songs, folklore in general, the autonomous creation of the people as distinct from the written products of learned tradition, came to be seen as a precious "patrimony," a "treasury" to collect and protect from impending destruction. It was indeed a new attitude. For centuries, popular culture had been despised, ridiculed, or severely criticized by the dominant classes. The Romantics turned with enthusiasm to the very thing that had conventionally been regarded with hostility or indifference. What brought about this shift of attitude?

Recent European historiography on the early modern period has focused on the relationship between learned and popular cultures—the culture of the dominant classes, the aristocracy, the clergy, the bourgeoisie, on one side, and that of the subordinated classes, peasants and craftsmen, on the other.[5] On the ground of this new body of research, we can sketch the fundamental processes that led to the Romantic change of mentality.

From the Reformation to the Enlightenment, popular culture was under attack, subjected to a constant process of repression and effacement. At first, this attack arose out of the Catholic and Protestant churches' effort to reform popular religion, and it was led mainly by the clergy. Later, with the Enlightenment, another phase followed, in which the laity took the initiative; popular culture, once attacked on religious grounds as immoral and superstitious, was then dismissed with secular arguments as superstitious and irrational. In this respect, the development of science and the Enlightenment only continued a trend that had started much earlier, in the conflict between established church religions (both Catholic and Protestant) and the religions of the people.

An important consequence of this was a constantly widening gap between the culture of the educated minority and that of the great masses of the population. Whereas medieval and postmedieval periods had been characterized by a complex exchange of reciprocal influences between learned and popular cultures, the age after the Reformation was marked instead by an increasingly rigid boundary between the culture of the dominant classes and that of the people. The upper classes rejected more and more explicitly the popular worldview. In 1500 educated people could despise the common people but still, to a certain extent, understood and shared their culture. By 1800, however, in most European countries, the clergy, the nobility, the merchants, the professional men had withdrawn from popular culture, abandoning it to the lower classes, from which they were now separated, as never before, by profound differences in worldview. By then, from the viewpoint of the learned, popular culture had become a thoroughly alien world. In fact, the Romantics saw themselves as engaged in "discovering" the people, their customs and beliefs, their poetry and art, as something totally unknown. The Romantic movement can be understood, against this background, as a recognition of the estrangement and, at the same time, as a powerful urge to overcome it. But what prompted this urge?

Romanticism was also a reaction to the social disruption brought about by the industrial revolution and to the ravages it created in the traditional, communitarian ways of life. The common culture of peasants and artisans was "discovered" at the very moment when the development of capitalism was undermining its conditions of existence and inflicting on it, in spite of its resilience, irreparable devastation. The Romantic act of recognition of popular culture was triggered by the keen sense of this impending and possibly irretrievable loss. The Romantics were not only the enthusiastic and often naïve transcribers of folk songs and collectors of ancient customs. Their poetry also contained a passionate denunciation of the destructive power of the new social and economic forces. To some Romantic poets—to William Blake or John Clare, for example—we owe the most stringent description and criticism of the human costs exacted by capitalist "progress"; the loss of sense of place and community produced by the enforced enclosure of the common lands; the degradation of work in the factory system.

Romanticism was thus the beginning of a controversy over the price of economic progress and of capitalist development that was to have far-reaching consequences on European consciousness. In the course of the nineteenth century, the criticism of the new industrial world contained in Romantic art filtered into political thought and action. It influenced what is called "utopian" or pre-Marxist socialism, from Charles Fourier to William Morris.[6] It would have been present, as a half-repressed but undeniable component, in Marxism itself. But it is with populism that it came to an especially clear and powerful political expression. The intellectual roots of populism stemmed directly from the Romantic protest against a society that, in the name of commodity production, was ruthlessly destroying the common ways of life. A significant circumstance, in this context, is the fact that populism assumed a massive importance, as an intellectual and political movement, in nineteenth-century Russia. Russia was then, in terms of economic development, one of the most "backward" of European countries. Its social and political structure had severely limited the possibility for capitalism to encroach into the traditional ways of life, especially in the countryside. This meant that a fundamental aspect of popular culture, all the complex world of the peasantry, with its economic, communitarian, and religious customs, had remained relatively untouched by external change.

It was to this peasant world that the members of the "go to the people" movement went in pilgrimage. Under their young and eager eyes, the peasant world revealed itself as an immense reservoir of forces that could resist the impending capitalist aggression. They reacted with fervid admiration, even to the point of idealizing it, to the peasant commune (*obshchina*), with its egalitarianism firmly grounded in the collective and communal property of the land.[7] Through centuries of serfdom and after emancipation (1861) the Russian peasants had clung tenaciously to this traditional form of organization. The commune was a self-governing community that held in common most of the land used by its households. Along with communal ownership of the land, its structure implied the cooperation of all the members at each major stage of the farming year. The egalitarian impact of the commune was especially evident in the periodic redistribution of land: much of the land was redivided at stated times among the members of the village on the basis of egalitarian principles (such as, for example, division by the number of mouths in each household).

The peasants' egalitarianism had derived in part from their very position as serfs. They thought that the land had been assigned to them permanently and that they themselves ought to redistribute it so that the burdens attached to it should fall equally on all. But for the Russian radical intellectuals, aware of the ongoing debate on capitalism and socialism in western Europe, the faith in the *obshchina* took a new, prospective meaning. Everywhere in western Europe, capitalism was destroying the last remnants of the "commons," the ancient custom of communal use and ownership of the land. Western socialist thinkers, however, believed that a new and higher form of communism could be achieved on the basis of the technological advancement produced by capitalism and the establishment of a socialist society, based on the collective property of the means of production. But in the remote and immense Russian countryside the ancient communal tradition had preserved most of its integrity and strength. Could not this tradition be spared the ruinous impact of capitalism? If socialism meant a higher form of communism, could not socialism be built in Russia on the foundation of its ancient, but still vigorous, agrarian communism?

Thus the Populists developed the idea that a way into the future could be found that would not destroy the ancient folkways but rather give them new value and meaning. With Russian Populism, the Romantic protest against the seemingly irresistible "progress" that was showing such destructive force took the form of a political program. The Populists advocated the defense of the Russian agrarian tradition and of the Russian village life, with its spirit of equality and solidarity; they proposed a possible autonomous path to Russian socialism, a path that did not imply capitalism as an inevitable stage.

Although this program was clearly shaped by Russia's specific situation, it held a more general significance in the broader context of European politics. The Populists called into question one of the most basic tenets of European political thought—the belief in progress. Some of the most representative of Populist writings—for instance, Mikhaĭlovskij's *What Is Progress?* and Lavrov's *Historical Letters*, both published in 1869—turn around this issue. Mikhaĭlovskij's discussion of progress questioned especially the liberal notion of individualism. While liberal thought regarded individualism as one of the most positive achievements of the new bourgeois society, Mikhaĭlovskij saw in bourgeois individualism only a negative state of alienation. "Individuality" meant for him "human wholeness," the harmonious copresence of many faculties and abilities in each single individual. This wholeness had been destroyed by capitalism, with its highly developed division of labor, which forced individuals into one-sided specialization instead of harmoniously developing all their potentialities. Authentic individualism, argued Mikhaĭlovskij, was to be found instead in the peasant community. There, where the social fabric was held together by "simple cooperation," without one-sided specialization and functional hierarchies, individuals were endowed with differentiated, many-sided individualities. It was thus utterly unjustified, for Mikhaĭlovskij, to say that economic progress had liberated the individual. Certainly individualism, in the sense of setting a central value on each person, was difficult to reconcile with the social consequences of liberal economy.[8]

In many respects, Mikhaĭlovskij, together with other Populists, was deeply indebted to Marx's vivid description of the atrocities of capitalist "primitive accumulation." He further shared with Marx the notion that a society dominated by commodity production generates alienation. He was especially influenced by Marx's criticism of the division of labor in the factory system as a "crippling of body and mind." But in Marx the strong

35

tone of moral denunciation against the evils of capitalism implied a completely different attitude to "progress." For Marx, capitalism was intrinsically progressive and historically unavoidable. Only the unprecedented development of "productive forces" that it brought about could furnish an adequate technological basis for the realization of socialism. Around the issue of the inevitability and progressive character of capitalism, Populists and Marxists parted ways.[9]

This difference was going to be more and more sharply marked with the development of the socialist movements in Russia and in the rest of Europe in the 1880s and 1890s. The development of Marx's thought involved a noticeable shift toward a more "scientific" theory, in which economic determinism and evolutionism (and, with them, the concept of "historical necessity") played a more prominent role. Furthermore, the revision of Marxism by the right wing of the Social Democratic parties emphasized the theory of "historical necessity," so that the idea of capitalism as a necessary stage on the way to socialism became even more rigid than in Marx's original formulation.[10] In the 1890s, the Populists still upheld the idea that Russia could bypass the capitalist stage and proceed directly to socialism on the basis of the peasant commune, but by then this meant an explicit rejection of Marxism.

Populism and Marxism thus came to represent two contrasting positions in the controversy over capitalism. They differed not only in their views on the possible paths to socialism, but also on which social class was to be the principal agent of the revolution. For the Marxists, the revolutionary class could only be the proletariat, the new class of dispossessed that had learned, through capitalist factory discipline, new forms of social organization. The peasants, on the other end, were not expected to play a crucial revolutionary role. While capitalism was constantly increasing the bulk of the proletariat, by the same process it reduced the peasant population. From the Marxist point of view, the peasants as a class were "doomed" by the very nature of historical "progress." In 1891 the Erfurt program of the German Social Democratic Party, for instance, recognized the ruin and disappearance of small, independent peasants as a "natural necessity" of economic development.[11]

For the Populists, the peasantry was the revolutionary class. The class that for others was the symbol of a "doomed" past—"the class that represents barbarism inside civilization," according to Marx's hostile definition —constituted for them the leadership of the struggle for a better future. This was consistent with their whole attitude toward "progress." In Mikhaĭlovskiĭ's theory, for instance, the persistence of enclaves of traditional, "individual" labor enables people to preserve an ability to struggle against the "divided" labor introduced by capitalism.[12] Significantly, the first Populist attempts to organize the urban working class were directed at those workers who had not yet broken their links with village life—the workers in the textile industry, for instance, who worked part of the year in the factory and went back to the fields at harvest time.[13] Marxist organizing was directed instead at the highly skilled working class of the more advanced industrial sectors. From the Marxist point of view, workers who were still half-peasants could only be the "rearguard" of the proletariat, still imbued with backward peasant mentality. For the Populists, precisely these residues of traditional values and attitudes enabled the workers to fight against capitalism. Through the remnants of peasant mentality in the working class, the past could still be a living, transforming force inside the present. As Lenin would have said in later years, with an intention at sarcasm, "in matters of theory, Populism is just as much as Janus, looking with one face to the past and the other to the future."[14]

Lenin's position on Populism in the late 1890s can be taken as the clearest example of what was going to be the predominant attitude to Populism among Marxists. Populism was seen by him as a protest against capitalism from the point of view of the small producers who, being ruined by capitalist development, saw in it only a retrogression. Although justly denouncing the tragic contradictions inherent in capitalist development, Populism idealized the precapitalist forms of production (in particular, the peasant commune). Its effort to preserve them from destruction was reactionary. The idea of building socialism on the basis of the peasant communitarian traditions was in fact a backward-looking utopia. Populism was, in Lenin's own words, a form of "economic Romanticism." But in this phrase "Romanticism" had a clearly disparaging meaning; it suggested a nostalgic, irrational, idealizing attitude toward the past.[15]

Lenin's interpretation thus cast a heavy shadow of condescension on the Populist political program as sentimental, utopian, and reactionary. With the consolidation of Marxist hegemony over the European socialist parties, this view was going to become a widely held and unexamined truism. Still, the course of historical events in the first decades of the twentieth century showed once again the centrality of the peasant question and therefore confirmed the relevance of the political problems raised by the Populists. For that very reason Populist ideas remained central to the political debate inside socialist and communist parties up to the 1930s. In

Russia, in fact, the first decade after the 1917 revolution saw a flourishing of neo-Populist ideas.[16]

Though proposing different solutions to the problems of the transition to socialism, Populism and Marxism had been closely intertwined in European experience. Although divided by profound differences in political outlook, Populists and Marxists had often fought side by side in the same revolutionary milieu. Sometimes Populist and Marxist ideas had coexisted inside the same individual, or the same political group, as a more or less conscious internal contradiction. This conflictual but strong bond was severed in the Stalinist era. Till Lenin, Populism, though criticized, was still recognized as a significant intellectual legacy and as part of an ongoing political debate. Stalinist dictatorship broke violently with this tradition. The official doctrine, as expressed by a Stalin mouthpiece, was "to annihilate the influence of Populism as the worst of the enemies of Marxism and of the whole cause of the proletariat."[17] All the men, ideas, and journals connected with neo-Populism disappeared in 1935–36. The security measures adopted by Stalin dealt not only with the living but also with the dead: even the editing of the works of the historical leaders of nineteenth-century Populism—Lavrov, Mikhaĭlovskiĭ, Bakunin—was stopped. An impenetrable silence fell on Populism not only in the political debate, but even in Soviet historiography.

There is no mistaking the meaning of this silence; it coincided with the forced collectivization of the countryside. With this step Soviet Russia embarked on a path to socialism very different from the one envisaged by the Populists. As in the case of capitalist accumulation, the costs of this choice would have been borne most heavily by the peasants. The revolution that had seemed at first to vindicate the Russian peasant world turned into a tragic crushing of the peasants' hopes and of their deepest, most valued traditions.

With the suppression of the Populist voice, a sharp tear was made in Russian, and indeed European, historical memory. Populist ideas had been alive in western Europe wherever the peasant question had been a central political issue, such as in Germany, Italy, Spain. Stalinist control over Western communist parties meant that there, too, the political tradition and debate were distorted and mutilated by the enforced silence on Populism. Only after World War II did Western historians start to reconstruct the historical record of the Populist movements. They had to confront, first of all, the orthodox Stalinist doctrine on Populism—a few sentences of Lenin's, mechanically repeated. Not surprisingly, they felt that in order to understand Populism, the first step was to leave Lenin aside. Franco Venturi, the Italian historian whose work (1952) was one of the first to break the silence on Populism, deliberately abstained from even mentioning Lenin's name in his book except once, "to thank the library in Moscow that bears his name."[18]

For European historiography, the task of recovering the historical significance of Populism is as yet far from being completed. What urgently requires critical examination is especially the stereotype that contrasts Populism as "utopian" and backward-looking to "scientific" and "progressive" Marxism. This stereotype is often indirectly conveyed by referring to Populism as a "Romantic" attitude. In a sense, as we have seen, this is accurate enough. Populism did develop out of the Romantic tradition. But this tradition itself was indeed much more manifold and complex than is assumed by characterizing it as a naïve idealization of the past and a sentimental wish to restore it. We belittle our own history when we attribute to the word "Romantic"—as too often we do—this impoverished and disparaging meaning. Apparently innocent, this commonplace notion is perhaps one of the most insidious obstacles to a fuller recovery of the historical legacy of European populism.

In the European case, persistent ideological divisions have made it difficult to piece together the fragmented history of populism, by obscuring the perception of the links and common themes among the movements in various national contexts. It seems even more difficult, at first sight, to find a common ground between the tradition of European populism and the Populist experience in the United States.

In the last decades of the nineteenth century the American Populist movement had an enormous political significance, paralleled probably only by the Russian case. In the 1880s and 1890s the farmers of the South and the Midwest (the cotton- and corn-belts of the United States), organized in the Farmers' Alliance and later in the People's Party, engaged in what was perhaps the most radical confrontation with capitalism attempted by any mass movement in American history. Through a network of cooperatives they tried to resist the strangling pressure from the financial system that was eroding their status as owners of the land, making them helpless in the face of fluctuating agricultural prices and pushing them more and more heavily in debt. Their party's platform challenged

39

American capitalism by advocating a radical reform of the credit system and of national monetary policy.

Comparisons of American and Russian populism have consistently led scholars—both historians and social scientists—to contrast the two as basically very different movements, not sharing much else beyond their name. Especially sociologists and political scientists, in search of a coherent pattern in the variety of movements that called themselves populist, have typically come to the conclusion that the Midwest farmers in nineteenth-century America would not have recognized any similarities between their own movement and the Russian one, and that, in general terms, the two movements "could hardly differ more from one another." [19]

On one side, it is recognized that both movements concentrated on the rural scene and on the most vulnerable part of it (the rural small producers). Both tried to resist "urbanism, centralization, industrialism." Both saw monopoly, finance-capitalist industrialism, and irresponsible government as the chief enemies of the commonwealth.[20] Both can obviously be seen, in general terms, as instances of "agrarian radicalism." Still it is maintained that "their similarities tend to dissolve upon closer inspection." [21]

Let us examine these alleged differences in detail. It is argued that whereas American Populism was a mass movement of farmers, an essential trait of Russian Populism is that it never had a mass basis among the peasants; it was the movement of "a tiny group of intellectuals, alienated from the people, on whom they projected their hopes and dreams"—an ideology about the peasants, not one created by them or rooted in them.[22] On the other hand, a leadership of intellectuals was absent in the American case; if anything, American Populism has generally been associated with a strong anti-intellectual attitude. In the American case, in contrast with the Russian, it is argued that if any intellectuals were among the Populists, they were a local, not a national or cosmopolitan intelligentsia. They did not have to "go to the people" because they were already living in their midst.[23] In summary: whereas the American movement had a mass basis of farmers, such basis did not exist in the Russian case. Whereas the Russian movement was strongly marked by the leadership of the intelligentsia, the American movement was not led by intellectuals. Furthermore, whereas Russian Populism upheld the practice of communal land tenure, in the American case the farmers' radicalism had a marked individualistic bent.

However plausible at first sight, this contrast is worth reconsidering. Many points in it should be questioned on the basis of a more accurate historical perception of both the American and the Russian forms of populism. Particularly in the American case, the image created and handed down by conventional historiography has newly been the object of close critical scrutiny on the basis of more recent and thorough research.

In the United States the continuity of historical memory on populism, though not violently broken as in the European case, does bear the traces of gaps and restrictions imposed by the dominant culture. What we seem to find in this case is not so much a suppressed as a half-forgotten legacy. Lawrence Goodwyn, the historian whose work has raised a general rediscussion of the American farmers' movement, has observed that a "heavy shadow of condescension" has hindered a serious appraisal of the history of American Populism.[24] According to Goodwyn, this condescending attitude especially characterized American liberal historiography, until recently enormously influential and substantially unchallenged. Liberal historiography emphasized those features of the Populist movement most easily reconcilable with a "progressive," liberal view of American history. Thus the Populist movement was seen mainly as an attempt to defend a competitive, fair-market system against the "un-natural" interferences of monopoly and big corporations. The political program of the Populists was described as substantially devoid of socialistic (or anticapitalistic) overtones and dominated by a narrow concern with monetary issues. (In fact, in this conventional view the farmers' movement was seen as practically indistinguishable from the movement for "free silver").[25]

According to Goodwyn, this image fails to reflect the actual complexity of the Populist movement; in fact, it systematically impoverishes its relevance and meaning. Goodwyn's own research, conducted chiefly on primary sources—the voices of the Populists themselves, such as their press, the records of their meetings—shows how earlier historical accounts have consistently neglected the radical core of the movement (privileging instead what he calls the "shadow movement" of the silver interests). Especially ignored has been the enormous democratic import of the movement, "the culture of self-respect and aspiration" generated by the farmers' crusade.[26]

In the light of this reappraisal, we may try to reconsider some points in the contrast of American and Russian Populism. A debatable issue is the asserted anti-intellectual character of American Populism. This image

41

comes directly from the liberal reading of the movement, which has repeatedly imputed "irrational" traits to the Populist mind. The Populists have been accused of a "conspiratorial theory of history" (the attribution of demonic traits to their perceived enemies, especially the money interests; a "manichaean" view of the social order as divided between exploiters and producers, "the robbers and the robbed," "those living by honest labour and those living off of honest labour").[27] These traits are not even discussed; they are simply snubbed and treated as plain evidence of the coarse, mobbish flavor of the Populist mind. They are sometimes condensed in the view of American Populism as a "primitivist" movement, yearning to return to a mythical golden age—a utopian attempt to "escape the burden of history" and, as such, intrinsically "apolitical" and "anti-intellectual."[28] These views betray a deeply suspicious and at best condescending attitude to popular culture in general, along with a very narrow and elitist conception of "intellectual" activity. As a consequence of this attitude, the intellectual content and development of Populist ideas has been ignored as not worth serious consideration.

In his description of the organizational structure of the Farmers' Alliance, Goodwyn gives us a vivid glimpse into the social interaction through which the Populists' ideas came into being. The Alliance was organized by means of a grassroots network of "lecturers":

> Day after day, the lecturers traveled through the poverty-stained backwaters of rural Texas and met with farmers in country churches or crossroads schoolhouses. The small stories of personal tragedy they heard at such meetings were repeated at the next gathering, in an atmosphere of genuine shared experience. . . . The lecturers themselves were altered by these experiences. They were, in effect, seeing too much. Hierarchical human societies organize themselves in ways that render their victims less visible. . . . But the very duty of an Alliance lecturer exposed him to the grim realities of agricultural poverty with a directness that drove home the manifest need to "do something." Repeated often enough, the experience had an inexorable political effect: slowly, one by one, local Alliance lecturers came to form a nucleus of radicalism inside the Texas Alliance.[29]

What is described here is a movement of knowledge from the bottom up—something indeed difficult to conceive for liberal intellectuals, accustomed ever since the Enlightenment to view knowledge as proceeding only from the top down in the social structure. The internal lecturing network of communication, comments Goodwyn, "made possible this expression of pain from below."[30] It was however more than the expression of mere pain; it was a sharing of experience, a transmission of information on how people lived and labored. Far more than just an organizational success, it was a diffusion of awareness and knowledge.

All this is strikingly parallel to what happened with the "go to the people" movement in Russia. Any account of Russian Populism that sees it as an ideology of the intelligentsia forgets that the ideas and political program of the Populists were developed through their exposure to peasant culture and peasant life. To a certain extent they tried to make themselves into a vehicle for the peasant worldview. In fact, when we ask: Where did the Populist ideas spring from? the most illuminating answers do not come from historians of political movements but from historians of the world of the Russian peasants.[31] And indeed, when the peasants arose in 1905 and 1917, Populism was the ideal of millions of them, the direct ideology of peasant democracy in Russia. The years after the revolution of 1917 saw a tremendous resurgence of the peasant tradition of communal egalitarianism celebrated by the Populists. The peasant commune proved not to be the idealized utopia of a bunch of intellectuals but the center of autonomous peasant organization.[32] An undeniable trait of Russian Populism must then be seen in the diffusion of peasant ideas upward in society. Also in this case we find a transference of ideas from the bottom up—a process that is one of the most important springs of radical social change.

But the crucial point of difference between American Populism and Russian Populism is the assumption that, although both were agrarian movements, they involved two very different kinds of producers: peasants in Russia, farmers in the United States. The backward Russian peasant is perceived as different as possible from the American farmer, pictured basically as an agrarian "entrepreneur." Again, this view of the American farmer derives from the liberal interpretation of the Populist movement. This interpretation has underlined the "dual character of the American farmer"—independent yeoman, on one side, but also "businessman, speculator, involved in the commercial ethos," on the other. This characterization of the American farmer has led to the conclusion that the Populist movement derived in great part from the American tradition of "entrepreneurial radicalism": "This tradition was entrepreneurial in the sense that it accepted the basic principles underlying private capitalism,

43

and tended to argue that its specific programmatic proposals would strengthen the capitalist order by broadening opportunities."[33]

This picture is certainly misleading insofar as it obliterates the radical criticism of American financial capitalism expressed by the Populist movement. And furthermore: can we really see the members of the Farmers' Alliance, chronically in debt, desperately struggling in the clutches of the credit system, as businessmen or entrepreneurs? These were the farmers who, in the following decades, would descend, in thousands, then millions, into the world of landless tenantry. A contemporary described their state as "helpless peonage"—and historians have verified that this was not an overstatement.[34] Sure, they were not subsistence farmers; they grew corn or cotton for the international market. But from this it does not necessarily follow that they had an entrepreneurial capitalist mentality. As a matter of fact, peasants in serfdom or plantation slaves can also grow crops for international markets. It is certainly erroneous, as economic history shows us, to call any orientation to the market "capitalist." A peasant economy has typically a double orientation, to subsistence and to the market, at the same time. Historically, and precisely because of this double orientation, peasant economy has resisted the pressure to transform itself into capitalist agriculture. In capitalist agriculture, on the other side, the subsistence sector is bound to disappear. Besides being primarily production for the market, capitalist agriculture is, first of all, capital intensive. It is an agriculture that requires capital and that, therefore, is highly dependent on credit. This dependency erodes the traditional independent status of the farmer, making his behavior more conditioned by the cash nexus and the credit system. He cannot devote part of his work to subsistence crops that would make him less dependent on the market for the daily maintenance of himself and his family; he is forced to work exclusively for the cash crops that will assure him credit. This is precisely the dilemma in which the southern farmers were finding themselves in the years of the Populist Alliance. They did not choose to grow only cotton because of entrepreneurial profit-maximization standards. They grew only cotton—instead of diversifying their crops, adding food supplies for themselves—because that was what their creditors demanded. "No cotton, no credit" was the rule. Their state of chronic indebtedness left them no choice.[35]

The period of Populist struggle in the history of the United States saw precisely the transition from the independent farmer to the farmer permanently in debt because of the increasing need of capital for farming and because, as a Populist said, "he buys everything now that he produced at one time himself."[36] Indebtedness marks the decline of the traditional figure of independent farmer. On him hangs the menace of becoming a landless tenant. Besides, the requirements of maximizing profit, output, and productivity, inherent in capitalist agriculture, make large numbers of small, independent farmers economically redundant as such. The American farmers reacted precisely against the pressure that an economy based on profit-maximization standards was exerting on traditional agriculture. Far from expressing an entrepreneurial capitalist mentality, the Populist revolt expressed the fact that the economic values imbedded in the tradition of small, independent farming were not easily reconcilable with those of a full-fledged profit-oriented economy.

Seeing the traditional independent American farmer as an entrepreneur exposes the typical inability of liberal thought to grasp forms of economic behavior other than capitalist. This inability is particularly evident in the case of peasant economy, or traditional agriculture. Peasant economy cannot be fitted into the categories of liberal economic thought. Historical evidence shows that, unless forced to do so by external pressure, peasants and traditional farmers do not tend to behave as entrepreneurs. Their behavior is not dominated by the goal of profit-maximization. They are not, in a word, a variant of "homo oeconomicus."[37]

This inability to understand peasant economy on its own terms and the tendency to assimilate it to the conceptual framework of capitalist economy is shared by Marxism. As is well known, Marx saw the peasant as a kind of puzzling monster, not fitting neatly into any economic category: "As owner of the means of production, he is a capitalist; as worker he is his own wage-worker."[38]

Interestingly enough, an effort to conceptualize peasant economy on its own terms, as an alternative to the liberal or Marxist views, has been made by a neo-Populist school of thought, a group of economists and statisticians active in Russia in the 1920s. This school is especially associated with the name of A. Chayanov.[39] Chayanov criticized the Marxist notion of the double nature of the peasant (combining in one person the roles of capitalist and wage-worker) as an "entirely capitalist fiction," a deformation of reality produced by the need to apprehend it through capitalist spectacles. According to him, we fundamentally misunderstand peasant economy when we see it as a commercial enterprise of a capitalist kind. How does peasant economy differ from capitalist economic behavior? First of all, peasant economy is based primarily on family work

45

and family needs; the family is the economic unit of production and consumption. Whereas the aim of capitalist behavior is maximum income, the training force of peasant family economy, according to Chayanov, is the balance of consumption and work—in other words, the balance between the satisfaction of family needs and the amount, or "burden," of work. If the family needs do not grow (as in the case, for example, of an expansion of the household size), the peasant family does not tend to increase its "burden" of work. The balance between consumption and work expresses the wish of keeping a stable level of well-being. In striking contrast with capitalist economy, the peasant family economy is therefore not committed to constant growth.

The Soviet economists of the late 1920s accused Chayanov—"this last of the Mohicans of the Populist ideology," as they called him—of idealizing peasant economy.[40] In their commitment to economic development, they also—like American liberal historians—could not conceive that the peasant economic mentality differed from the capitalist, profit-maximizing attitude. Chayanov's theory was developed, of course, with immediate reference to the Russian peasant economy of the period, but it was aimed at a more general application. In fact, historians and anthropologists, in their effort to understand peasant economy, have increasingly found it useful also in other contexts.[41] It could be suggested that it might also help us understand the crisis of the American farmers in the last decades of the last century. The fact that American agriculture is now, in all the world, probably the most closely dominated by purely financial imperatives, the least like peasant agriculture (if by peasant agriculture is meant family-operated farming), should not make us forget that the family farm, producing both for the market and for subsistence, was for centuries one of the most characteristic American institutions. It could be suggested therefore that, instead of seeing the American Populist farmers as entrepreneurs, we could see them as caught in between the traditional family economy, aimed at keeping a stable work/consumption balance, and the external pressure (from the financial system) to adapt to profit-maximization standards or just disappear, as not economically viable units.

In spite of all the obvious differences between the American and the Russian case, the history of populist movements at the turn of the century could then be seen within a common frame. It could be seen as a page in the history of the opposition of peasant family economy, with its non-capitalist values (the orientation to customary needs and not to profit; the

46

orientation to equilibrium and not to growth), to the social choices that, in both the American and the Russian case, were justified under the convenient anonymity of "progress."

What meaning can the historical memory of Populism have for us today? One century ago, the men and women who called themselves Populists found in themselves and in solidarity the resources to stand up to overwhelming social forces. They questioned, politically and morally, the value and inevitability of "progress." It is in the name of progress, or "historical necessity," that people in contemporary society, in both the lands of democratic and socialist dreams, have been told over and over again that they had better give up the hope of altering a course of events ruinous to them—the hope of shaping their fate, instead of resigning themselves to be the casualties of history.

Discussing the difficulty of rekindling the historical memory of Populism in the case of the United States, Lawrence Goodwyn has written: "It may be that the Populists have never been made a seminal part of the national heritage because to do so would diminish the present, and the people who live in it, too profoundly."[42] The mixture of amnesia and condescension in the current attitude to Populism may be a thin covering for our sense of inadequacy in the face of a past having standards—of courage, lucidity, capability for struggle—we are not up to. Some responsibility, however, falls on those whose task it is to keep memory alive and teach us to remember—the historians. Historians have generally had two attitudes to what is called "progress." One is, of course, to side with it and be its apologists. The other one is to recognize its destructive aspects but to view them with an attitude of passive contemplation, which again confirms the inevitability of it all. This attitude can be described as the one in which an European writer, in a spirit of parable, has portrayed the angel of history:

> This is how one pictures the angel of history. His face is turned
> towards the past. Where we perceive a chain of events, he
> sees one single catastrophe which keeps piling wreckage upon
> wreckage and hurls it in front of his feet. The angel would
> like to stay, awaken the dead, and make whole what has been
> smashed. But a storm is blowing from Paradise; it has got

47

caught in his wings with such violence that the angel can no longer close them. This storm irresistibly propels him into the future to which his back is turned, while the pile of debris before him grows skyward. This storm is what we call progress.[43]

As an alternative to this fatalism, the history of populist movements reminds us that still another attitude to progress is possible—that it is possible to find a way beyond resignation and despair. This simple reminder, with its message of hope, is perhaps the most precious core in the meaning that the historical memory of populism can have for us today.

Notes

1. F. Venturi, *Roots of Revolution: A History of the Populist and Socialist Movements in Nineteenth-Century Russia*, 2nd ed. (Chicago and London, 1983), pp. 504–505.

2. S. Kravchinskij, *Underground Russia* (London, 1883), pp. 25–26, quoted by A. Walicki, *The Controversy over Capitalism: Studies in the Social Philosophy of the Russian Populists* (Oxford, 1969), p. 89.

3. Venturi, *Roots of Revolution*, pp. 500, 498–99.

4. Ibid., p. 505.

5. For a general overview, see P. Burke, *Popular Culture in Early Modern Europe* (New York, 1978); for a more specific discussion, C. Ginzburg, *The Cheese and the Worms: The Cosmos of a Sixteenth-Century Miller* (Harmondsworth, 1980), esp. pp. xiii–xxvi.

6. E. P. Thompson, *William Morris: Romantic to Revolutionary* (New York, 1961).

7. On the peasant commune, see Venturi, *Roots of Revolution*, pp. 70ff.; T. Shanin. *The Awkward Class: Political Sociology of the Peasantry in a Developing Society: Russia 1910–1925* (Oxford, 1972), pp. 32–38.

8. For a discussion of Mikhaïlovskij's thought, see Walicki, *Controversy*, pp. 26, 46–59. A fundamental contribution to the history of individualism in Western thought is L. Dumont, "The Modern Conception of the Individual: Notes on its Genesis and that of Concomitant Institutions, in *Contributions to Indian Sociology*," Oct. 1965; and, of the same author, *From Mandeville to Marx: The Genesis and Triumph of Economic Ideology* (Chicago, 1977).

9. Walicki, *Controversy*, pp. 132–92.

10. Ibid., pp. 188–91.

11. Ibid., pp. 172–73. See also D. Mitrany, *Marx Against the Peasant* (London, 1952), Part I.

12. Walicki, *Controversy*, p. 52.

13. Venturi, *Roots of Revolution*, pp. 511–12.

14. Quoted by Walicki, *Controversy*, p. 22.

15. Ibid., pp. 6, 17–22; for a criticism of Lenin's view of Populism, see Walicki, "Russia," in G. Ionescu and E. Gellner, eds., *Populism: Its Meaning and National Characteristics* (London, 1969), pp. 90–91.

16. Shanin, *Awkward Class*, p. 46.

17. Venturi, "Russian Populism," in *Studies in Free Russia* (Chicago and London, 1982), p. 218, and passim, pp. 216ff.

18. Ibid., p. 217. For Venturi, reconstructing the history of Populism meant a deliberate attack against the Marxist hegemony of socialist tradition: "The history of Populism leads to a historical confrontation with Marxism: for the past two centuries Socialist thought and movements in all Europe have been too rich and varied to be monopolized by one trend, even if the trend is Marxism. Every attempt to establish in the context of Socialism a so-called scientific trend that is considered authentic and opposed to the other utopian and false trends, is not only historically wrong but eventually leads to a voluntary mutilation and distortion of all Socialist thought" (ibid., p. 275). A definition of Populism as "an early version of the Marxist movement" can still be found in *An Encyclopedic Dictionary of Marxism, Socialism and Communism*, ed. J. Wilczynsky (Berlin and New York, 1981), p. 448.

19. P. Worsley, "The Concept of Populism," in Ionescu and Gellner, *Populism*, pp. 218–19; M. Canovan, *Populism* (New York and London, 1981), p. 3.

20. Worsley, "Concept," pp. 221–23.

21. Canovan, *Populism*, pp. 96–99.

22. Ibid., p. 60; Walicki, "Russia," pp. 30–31.

23. Worsley, "Concept," p. 221.

24. L. Goodwyn, *Democratic Promise: The Populist Moment in America* (New York, 1976), pp. viii, 600–614.

25. For this view of American Populism, see R. Hofstadter, "North America," in Ionescu and Gellner, *Populism*, pp. 9–27.

26. Goodwyn, *Democratic Promise*, p. 605.

27. Hofstadter, "North America," p. 18.

28. D. MacRae, "Populism as an Ideology," in Ionescu and Gellner, *Populism*, pp. 153–65.

29. Goodwyn, *Democratic Promise*, pp. 74–75.

30. Ibid., p. 126.

31. On the world of the Russian peasants, see the important work of Pierre Pascal, *Civilisation paysanne en Russie* (Lausanne, 1969).

32. On the revival of the peasant commune during and after the 1917 revolution, see Shanin, *Awkward Class*, pp. 151ff.

33. For this view, Hofstadter, "North America," pp. 9, 14, 25.

34. Goodwyn, *Democratic Promise*, pp. 28ff.; P. Daniel, *The Shadow of Slavery: Peonage in the South, 1901–1969* (Urbana, 1972).

35. Goodwyn, *Democratic Promise*, pp. 30–31.

36. W. A. Peffer, *The Farmer's Side: His Troubles and Their Remedy* (New York, 1891), pp. 56–57, quoted by R. Luxenburg, *The Accumulation of Capital* (New York, 1968), p. 398. Rosa Luxenburg's pages on the American farmers' crisis are still useful.

37. Classical economic theory and, with it, liberalism started precisely over the issue of reconceptualizing agriculture around the figure of the farmer-entrepreneur; see L.

Dumont, "Agriculture and the Birth of Classical Economics: The Docteur Quesnay," in E. J. Hobsbawm, W. Kula, A. Mitra, K. N. Raj, I. Sachs, eds., *Peasants in History: Essays in Honour of Daniel Thorner* (Oxford, 1980), pp. 271–82; see, also, in the same collection, E. J. Hobsbawm, *Scottish Reformers of the Eighteenth Century and Capitalist Agriculture,* pp. 3–29.

    38. K. Marx, *Theories of Surplus Value* (London, 1951), p. 192.

    39. D. Thorner, "Une théorie néo-populiste de l'économie paysanne: l'École de A. V. Čajanov," in *Annales E.S.C.* 21, n. 6 (Nov–Dec. 1966): 1232–244.

    40. B. Kerblay, "A. V. Čajanov: un carrefour dans l'évolution de la pensée agraire en Russie des 1908 à 1930," in A. V. Čajanov, *Oeuvres choisies,* 1 (The Hague, 1967): 456–57.

    41. D. Thorner, "L'économie paysanne: concept pour l'histoire économique," in *Annales E.S.C.* 19 (May 1964): 417–32.

    42. Goodwyn, *Democratic Promise,* p. 612.

    43. W. Benjamine, *Illuminations* (New York, 1969), pp. 257–58.

Two

THE POLITICS
OF EMPOWERMENT

Two

THE POLITICS
OF EMPOWERMENT

two

THE POLITICS
OF EMPOWERMENT

Three

Frank Riessman

THE NEW POPULISM
AND THE
EMPOWERMENT ETHOS

In the last two years a wave of support has arisen for a new populism.

The Fingerhut/Granados Opinion Research Report found that "Democratic populism attracted Reagan Democrats (swing voters)" in the 1984 elections. Seventy-five percent of this group agreed with the statement, "Government should do more to protect ordinary Americans from the power of banks and big corporations."

Self-styled populists held their seats in Congress often in the face of huge Reagan margins in their districts.

Iowa's recently elected senator, Tom Harkin, formed a congressional Populist Caucus that includes twenty-two members of congress. This group has now formed a Populist Forum that plans nationwide organizing.

Local politicians like Raymond Flynn of Boston have been espousing the new creed. And so too have right-wing fundraiser Richard Viguerie, conservative political analyst Kevin Phillips, and Republican Congressman Jack Kemp.

Why Now?

What does the new populism mean and why is it resonating so strongly now? The essence of populism is ordinary people getting involved with others to collectively control their lives. Opinion polls indicate that some two-thirds of the American people feel powerless and ignored, buffeted by big institutions.

The new populism reflects a spirit, a mood, in search of an ideology. A number of important developments have taken place in the last decade that lack a unifying political theme or conceptualization, and the neo-populist perspective has emerged to fill this gap. Large numbers of people feeling submerged and overpowered by big institutions and big government are attempting to get some control over their lives. They are struggling for empowerment. This is expressed vividly in the new movements: tenants', anti–toxic waste, women's, consumer, gay, environmental. Organizations like Citizen Action and National Peoples Action are highly responsive to this mood. Their action agendas revolve around issues such as utility rates, toxic waste, and rents. The stress is on identification with the little guy, the underdog.

Historically, populism was largely an agrarian movement flourishing in the South and West. In the 1930s its themes were reactivated by Huey Long and Father Coughlin with strong right-wing, racist overtones. Nevertheless, much of the populist spirit has a strong progressive potential. It is directed at big concentrated power, both business and government. This is used by conservatives to argue against the role of government in providing needed services for the poor and all of us. Clearly, progressives must disentangle the negative role of government as a controlling, bureaucratic, dependency-producing force from its positive role, both in providing services and assisting the local self-help creation of services. (The government has other roles in terms of ensuring equity and perhaps monitoring the decentralized services.) In this area right-wingers have an easier task in using populism as a global attack on government.

Another feature of populism is its emphasis on traditional values like family, neighborhood, religion, and patriotism. While recognizing the significance of these roots, we must distinguish between traditions that have a progressive potential and those that are narrow, provincial, parochial, chauvinistic, sexist, and racist. And, here again, right-wing populists have an easier task as they can more uncritically accept traditions.

54

A third leg in the populist ideology is the emphasis on communitarian, cooperative, self-initiated activities emanating at the grassroots level. This bottom-up participatory approach is rooted in American traditions and has been powerfully reactivated. The town meeting and participatory democracy are central to this theme. They breed a healthy concern for local issues, sometimes moving from there to a national agenda, albeit somewhat slowly. Participatory democracy, while occasionally utilized by the right as in the tax reform movement, has significant potential for progressives, particularly if it can be united with an anti-elite, anti–big corporations thread. The neighborhood movements' attack on redlining is an outstanding illustration.

The new populism has the potential of resonating with large numbers of people who have become concerned with empowerment, with having a say over their own lives and control over what happens to them. This desire for empowerment is reflected in the numerous movements of the past twenty-five years: The civil rights movement, the peace movement, the women's movement, and later, the consumer and environmental movements, and the self-help and neighborhood movements.

All of these movements have qualities that are rooted in populist traditions mixed with some that are new. The new dimensions originate from an ethos that emerged in the 1960s, an ethos that emphasized both self-actualization and participation. One form of the self-actualization appeared in the "me-ism" of the 1970s with its excesses and narcissism. But as noted in Yankelovich's *New Rules*, this "me" orientation has been giving way to much more mutuality and new forms of social concern. This is reflected particularly in the mutual-aid movement, where altruism and egoism are typically united—giving help is helpful—helping helps the helper. This unity is very powerful and potentially important at the political level, as we need a political program that is not a zero-sum game where some lose and others gain, but, rather, universally beneficial programs such as social security and national health insurance.

Sources of the New Quest for Empowerment

It would be easy to say that the demand for empowerment arises because people have been unempowered, because of the need. However, demands do not simply arise from needs. Revolutions typically do not appear at the lowest point, but rather when there are rising expectations based upon changed conditions and new possibilities. The civil rights movement emerged in the 1960s in a period of economic expansion, coming after World War II when blacks served in the armed forces and worked in the factories. Their new expectations arose from this experience.

What then are the new conditions that have emerged to give rise to the quest for empowerment—the desire to increase control over one's life? There seem to be some more immediate factors and some deep, underlying roots.

1. A long-range underlying cause relates to the significance of the consumer role in an advanced capitalist society. Consumers are needed to absorb the goods arising from the vastly expanded productive capacity. Selling and advertising become central enterprises directed at the consumer. And although it is conventional to emphasize the exploitation and manipulation of the consumer, there is another side that is, to some extent, taken for granted and understated, namely, the fact that the consumer has choices, perhaps limited choices, but nevertheless the consumer is involved in appraising, questioning, choosing, and evaluating. *Out of this choosing process, the consumer develops the beginnings of feelings of power* (perhaps sometimes exaggerated), plus various skills in making choices. Consumerism and the consumer movement arise as a way of strengthening the consumers in their choices (and practically all of the movements of the past twenty-five years have been consumer-based and built around consumer issues—rents, crime, human service, and self-help problems). This choosing dimension is the forerunner of the empowerment orientation. Empowerment obviously is more than choosing at the marketplace and more than the power of choice alone. But the underlying feeling and the skills associated with choosing form an important base, which together with other dimensions serve to stimulate an increase in empowerment.

2. In our service society, most services are very near the consumer. This is true not only in the human services such as health, education, mental health, but also in sales, where frequently the consumer is involved fairly closely with the seller and sometimes involved with service production itself. For example, consumers do their own shopping in the supermarket, fill out their own bank deposit slips in banks, participate closely in their own health practice. The human services particularly are consumer intensive: that is, the consumer potentially contributes to the pro-

ductivity of the service. This could be far better developed, were it not for the ambivalence of the providers of the service. Nevertheless, consumer power does expand—the feeling of choice, the feeling of some control, some involvement, and perhaps the wish for more.

3. The tremendous expansion of education, both formal and informal, is also critical to the empowerment theme. There has been a tremendous growth of education in the last twenty years as far greater numbers graduated from high schools, community colleges, and colleges. In 1985, 45 percent of 20- to 30-year-olds had some college education, compared with 28 percent of the same age group in 1970. But perhaps even more important is the enormous expansion of informal education arising from the media, particularly television. Whatever the limitations of the media, they impart information, verbal skills, models, and do so in a pervasive, entertaining fashion. Education is potentially empowering. It can increase the desire for control over one's own life.

4. Major political events in the past two decades have contributed to a decline in respect for authority, experts, and an increase in respect for experiential knowledge. Watergate and Vietnam, of course, were major to the debunking of big authority. The free speech, student, and new left movements of the 1960s were also contributing factors. Investigative journalism and the media's interest in muckraking also play a role.

Until recently, all the polls showed a decline in trust for big institutions, government, the professions, business, and the like. Distrust of big power dovetails with increased respect for the layperson, for experience, for peers. All of this is expressed in the self-help movement with its anti-expertism, critique of professionalism, and concomitant respect for the average person.

5. Some other developments that took place in the 1960s were further contributors to the empowerment theme. The participatory emphasis emanating, in part, from inside the government in the antipoverty program with the stress on maximum feasible participation is an important factor. The 1960s also, of course, brought with them a great deal of external protest—for example, in the welfare rights movement, reflecting the main model, the civil rights movement. The 1960s also emphasized self-expression, self-actualization, personal liberation, and in the 1970s this was expressed perhaps in one of its more negative forms—"me-ism," with its narcissistic overtones. But the positive aspect of me-ism is the concern for control over one's own life, freedom of self-expression. A

crucial aspect of this is expressed both in individual and collective forms, in the women's movement, in books such as *Our Bodies, Ourselves*, which sold over 4 million copies in its first edition, in the women's health movement, consciousness-raising groups, and ultimately its more advanced political forms.

Underlying all these themes is the fact that overall, the majority of people in our society have not felt able to cope with or even to understand large issues, such as foreign policy or national economic policy. People feel a lack of control in these matters and they are mystified by the processes involved. For the most part they have retreated from this larger agenda and have moved their demands for empowerment to local issues and more narrow interest group questions. As people gain strength, experience, and competence on these local issues, to some extent they move back to the larger agenda, as is illustrated in the nuclear arms freeze movement and may be furthered in a populist movement directed at economic issues on a national scale as well as a local scale. This is the opening for the new populism.

The Self-Help Ethos in Populism

A current dimension relevant to the new populism, not typically found in historic populism, relates to anti-expertism and antiprofessionalism. This reflects the enormous expansion and significance of services in the welfare state. People have been made to feel dependent, as clients (patients) and passive students, rather than active and independent, as consumers. Experts, professionals, and political leaders have frequently mystified not only the political processes but the services they "deliver." A whole informal structure has arisen as a reaction to this development — self-help mutual aid groups, natural helpers, neighborhood groups, peer groups. The self-help ethos emerging here must inform the new populist ethic.

There are many themes in the self-help pattern, well depicted for example in the television movie "Adam" about parents' reactions to the death of their missing child. (The same theme is expressed by a whole host of self-help groups — MADD, Association for Retarded Children, Victims for Victims, and so forth.)

58

In "Adam" the parents first experience enormous personal suffering in their loss. Then they discover that others have experienced and are experiencing a similar loss. They share, they understand from the inside (indigenously) from their own experience, as no one else can understand. They then begin to reach out and help these others, using their own experience. And, lo and behold, they find new strength from giving this help and care. Altruism and egoism are fused. They are helped from helping. They are transformed. They are no longer simply victims.

Then they move to the next stage, changing legislation. They go up against the FBI as they fight for a national program to involve the FBI in the search for missing children. Finally, they appeal to even the president of the United States and begin to affect the consciousness of masses of people through the use of the media. Especially ingenious is their use of milk containers to circulate pictures of missing children. Their advocacy enriches their competence as they struggle with powerful opponents. Their transformation truly empowers them. And they build a new type of organization, a nonbureaucratic one, which again is characteristic of the self-help mode.

Bureaucratic organization is characterized by hierarchy, impersonal rules, a division of labor that emphasizes technical competence. Self-help mutual aid is highly personal. The competence is based upon experience; it does not have a highly differentiated division of labor and is typically nonhierarchical, highly participatory. Moreover, the help given and taken is free. It is not a commodity.

One of the most important reasons for the rapid spread of the self-help movement is the self-help ethos or spirit. This ethos has the following dimensions:

☐ a noncompetitive, cooperative orientation;

☐ an anti-elite, antibureaucratic focus;

☐ an emphasis on the indigenous—people who have the problem and who know a lot about it from the "inside," from experiencing it;

☐ a goal of doing what you can do, taking one day at a time, not trying to solve everything at once;

☐ a shared, often circulating leadership;

☐ being helped through helping (the helper-therapy principle);

☐ no necessary antagonism between altruism and egoism;

☐ offering help not as a commodity to be bought and sold;

☐ an accent on empowerment—control over one's own life;

□ a strong optimism regarding the ability to change;

□ a recognition that small may not necessarily be beautiful, but is the place to begin and the unit to build upon;

□ a critical stance toward professionalism, which is often seen as pretentious, purist, distant, and mystifying; a preference for simplicity and informality;

□ an emphasis on the consumer, or, in Toffler's term, the prosumer — the consumer as a producer of help and services;

□ placing helping at the center — knowing how to receive help, give help, and help yourself, that self-victimization is antithetical to the ethos;

□ a recognition that the group is key — de-isolation is critical.

Transforming Prepolitical People

For the most part, although there has been a significant increase in their orientation toward advocacy, self-helpers are prepolitical. As they become more political, they appear to progress through three stages:

1. The very process of mutual help begins to develop competencies of working together and sharing, which can be applied to larger issues. The beginnings of empowerment emerge as people feel able to control some aspect of their lives.

2. An advocacy focus may appear as the self-helpers discover the external causes of their problems. In some cases this takes the form of criticism regarding the provision of services, in other cases it is concerned with the media and the images presented of the self-help problem or condition. Underlying all of this is the basic self-help ethos that emphasizes the indigenous strengths of the people involved in contrast to a dependence on external, elite experts. These attitudes are unlike a lobbyist form of advocacy, in which representatives speak for the constituents who remain passive and inactive.

3. From these prepolitical forms there may begin to emerge a consciousness of the interconnections of issues, and coalitions of self-help groups may surface, at first in the form of subgroup alliances (either by region or topic), perhaps ultimately evolving into a national coalition — such was the development of the anti–toxic waste movement that arose out of neighborhood self-help.

60

As self-help groups are typically prepolitical, it is often difficult to predict the political forms their action will take as they become more focused on advocacy and concerned with larger issues. As these groups become politically active, they do not necessarily move in a straight line to political positions that progressives might espouse.

For example, MADD's emphasis on raising the drinking age may have some antiyouth components; and we know that some neighborhood groups have had, on occasion, segregationist orientations. On the whole, however, the self-help groups that have become more politically focused have moved in a direction that progressives would generally support, e.g., with regard to the disabled, crime victims, women.

It should be noted that self-help groups are not developing advocacy in a vacuum; rather, they reflect the mood of the country with its interest-group focus. Moreover, there are a number of organizations with a progressive orientation strongly interested in reaching and moving the self-help groups: for example, Citizen Action and National Peoples Action. These groups are very adept at connecting to the prepolitical mentality and politicalizing it step by step, as well as learning from the grassroots indigenous base. The prepolitical people respond in a variety of ways. Some are politically active episodically. Some leaders emerge and remain continuously active, feeding not only new issues and themes into the political mainstream, but also adopting a new style of political activity. Both ways are badly needed.

Obviously there is a battle to win over the prepolitical self-helpers. Progressives have a potential edge in this battle, particularly if they are open to the new populism emerging from the grass roots. The problems of the self-helpers, both neighborhood and human service, cannot be resolved by their self-help action alone; as they become involved, they are increasingly drawn to the larger external causes of their locally felt concern. It is at this point that the new populism can play a powerful role in connecting ethos to politics.

What Is New about the New Populism

1. It is taking place in the context of a wave of empowerment—the demand by a variety of groups and movements for some control over

their lives. This includes the neighborhood and self-help movements, tenants, women, consumers, environmentalists, gays, and others. Present-day populism builds on the ethos and the movements of the 1960s with their emphasis on participation, which derived in part from the anti-poverty programs' credo of maximum feasible participation.

2. The new populism is arising at a time when liberalism and radicalism have come under severe attack.

3. The new populism is occurring worldwide, particularly in the developing countries (but also in Europe), as is surprisingly documented in a book by a Soviet author, V. Khoros, *Populism: Its Past, Present and Future* (see the Bibliography at the end of this volume).

4. Current progressive populists like Lane Evans of the congressional Populist Caucus are committed to foreign policy stressing America's interdependence in the world. Evans states, "That's why we call it new."

5. The new populism, surfacing in a highly developed welfare state where professionalism and expertism are very prominent, is critical of the mystification and dependence often fostered by elitist professionalism.

6. Finally, the new populism is converging with a number of other important developments such as the Jesse Jackson phenomenon, the voter registration strategy, the appeal of the Catholic bishops, and the nuclear arms freeze movement.

The new populism is a political response to a number of current developments, perhaps the most important of which is the demand for empowerment. But potential problems arise here. For example, the empowerment ethos is reflected in the demands of people for control over their personal lives—women, for instance, having a choice with regard to abortion, gays having a choice with regard to sexual preference. In many ways, the values reflected are antithetical to traditional values to which populism is particularly responsive. Thus, problems will emerge that need to be considered and dealt with carefully. If the new populism is to be successful, it will have to face these contradictions.

Populism traditionally has been responsive to farmers, the middle- and upper-working classes and small business groups. This seems to be the immediate thrust of the new populism, as well. The empowerment movements, on the other hand, are much more inclusive of minorities, women, and, in some cases, upper-middle-class groups (what Kim Phillips calls elitist liberals) concerned with consumerism and the environment, quality-of-life issues, the nuclear freeze, peace. This apparent contradiction also will need to be resolved in order for the new populism to sustain wide support.

Another problem for the new populism is the fact that most people at the grassroots level do not really know what populism stands for, despite Reagan's emphasis on populist positions. Much more attention will have to be given to popularizing populism—relating it to people's power, grassroots democracy, and the empowerment motif.

An historic danger of populism, referred to as democratism, will also have to be considered. Democratism was at work in the most widely publicized political development of 1978, when California's citizens went to the polls to approve Proposition 13, a tax-cutting measure put on the ballot because 1.2 million people signed a petition to put it there. Similarly, various citizens' initiatives in the 1970s and 1980s have opposed homosexual rights. Populism powerfully supports direct democracy, the referendum, local initiatives, and is often impatient with representative democracy.

In the present period, when representative democracy has been distorted by big-power interests, and where the common man and woman often goes unheard, a new balance is needed, and this is why the emphasis on direct action and local initiatives has come about. But we need to be alert to the democratist danger (the dark side) in the populist ethos that often leads it in rightist directions, when it is manipulated by demagogues. This happened in the 1930s, with Huey Long and Father Coughlin, and in the 1980s with Reagan. The new progressive populism will have to tread a careful path, avoiding the errors of democratism and overresponse to the moment, while attempting to redress the imbalance that has been produced by big institutional power, particularly big business.

Four

Julian Rappaport

COLLABORATING FOR EMPOWERMENT:

CREATING THE LANGUAGE OF MUTUAL HELP

The professional has much to gain from genuine collaboration with members of the self-help movement, and in turn has something to offer. On the pragmatic side, those who are interested in more than obtaining third-party payments by selling themselves as health-care professionals can gain a constituency of allies for support in the allocation of mental health and social welfare resources at a time when government and policymakers are making such resources scarce. On the scientific and knowledge-base side, professionals have a unique opportunity to learn about basic human processes and relationships by observing the helping phenomena *in vivo*. However, in order for helping professionals to be useful to grassroots mutual help organizations, they need to develop a language that communicates a sense of respect, and acknowledges the power and competence contained in organizations that bring people together to help one another. This chapter suggests that the language of empowerment is more appropriate for such work than is the language of medicine.

Anyone who has experienced joining a group or an organization to look for help and discovers that he or she can help others as well knows something of what it feels like to begin a journey toward what I call empowerment. That person knows what it is like to gain psychological control over one's self and to extend a positive influence to others, ultimately to reach out to influence the larger community.

The cognitions, motivations, and personality changes experienced by those who gain a sense of control may be the essence of empowerment, and it is useful to flesh out the idea of empowerment as a metaphor and a symbol of the goals of helping. It is important to talk in empowerment terms, rather than in the traditional medical terms of the helping professions, where words like "health" and "illness" and "prevention" and "disease" and "cure" are used.

The Power of Empowerment Language

To understand the importance of thinking in empowerment terminology, or at least to see the importance of learning to speak in other than traditional medical terminology, it is useful to be aware of the hidden consequences of thinking and speaking about the process of helping in traditional ways. Medical thought and language, which has now extended itself to encompass not only our views of physiological and neurological processes but also our views of interpersonal relationships, tends to have an iatrogenic effect on our ability to handle our problems in living in the absence of expert advice.

Iatrogenesis

The concept of iatrogenesis has received only scant attention in the field of social relations. The term, which refers to a negative effect of a treatment, is most well developed in the field of clinical medicine. Its most familiar form is in discussions of the "side effects" of medication and surgery. As is well known, it is not uncommon for a treatment to cause an adverse reaction that is worse than the original malady. However, Illich has extended the concept to include what he calls "social and cultural iatrogenesis."[1] He views as socially iatrogenic those effects of medicine that are created by a medical bureaucracy that increase stress and dependence while reducing individual choice and self-care. It is, in his view, the medical monopoly itself that has a negative impact on individuals—quite independently of any positive or negative clinical effects of a given treatment—by depriving people of control over their own bodies. Cultural iatrogenesis is more subtle; in the context of medicine it refers to a society that is robbed of the will to understand its own pain, sickness, suffering, and dying. An essentially moral enterprise has been turned over to a technocracy rather than retained by every person.

In a book bringing together contributions from psychologists, physicians, sociologists, economists, philosophers, and journalists, Robert F. Morgan suggests that "if we enlarge the word iatrogenic to include any disorders caused by members of the *helping* professions in the process of helping, then we may hold accountable a more comprehensive range of disciplines and services actually affecting the consumer."[2]

The helping professions create iatrogenic, that is, unintended negative effects, in the very words they use to describe what helping is about. If we are to reject a culture of dependency on experts, we need to use a different vocabulary, to give ourselves a way to express new meanings, new beliefs, and a new faith in ourselves and in one another, rather than in experts. We need our own language, rather than one borrowed from a model of the physician as healer in whom we must have faith. We need to break down the strongly held belief in the doctor-patient relationship as the crucial ingredient in healing. We need to substitute a healing concept that is self-generating and regenerating rather than one that is controlled by others and scarce.[3]

It is not easy to get a handle on such ideas in a way that expresses them to the established professions, to government officials, policymakers, and to a general public raised in our culture of dependency on experts and technologies. The very language available is meager. To do so requires collaboration among mutual-help practitioners and social scientists. There are many millions of people who are in need of help. A recent epidemiological study by the National Institute of Mental Health suggests one of five Americans suffer, at some time in life, from some form of emotional difficulty;[4] and this does not take account of the myriad other problems in living. But most of these sufferers will suffer alone. Many will rely on their own individual and isolated efforts, all the while thinking they should seek professional help if they cannot solve their problems alone. Those

66

who do seek help will often be encouraged to accept blame for their failures and to attribute their successes to expert advice.

If we are to make it possible for more people to have access to alternative ways of dealing with their problems in living—ways that take them away from an excessive dependence on the scarce commodity of professional helpers and on a professionalized helping system—we need to provide people with a vocabulary and ideas that communicate something about their own ability to help themselves, and even to help others, independently of the formal professionalized helping systems.

We need a language that conveys a different set of beliefs, images, and realities about the relationship of the sufferers to themselves and to others. This is needed because the current language of helping is steeped in the iatrogenesis of dependency on scarce experts as a consumer item. That is, the language of helping itself, developed in both a medical and an independent business context, is iatrogenic because it suggests that we are dependent on experts whose help we must purchase. We need instead a language for helping that is steeped in symbols that communicate the powerful force for change contained within ourselves, our significant others, and our communities.

Placebos: Trivializing the Power of Self-Healing

An example of the problem we are facing is in the way medical and social science have interpreted so-called placebo effects. This is the name given to a wide variety of cures, changes, and processes, when there is found a positive impact of a supposedly inert or nonuseful treatment; that is, a positive effect when there is no real (professionally sanctioned) treatment. Given a belief in only professionally acceptable treatments, accounting for such effects in the absence of professionally correct treatments is a serious problem for scientific explanation. It is handled by the language of medicine in two ways: one is by denying that the effect is real, unless it can be attributed to the professional. The denial takes the form of calling it a "placebo effect." This choice of words is very powerful. It denigrates the effect as unimportant, as an "artifact," because it came from someplace outside the sanctioned treatment approaches. Rather than studying it, professionals and researchers generally exclude it from consideration as either not interesting or a confound. The second way it is handled is to attribute the placebo effect to the relationship between the

67

professional and the patient, so that the professional, or sanctioned treatments, are viewed as a necessary part of the process. Presumably, without
the existence of a relationship to a professional the effect would not occur.
If it does occur outside such a relationship, it is often called "spontaneous
remission," again, a denigrating term.

Ann Weick has recently presented an analysis of how the traditional
model of diagnosis and treatment forces us to rely on the relationship
between the healer and the sufferer, even to explain the placebo effect.[5] In
order to understand the effect, we are asked to rely on the healer's ability
to mobilize forces within the sufferer. She points out that the way we are
taught to think about healing is to focus our hope on, and belief in, the
person designated as healer. In the course of scientific experiments this
force or belief is found to be so strong that it is necessary to "control" for
placebo effects. In this context what is sought is to eliminate from consideration those effects that are presumed to be due to the patient's belief
in a treatment or a treater, rather than those that are a consequence of the
drug administered or the therapeutic technique per se.

Weick suggests that in most of the explanations of the power of the
placebo effect the professional healer is given credit. It is assumed that the
change is best accounted for through the real or imagined power of the
professional caregiver, in the eyes of the patient. The caregiver is seen as
the most salient feature in the dynamics of getting well, because the patient
believes in him or her. Attribution "of the effect to the caregiver is simply
an expression of a belief in the medical model which is based on the
concept that professional treatment is the vehicle for change and that
without it good effects can not be achieved."[6] To the extent that this view
is held, all of the people who have not received professional help — because
they can not afford it, are intimidated by the system, or have had bad
experiences with it—are deprived not only of faith in the professional
caregivers but also of the possibility of faith in alternative methods of help.

Most important is Weick's suggestion of an alternative way to think
about the so-called placebo effect, not as an artifact or as a demonstration
of the power of belief in the professional, but rather as a demonstration of
the reality that individuals can be the source of their own healing. In her
words: "It suggests that the capacity to 'get well' is inherent in individuals
and exists whether or not there is an external agent such as a professional.
. . . In essence this view is based on the belief that human beings have the
innate capacity to be the source of their own change and that the process
of self-healing is one expression of that capacity."[7]

Weick argues that "because of cultural conditioning, self-healing is generally activated only in conjunction with standard medical or therapeutic practice. . . . one could assume that the capacity for change is inherent in people and can be self-motivated." [8] To this I would add that it might also be found to be activated by significant others in our life. We already know, from many studies, that there is good evidence that social support can serve as both a buffer and a reducer of the effects of life stress. [9]

One step toward making this kind of assumption about self-healing accessible to people, i.e., to make it more a part of our culture, is to begin to talk about empowerment as the vehicle for handling problems in living and for releasing a positive self-healing force. Let us talk in terms of empowering one another, not in medical language with words such as "cure" or even "prevention" (which assumes prevention of a disease by an expert). We need to develop a cultural alternative and to create both symbols and a language of belief in the power of ourselves to both help ourselves and to help others. If the force contained in the so-called placebo effect is seen to reside in the person, and if it is released by belief, then we can—we must—develop a language and a symbolism that fosters belief in each other, rather than in powerful others. Empowerment is potentially one such symbol because it does not have a history of being used in reference to an expert. "Empowerment" is, rather, a word that conjures up a different imagery.

Defining Empowerment

Empowerment is like obscenity; you have trouble defining it but you know it when you see it. It seems to be missing in people who feel helpless. Although it is easy to intuit, it is a very complex idea to define because it has components that are both psychological and political. The word is used by psychologists and social workers, and by sociologists and political scientists, as well as by theologians. It suggests a sense of control over one's life in personality, cognition, and motivation. It expresses itself at the level of feelings, at the level of ideas about self-worth, and at the level of being able to make a difference in the world around us, and even at the spiritual level. It is an ability that we all have, but that needs to be released, much the way our bodies can be self-healing when endorphins are released. We all have the potential. It does not need to be purchased, nor is it a scarce commodity.

The outcome of empowerment is difficult to define because it is not in itself consistent with any particular goal or political point of view. It is easy to see its absence: powerlessness, real or imagined, learned helplessness, alienation, loss of a sense of control over one's life. It is more difficult to define positively because it takes on different forms in different people and contexts. Empowerment for a poor, uneducated black woman can look very different than for a middle-class college student or a thirty-nine-year-old businessman, a white urban housewife, or a single elderly person resisting placement in a nursing home.

Nevertheless, using "empowerment" to name the force that releases powers of self-cure is very different from saying that the change in the absence of professionally sanctioned help is a "placebo effect." One suggests powerful processes at work; the other trivializes. When the idea of empowerment is combined with the goal of mutuality, an even more exciting idea emerges: mutual empowerment enhances the possibilities for people to control their own lives and has serious implications for professionals.

If empowerment is our aim, we will find ourselves questioning both our public policy and our relationship to dependent people. We will not settle for a public policy of programs designed, operated, or packaged for social agencies to use on people, because we will require that the form and the unspoken implications, as well as the content, be consistent with empowerment. It will cause us to confront the paradox that even the people who are most incompetent, in need, and apparently unable to function require more, rather than less, control over their own lives; and that fostering more control does not necessarily mean ignoring them. Empowerment presses a different set of metaphors upon us than the traditional helping model.

An empowerment ideology has at least two requirements. First, it demands that we look to many diverse local settings where people are already handling their own problems in living so that we can learn more about how they do it. Second, it demands that we find ways to take what we learn and make it more, rather than less, likely that others not now handling their own problems in living, or shut out from current solutions, gain control over their lives. For both of these requirements, self- and mutual-help groups are a potential source for intervention and learning.

70

We must begin to develop a social policy that gives up the search for one monolithic way of doing things according to *the* certified expert. A bottom-up mapping of social policy rather than a top-down process starts with people's telling officials what social policies and programs are necessary.[10] This means that empowerment will not only look different, depending on what sort of problems in living one is confronting, but it may even look different within each setting that it operates. Diversity rather than homogeneity of form should dominate if the operating process is empowerment.

Marc Zimmerman, a graduate student at Illinois, defines empowerment for his dissertation research. Empowerment, he finds,

> links individual strengths, and competencies, natural helping systems, and proactive behaviors to social policy and social change. . . . empowerment can be understood at different levels of analysis. For example, organizations can be empowering because they influence policy decisions or because they provide settings for individuals to feel in control of their own lives. A community can be empowered because the citizens engage in activities that maintain or improve the quality of life and respond to community needs. . . .
>
> Psychological empowerment logically includes beliefs about one's competence and efficacy as well as one's involvement in activities for exerting control in the social and political environment. The construct assumes a proactive approach to life, a psychological sense of efficacy and control, socio-political activity, and organizational involvement. To understand empowerment one must understand how people integrate themselves into their community so it is seen to work for them not on them. . . .
>
> Self and political efficacy, perceived competence, locus of control, and self-esteem appear to be logically related to the construct of psychological empowerment. The empowered individual is also thought to be one who can critically analyze the social and political environment. This enables the person to make choices to effectively engage conflict and change. Consequently, psychological empowerment may be seen as both a feeling of perceived control and the critical

71

awareness of knowing when to confront powerful others and when to avoid them.[11]

Empowerment is not something that can be given; it must be taken. What those who have it and want to share it can do is to provide the conditions and the language and beliefs that make it possible to be taken by those who are in need of it. That is one role the mutual-help organization can play.

Community Mental Health and Mutual Help through Empowerment

The role of the professional involves providing first, the sense of purpose and direction for people's efforts in a cultural context, and, second, a metaphor, a rationale, a set of symbols like empowerment, which differ from the kind of symbols and context Illich critiques in the medical industry. It is consistent with the kind offered by the self- and mutual-help movement.

It is also consistent with the ideal of community mental health, and it is now possible for self-help leaders and community mental health leaders to come together on common ground, especially if they both seek empowerment. The ideology of the community mental health movement can be consistent with the rise in legitimacy of self-help groups. In many ways people coming together out of mutual concern—not for pay, nor as volunteers, but rather as peers mutually sharing their lives, without professional intervention—is the ideal of a strength-based, preventively oriented, empowering mental health system. In many respects community mental health professionals and self-help organizations are natural allies.

My own recent work with colleagues at the University of Illinois, who have developed a close working relationship with members of a large mutual-help organization, is an example of this sort of collaboration in research.[12] We are participant-observers and colleagues, as well as evaluation researchers. As researchers, we have found that our collaboration has enhanced our ability to understand how a mutual-help organization achieves its aims with many people for whom the traditional mental health system of in-patient and out-patient services has been of little help. They have assisted us in the formulation of research questions, and we have been feeding back our results and observations. We are discovering how an organization of lay people, in this case an organization called GROW, which targets its membership at those with a history of mental illness, could expand in Illinois from six to almost one hundred groups in four years.

Although this research project is still in progress, one of the things we think we are finding is that the ability of the organization to reach people who are outside the mental health system can be improved, or hindered, by the attitudes and behaviors of the local mental health professionals. It is *not* that the organization is controlled by the mental health professionals so much as that the professionals can either be useful or serve as barriers to the mutual-help organization. For example, GROW has developed at very different rates in different parts of the state, largely, we think, as a function of professional support or resistance, which, not incidentally, includes financial support.

By simple weight of referral, or refusal to refer, from people who are seen by others as mental health authorities; by encouragement or discouragement of individuals and groups; and by advocating for or against them with local governments and mental health officials, newspaper, television, and radio people, professionals enhance, or harm, their credibility and reach. That encourages or discourages people and policymakers from supporting or joining self-help groups.

I am also convinced that this is, or can be, a mutual process. If professionals advocate for self-help group members, they gain potentially important allies for their own future battles. It is important, in the fullest sense of empowerment, for members of self-help organizations to recognize their potential for social and political influence, and to use it.

Mutual-Help Organizations and Political Power

Mutual support is not a one-way street. The same principles that apply to members' relationships with one another also apply to relationships with professionals. It is important to recognize, in the best traditions of acknowledging the strengths of those with problems in living and in the full sense of empowerment, that there are over 500,000 self-help groups in the United States, with 15 million people.[13] If those in community mental health can bring their organizations, professional societies, staff, and resources to the service of those in the self-help movement, they will build a constituency. But to do so will require learning a lot about how to be genuine colleagues, and the only way to learn it is to do it. Collaboration is not control. Both sides can be empowered by a genuine mutual relationship. They can advocate for each other.

The Self-Help Ethos

The self-help ethos is not things being done *to* or *for* people, it is things done *with* people. "This does not preclude assistance from government or professionals, but it opposes a dependent orientation . . . it emphasizes giving help (and being helped by doing so), receiving help (and knowing how to receive help)." [14]

Similar relationships are found in places not normally thought of as self-help organizations. On any given weekend more people attend churches and synagogues than attend an entire season of NFL games. These settings are places where much help and community organization already takes place. Some of what goes on in religious settings is similar to what takes place in mutual-help organizations. For example, Ken Maton studied the activities of 150 members of a non-mainline religious community over nine months. He found that individuals who *both* provided and received material assistance from others reported greater life satisfaction than those who only provided or only received. [15] That is one of the basic tenets of mutual-help organizations.

Indeed, this finding has recently been replicated among self-help group participants. [16] A study of multiple sclerosis sufferers, Compassionate Friends, and Overeaters Anonymous found that those individuals who both provided and received social support obtained more benefits and satisfaction from their participation, had higher scores on a measure of self-esteem, and were less depressed than those who only provided or only received. This means that, in the realm of both material and social support, mutuality seems to have more positive outcomes than just providing or just receiving. The implications of this for professional caregivers are tremendous. Perhaps more of professional time should be spent in developing and supporting mutual rather than unilateral help.

Riessman points out that, unlike self-help, "professional help has been contextualized by the fact that the help provided is a commodity to be bought, sold, promoted, and marketed. . . . Since self-help does not have to encounter the constraints of the market, it can begin to develop helping combinations and patterns in novel, fresh ways unencumbered by professional assumptions." Self-help has fewer constraints of "time, place and format." And most crucially, "People in need are converted into resources . . . not only is the quality of help changed and viewed differently, but the quantity is enormously expanded."[17]

Again, our own work at Illinois has been finding research support for these observations. We have observed the GROW organization take people who were functioning in very limited ways, those with a history of previous emotional difficulties (about 75 percent of the Growers studied have been in a mental hospital prior to joining the organization), and provide roles and niches in which they become helpers for others.[18] We have seen them create what we have come to call, in Roger Barker's terminology, "undermanned settings."[19] These are settings which the organization purposely creates before they have enough people to handle the duties, i.e., new groups are begun before enough experienced leadership is available. These settings have fostered the development of their members because the members are needed to work in the settings, and are provided with a role, and supported in that role. It doesn't work for everyone, but it works for many who are the products of professional failures by the time they find the mutual-help organization.

With regard to the political potential of the self-help movement, Riessman has suggested that help obtained from joining with others who share in similar problems (mental health or neighborhood problems) creates a sense of control, rather than a sense of dependency. This empowerment, asserts Riessman, is energizing—it feeds on itself and has political relevance because it becomes contagious and spreads to other aspects of one's life.

There is already some research to suggest that this claim is correct, e.g., the work of Kieffer, who has followed the lives of people who have emerged from grassroots organizations.[20] Kieffer sees empowerment as a process of adult learning and development, and by a series of case studies has illustrated some of the process. In addition, there is the experience of people such as Judi Chamberlin and her organization, the Mental Patients Liberation Front. Their work suggests some of the potential for people who become empowered to teach professionals how to avoid applying to their clients the self-fulfilling prophecy of low expectations. Her "user-controlled alternatives" constitute an important challenge in terms of cooperation with community mental health workers. In some states, departments of mental health have already given this organization grants to provide a seven-day-a-week drop-in center and a teleconferencing system for organizing.[21] Community mental health professionals need to see such people as neither a threat nor competition, but rather as advocates for the same people on whose behalf professionals should be working.

Many (although not all) mutual-help groups seem to move naturally toward advocacy. Once this begins, the potential for social and political change is ripe. Many mutual-help groups have become involved in advocacy for legislative action such as MADD, the Gray Panthers, and the Association for Retarded Citizens. Neighborhood self-help groups that organize first on simple issues such as traffic lights can become citizen-action groups for environmental protection. Riessman describes this process of politicization as moving from the beginnings of empowerment, when people first feel they can control some aspect of their lives, through the development of advocacy roles, in which they discover external causes of their problems and learn to speak for themselves, to the emergence of a consciousness of the interconnections among issues.[22] Most crucially, he has pointed out that self-help groups do not necessarily become progressive political organizations, but rather, there is a battle to win their allegiance for a range of causes—from every part of the political spectrum. Yet Riessman sees progressives as having a real chance to win the support of the self-help movement through participation in "bottom-up" politics. I see this as a real chance for community mental health professionals to bolster the badly sagging community mental health movement. Again, members of self- and mutual-help organizations themselves will benefit from recognizing their own potential political influence.

If Riessman is correct, and I think he is, the self-help movement is part of a new populism. He sees several themes as important in that perspective: the "anti-big" theme, the "pro community" theme, and the emphasis on grassroots activity. In addition, the mutual-help theme stresses a contrast to individualism, and an obligation to help others. I believe this cooperative spirit harkens back to Nicholas Hobbs's original call for community mental health, and his plea for us to see that mental illness "is not the private organic misery of an individual, but a social, ethical, and moral problem, a responsibility of the total community."[23]

Finally, Riessman points out that government need be neither the enemy (as conservatives argue) nor the solution (as liberals argue). Rather, government can provide resources, listen, and monitor for equity. Here again is the need for collaboration among professionals, who often are the representatives of government-funded agencies and mutual-help organizations.

An Exemplary Program

A program of collaboration for empowerment described in a recent paper by Gallant, Cohen, and Wolff makes concrete much of what I have been saying.[24] Dissatisfied with traditional approaches to providing services for older people that are confined to individual, remedial interventions using professionals, these authors sought to develop, for an agency in Massachusetts, a program with the following motto: "Our best services are those that empower elders to discover their own strengths, their own talents, and their own solutions."

They sought to develop a system that would

combat stigmatization and ageism by fostering a positive sense of
aging and, . . . by promoting the concept that elders are
entitled to services as a result of being taxpayers . . . elders
themselves would be engaged in the process of program design
and in self-help so that they could become active advocates
for their best interests. Blaming the victim would be replaced by
consumer and political advocacy. . . . In sum, the system
would be designed to empower elders and endorse their
importance to society.

Starting with the definition of empowerment, these workers used it in their setting as a combination of political empowerment and provision of an array of choices of services, not a single option defined by others.

The agency, which blends local, state, and federal government elements, eventually used its discretionary funds to help support seven interlocking initiatives proposed by community residents and groups: a small research group to do economic needs and interests analysis, the Gray Panthers to strengthen advocacy, a cooperative food-buying club, a home energy assistance agent, a newsletter, a homemaker agency (including jobs development), and projects for physical and emotional health—all at a total cost of $50,000.

77

One of the most creative elements in the linked program of cooperative services was the building of a membership system. As they put it, "the membership system was envisioned as promoting empowerment, ownership, dignity, and entitlement by moving elders from a client status to a membership status. . . . The membership system automatically included every person over sixty in the 24 towns and communities covered by the agency. All elders were "entitled" to membership at no charge as a result of being taxpayers and elders."

In addition to sharing information and soliciting opinions via post-cards and newsletters, they developed several wellness programs that covered topics such as new images of aging, interpersonal skills, and exercise. The programs were structured so that members ultimately were trained to run groups in their own communities. Not only do they encourage self-help in terms of elders' health but also promotes a model whereby elders are empowered to become trainers of other elders in wellness. They added programs of statewide advocacy and political influence, including an organization representing 22,000 members that could talk to leaders of the business community about costs of food, fuel, and other commodities.

Such collaborative programming for empowerment is not only possible but is a reality. There are two keys to its success: One is the absolute commitment to an empowerment ideology in *both* language and deed, and the other is a genuine collaboration among the professional community and the members who are viewed, not as clients, but as resources. This venture is empowering in itself. It contributes to a new culture of mutual helping based, not on a dependence on experts, but rather on the power and dignity of people—power and dignity that only waits to be released by the proper circumstances.

Notes

1. Illich, *Medical Nemesis: The Expropriation of Health* (New York: Pantheon Books, 1976).

2. R. F. Morgan, ed., *The Iatrogenics Handbook* (Toronto: IPI Publishing, 1983), p. vi. For an expanded discussion of these issues, see also E. Seidman and J. Rappaport, eds., *Redefining Social Problems* (New York: Plenum, in press).

3. For a discussion of the implications for viewing helping as resource generating, or synergistic, rather than as a scarce commodity, see R. F. Katz, "Empowerment and Synergy:

Expanding the Community's Healing Resources," *Prevention in Human Services* 3 (1984):
201–26.

4. L. N. Robins, J. E. Helzer, and M. M. Weissman et al., "Lifetime Prevalence of Specific Psychiatric Disorders in Three Sites," *Archives of General Psychiatry* 49 (1984): 949–58.

5. A. Weick, "Issues in Overturning a Medical Model of Social Work Practice," *Social Work* 28 (1983): 467–71.

6. Ibid., p. 469.

7. Ibid.

8. Ibid.

9. S. Cohen and T. A. Wills, "Stress, Social Support, and the Buffering Hypothesis," *Psychological Bulletin* 98 (1985): 310–57.

10. R. F. Elmore, "Backward Mapping: Implementation Research and Policy Decisions," *Political Science Quarterly* 80 (1979): 601–16.

11. M. Zimmerman, "Empowerment, Perceived Control, and Citizen Participation: A Dissertation Proposal," submitted to the University of Illinois Psychology Department, Sept. 1985.

12. J. Rappaport, E. Seidman, P. A. Toro et al., "Collaborative Research with a Mutual-Help Organization," *Social Policy* 15 (1985): 12–24.

13. F. Riessman, "New Dimensions in Self-Help," *Social Policy* 15 (1985): 2–4.

14. Ibid.

15. K. Maton, "Economic Sharing among Church Members: Psychological Correlates and Evaluation of an Economic Barter-Sharing Service" (Ph.D. diss., University of Illinois at Urbana-Champaign, 1985).

16. K. Maton, "How Do Self-Help Groups Help?: Social Support, Organizational Characteristics, and Psychological Well-Being in Three Self-Help Populations" (MS in preparation, University of Maryland, Baltimore County).

17. F. Riessman, "New Dimensions," p. 2.

18. T. Reischl, L. McFadden, and M. Zimmerman, "GROW as a Social Movement Organization," paper presented at the Annual Meeting of the American Psychological Association, Toronto, 1984.

19. R. Barker, *Ecological Psychology* (Stanford, Cal.: Stanford University Press, 1969).

20. C. H. Kieffer, "Citizen Empowerment: A Developmental Perspective," *Prevention in Human Services* 3 (1984): 9–36.

21. J. Chamberlin, *On Our Own: Patient Controlled Alternatives to the Mental Health System* (New York: McGraw Hill, 1979); J. Chamberlin, "Concept Paper: Ex-patient Self-Help Groups," prepared for the Seventh CSP Learning Community Conference, Mental Patient's Liberation Front, P.O. Box 314, Cambridge, MA 02238.

22. Riessman, "New Dimensions."

23. N. Hobbs, "Mental Health's Third Revolution," *American Journal of Orthopsychiatry* 34 (1964): 822–33.

24. R. V. Gallant, C. Cohen, and T. Wolff, "Empowerment in Elders: Repositioning an Area Agency on Aging System," *Perspectives on Aging*, in press.

Three

POPULISM TODAY: THE MAINSTREAM APPEAL

Five

Robert Coles

A WORKING PEOPLE'S POLITICS:

BOSTON'S MAYOR FLYNN

Since 1932 the liberalism of the Democratic Party has been, significantly, an initiative of the well-to-do academic people, lawyers, and high government functionaries who have put their ideas into the political policies of a succession of national administrations. This liberalism has its origins not only in the minds of particular thinkers, writers, advisors, and candidates but in the genteel streets where one can express sympathy for a suffering, exploited "them," can think up solutions for "their" problems, all the while feeling no need to scrutinize one's assumptions or one's way of living. With respect to the so-called social issues, this liberalism was easy-going; indeed, was often indifferent. The point was to help the poor, to take from capitalism its rough edges, to respond to the pain of the marginal, the vulnerable, the dispossessed—and to let the intelligentsia, the upper bourgeoisie, go about their thoroughly influential business.

The populist tradition has quite different political and moral roots. The nineteenth-century populists were farmers and the urban poor who came together out of the immediate, concrete needs of their everyday lives. They were not organized by patrician politicians or well-off outsiders anxious to make a political and historical point. They organized themselves. They were at once radical and conservative. They denounced Wall Street and other important American social and economic institutions with a vehemence that embarrassed the "progressives" of their time, and they would not be especially attractive to today's liberals. They were also conservative on so-called family issues, and unashamedly patriotic. They often succumbed to racist innuendo and worse—the unrelenting frustration and bitter disappointment that can turn decent folk into mean and suspicious ones. This populism, localist and working class, disappeared as a cohesive political movement at the turn of the century, but its split heritage persists in both our parties—the Democrats in their call for economic justice, in their denunciation of the vested interests, the Republicans standing strong for the flag and their espousal of "traditional" family values.

Sometimes as I watched the 1984 Democratic convention, or have read the many, largely favorable analyses of or stories about Boston's Mayor Raymond Flynn, or New York's Governor Mario Cuomo, two so-called populist Yankee politicians who seem to offer hope to a political party said to be beleaguered and drifting, I remember how it was twenty years ago, when the nation's attention was very much directed south. A young president from Massachusetts had been replaced fatefully by his Texas vice-president. The Mississippi Summer project of 1964, an effort by hundreds of college students, many from Ivy League schools, to challenge the bastion of segregation, had captured the nation's moral imagination by late June, when three youths were missing and presumed dead at the hands of the Klan. At the end of the summer, Freedom Houses throughout the Delta had survived intense hostility, and the Democratic convention, sure to nominate President Johnson, nevertheless felt a strong rumble of black protest, a portent of what Jesse Jackson would later have to offer.

White southerners had their own reasons, of course, to mock the motives, not to mention the political purposes and ethical vision of these young northerners, most of whom were from a rather privileged social and economic background. In turn, those of us living and working in those Freedom Houses had our own ready-made explanations for any criticism or comment sent our way by the Mississippi press, or the ordinary white people we met in stores, banks, post offices. Those overheard remarks were racist, as were many of the editorials that appeared in local newspapers. As for the suggestion that we go home and tend to our own political problems, our own inequalities and injustices, it was not hard to summon a psychological response: the people so anxious to have us depart were rationalizing their real reasons with a sudden, counterfeit interest in Chicago's troubles, or those of New York City or Boston.

It was harder, however, to ignore the following observations, made one early August night in the Canton, Mississippi, Freedom House by a white southern youth (from Georgia) who had gone north to Yale, only to return as a full-fledged civil rights activist. Years afterward I would play segments of the tape I had of his strongly stated opinions—and note, always, how uncomfortable they made my Harvard students, not to mention me:

> This is all great for us. We're the young heroes who have come
> from our fancy colleges to change the world of these poor
> folks! We tell the colored folks we're going to help them out;
> we'll stand up for them. We tell the white folks to watch
> out, there's a new day coming, and we're ushering it in. The
> Negroes are suspicious, lots of them; they know we're
> headed home fast—in time to register in New Haven and
> Cambridge and Princeton and at the University of Chicago,
> or at the Berkeley campus, and when we're choosing our fall
> term courses, they'll be doing what they've been always
> doing, dealing with "the man," trying to get the most mileage
> possible with very little going for them.
>
> And "the man"—who's *he?* Have any of us this summer tried to
> see who these folks are? I know, I know—we're not even
> sure we'll survive the summer, because some of the white people
> in this county and in the other counties where we've come
> have told us right to our faces they'd like to see us dead. But
> what the devil have they got going for themselves? What
> kind of life are they living? Are they the ones who own and run
> the state of Mississippi? They rant and rave about the
> "niggers," but just look at the facts and figures about white

people in Mississippi, and my home state of Georgia:
there's the few who have a lot, and the many who haven't got
much—and if you ask me (if you ask *them*, actually!), the
one thing they've had going for them, through thick and thin,
mostly thin, has been their skin, their lovely white skin! It's
sadder than hell for them and their colored neighbors, and it's
sadder than hell for us, too. They tell us to go home and
tend to our own problems; and we say they're just a bunch of
no-good haters—and no wonder it's so hard to make
change here. The poor people and the people who just manage
to get by—they're at each other's throats, Negro against
white. I suppose we're helping to shake things up a little this
summer, but in the long run there's an even bigger problem
than race down here, and maybe there's the same problem up
North, too—the Populist dream that never worked out.

He had taken his fair share of history courses, knew that strictly
speaking the Populists were a predominantly southern and western alliance of small farmers who fought long and hard their considerable exploitation at the hands of the railroads and the banks in the form of high
transportation costs and interest rates. He knew, too, that in the late nineteenth century the Populist movement had rallied considerable political
support, but not enough to change the nature of American capitalism.
The farmers remained poor and vulnerable; the banks and railroads, as
powerful as ever. By the early years of the twentieth century, the Republican Party, once a voice of western egalitarianism that gave the nation
Abraham Lincoln, had become steadily more wedded to big capital and
an increasingly expansionist corporate life. The Democratic Party was
much the property of the traditional and conservative white South. There
the blacks were almost totally disfranchised, and poor whites voted again
and again for racist demogogues who, on economic matters, played cozy
with the handful of businesses and financial institutions that owned what
wealth there was in an essentially backward region.

Large immigrant populations were, of course, settling in our northern
cities, but they had yet to obtain political significance. It is important to
emphasize that the Populists of the nineteenth century regarded both the
Democratic and the Republican parties as unresponsive to their personal
needs, their moral outlook. Nor did those Populists embrace socialism, or

for that matter, the kind of progressive platform Theodore Roosevelt or Woodrow Wilson would soon enough propose. Populism was reformist, all right—but insistently suspicious of bureaucracies, be they private or public. Populists had seen the federal government sponsor and subsidize the railroads, whose excesses had eventually driven so many hardworking, perplexed, frustrated farmers to ruin. Populists espoused a localist cooperativism and, always, democratic principles. Populists worried prophetically that if the government can have the power to help the needy, it can also exert its authority over the poor or the not-so-poor, the working people of the country—as Raymond Flynn and Mario Cuomo discovered early in their careers. Still, those same Populists had nowhere else but Washington to go, really, for the kind of help they wanted and needed —the case today for compassionate political leaders such as Mayor Flynn and Governor Cuomo.

Some Populists fell victim to the accumulated failures of their political movement. They saw elections bought and sold. They saw newspapers lie, businessmen cheat, government officials deceive, and professors or doctors or lawyers ingratiate themselves shamelessly with those who had money and power. Soon enough Catholics and Jews were being blamed for everything; and there was, of course, the always convenient scapegoat, the blacks. This sad and ugly side of American Populism (the frustration of the down-and-out become their wild outpouring of hate), cannot be denied, only understood and, maybe, remembered today as the Reverend Farrakhan has his say—the way the historian C. Vann Woodward does in his classic, *Tom Watson: Agrarian Rebel*, wherein the moral decline of a bright, sensitive, and eloquent Populist leader is painstakingly chronicled. Watson's efforts as a young man to change Georgia's laws and commercial arrangements in order to help the poor of both races and to establish a more honest, equitable social order were thwarted at every turn, often by flagrantly manipulated elections. Eventually he soured on himself and his own years of outspoken good will. He became a bitter racist and dropped his earlier interest in changing a particular economic order. He was now "safe"—no threat to unregulated, greedy banks and railroad companies that were bleeding the South dry through soaring rates. His election victories were, thereupon, allowed to stand untouched by crooked manipulation. He became a great power in the South, in the United States Senate —or rather, a convenient instrument of the power possessed by others. His hysterical suspicion of blacks, Jews, and Catholics apparently offended

87

few of the genteel members of the Georgia upper class—glad, no doubt, to have all those white yeoman, or those country folk settled in towns and cities, enthralled by the excitements of religious and racial innuendo.

We all know what Franklin Roosevelt did as president, how he rallied all sorts of people to the cause of New Deal reformist politics, how he used the government resourcefully and insistently (to the screaming outrage of corporate leaders, bankers and brokers, newspaper owners and their editorial writing employees), and how he mobilized an unprecedented constituency that included hitherto strangers and antagonists— poor southern whites and black sharecroppers or tenant farmers, midwestern farmers and big-city working people who had just arrived here from Ireland and Italy and Greece and Poland and Russia. It was a miraculous political transformation, one still alive in certain respects, but without its earlier influence. When the Great Depression gave way to the prosperity of World War II, and then the Cold War (nearly half of our postwar budgets have gone to military expenditures), millions felt themselves newly comfortable and secure, less interested in a government that helps the needy and more interested in a government that might tax the relatively well-off a bit less, even hand them a few bonuses or breaks—so that, for instance, their children might go to private schools through the courtesy of a deductible expense.

Moreover, the same federal government that had helped distribute food to hungry people in the 1930s, that had tried valiantly to provide work for the jobless, build housing for those virtually homeless, clean out the liars and crooks from Wall Street, establish a reliable and honest banking system, encourage through loans small businesses and farmers, was now (in the 1950s and beyond) exerting its considerable leverage in new directions—the so-called social legislation of the past forty years, much of it a matter of enfranchising and then helping in various other ways (school desegregation, fair housing legislation) those minority groups whose general circumstances had been least affected by New Deal laws. No wonder the youth quoted above would add this comment a week or so later to his recorded remarks—the result of an intense exchange on the subjects of "populism" and "social change" by certain members of a particular Freedom House:

> I don't see how we'll get the kind of new voting coalition
> together we need. Lots of people deserted the Democrats

for Eisenhower, and only some of them came back to Kennedy.
They say Johnson will win in a landslide, but maybe so. . . .
But I hear my own parents talk, and others I know—people
only one or two generations away from their poor
immigrant ancestors—and I wonder what's happening, or going
to happen in this country. My father says he grew up
thinking Franklin Roosevelt was Jesus Christ, but frankly, my
father now talks more and more like the people who fought
Roosevelt all during the 1930s. I think our Southern politics
has moved up North.

The rest, so to speak, is our recent history—the twenty years that
proved the above-quoted youth, among others, all too far-sighted. I well
remember hearing, in the middle and late 1960s, ordinary working people
(never mind those as well-off as his parents) speak their discontent, their
apprehension, their outrage—not directed, by then, at Roosevelt's enemies (the "economic royalists" he would mention) but at those who,
ironically, regarded themselves as his heirs, namely—well, let a man who
(from 1967 to 1975) worked in the Lynn, Massachusetts, General Electric factory briefly spell out their characteristics and purposes.

All those people, they're always itching to help someone else,
but who picks up the check? It's us! We're the ones who
are supposed to be no good, or prejudiced. We're the ones
whose kids have to go through all the violence of
desegregation. Those rich liberals—they live in the nice, pleasant
suburbs, and send their kids to private schools, and give us
lectures on how we should behave. If we don't do what they
want, they try to get some government department to start
pushing, pushing, pushing on us. Look at what's happening to
this country! My son is fighting overseas for this country,
and these people are dragging the flag through the streets, the
American flag, and shouting swear words and behaving like
freaks. What do they all stand for? Not for what I was brought
up to stand for—my country, my home and my
neighborhood, my church. They want to change everything,
meddle in everything, and they think they can get the
government to do anything they want, through those federal

courts! How can you vote for that Nixon, my mother said.
I'll tell you how, I told her; and I did, twice!

For years I've heard such comments, some more eloquent and detailed
in their account of hurt feelings, deep suspicions—a sense that many
neighborhoods were being selectively branded as impossibly segregated or
racist, for instance, while the well-to-do and well educated had their own
ways of avoiding social pain or personal sacrifice, and as well, had their
own arrogant meanness, all unnoticed, it seems, by important and influential journalists or essayists, not to mention politicians. Nixon's phrase
"middle Americans" was meant to describe people like the man just
quoted and reach out to them politically. He succeeded. The second time
around he won every state but one. Only Watergate ended his dream of a
dramatically realigned politics—with millions of so-called working-class
Americans voting for him and, presumably, others like him, willing to
give voice to certain rising resentments in hitherto traditionally Democratic voters. Though Watergate set up the assertively pious and honest
outsider Jimmy Carter for the presidency, by 1980, with the election of
Ronald Reagan, the same politics Nixon saw to be promising had once
again won a strong victory.

Surely, in 1984 a similar politics of class and race, both, figured
prominently. Early in 1980 I saw Reagan stickers on the cars of families
long proud to be called Democrats—and heard from them comments
not unlike those quoted above. True, the high inflation rate had added
additional discontent, but for many traditional urban Democrats Carter
emerged as a curiously wooden, hesitant figure—indeed, an outsider.
Someone much given to moral abstractions, and someone clearly unable
in their minds to appreciate and respond to their neighborhood worries,
their fear that inflation was eroding not only their savings, but what little
social status they had, their patriotic passions, their everyday, concrete,
earthy lives, which they felt to be endangered by the self-righteous intru-
sions of federal judges, the liberal intelligentsia (with its control of television, the important newspapers and magazines), and the politicians who
took their cues from them.

Irony asserts itself in public life, however, as in other realms of human
experience—and so we have the interesting, present-day success of figures
like Mayor Raymond Flynn of Boston and Governor Mario Cuomo of
New York, two Democrats being hailed everywhere as able to bring to-

gether the old Roosevelt coalition. Both of these fine men possess personal and political backgrounds that surely qualified them, a decade ago, as leading spokesmen for the kind of social conservatism the Republicans were (and still are) anxious to assert.

In the early 1970s Ray Flynn was struggling on behalf of his native South Boston—trying hard to stop a federal judge from integrating through busing that neighborhood's high school. As a state representative and as a private citizen he was also fighting hard against newly legalized abortion—another court-ordered break with what had seemed to be a strong tradition in Massachusetts and other states as well. In the early 1970s Mario Cuomo was a Queens attorney who was trying to thwart the efforts of a liberal mayor (John Lindsay) and his political allies to further housing integration—build high-rise projects for poor people, many of them black and Puerto Rican, in neighborhoods where, again, working-class people (Italians, Jews, Irish, and Polish people) had been living for a generation or two. What has happened in one decade to make such obscure figures who seemed to be part of a "white backlash" (as it was called at the time) today's hope of many Democrats who once called themselves "liberal" and now favor "progressive"?

For Ray Flynn, who is forty-four years old, the answer is not all that hard to find. He does not see himself as having experienced some sudden, miraculous conversion. He sees himself as where he is because he has tried for many years to help his own neighbors, and others like them, get through all sorts of difficult times. He was born in South Boston to a poor struggling, hard-working Irish immigrant family. His father was a longshoreman who contracted tuberculosis when his children were young. He went to a Catholic elementary school, to South Boston High School, to Dominican-run Providence College in Rhode Island, on scholarship. He was an athlete, a potential professional basketball player. Instead he became interested in the troubled youth of his neighborhood and in 1965 became a probation officer in the Suffolk Superior Court:

> I did investigations; I was a case worker, a probation officer. I
> followed the progress of these people, and worked hard to
> get them on the honest, law-abiding road. I liked the work. I
> came to know a lot of families. It was this way that I first
> learned about the neighborhoods in Boston—what their
> problems were. You talk with someone who has gone

91

wrong, and soon you're finding out what's been happening to
others—the problems they have finding jobs, the sickness
in their family, and what it can take out of their pocket books,
their savings (everything!). I think I ran for office because I
kept realizing that there was only so much I could do, being a
case worker.

Not that he discovered himself omnipotent as a state legislator, or
later (1978 to 1983) a Boston City councilor. He was devoted to the
families of South Boston, mostly working people or poor people. In
1974, when a federal judge (who lived in the affluent town of Wellesley,
well to the west of Boston) ordered the children of mostly working black
people or poor black people to go to South Boston High School by bus,
and the white children of "Southie" to attend hitherto all-black schools in
Roxbury, also courtesy of a bus ride, the city of Boston exploded with
bitterness, anxiety, fear, and no small amount of hate. Nor was it only a
matter of whites feeling put upon, used, in the interests of what they saw
to be a grand social engineering scheme—while suburban folks enjoyed
the safety their moneyed situation provides, and too, received immunity
from public examination of *their* attitudes, *their* limitations, if not outright
animosities and prejudices. As I well remember, many black families I was
then visiting in the course of my studies of northern school children were
frightened and perplexed, too. They realized that they were being, yet
again, shuffled from one set of inadequate schools to another—and for
what? they kept asking. They realized, too, that the sympathy they received
from some liberals who resided outside the city of Boston, in towns where
few or no blacks lived, was essentially gestural in nature: "Their kids go to
private schools, even when they live in those high-class suburbs—and
then they say they're all for us black folks, and they're all against the racist
bigots over in South Boston. Great! But a lot of good their cheering does
us—because they're so far away from us, we can't even hear the noise!"
As for the white people Ray Flynn represented, they were (many of
them, at least) alarmed, indeed, if not fearfully, angrily out of control.
Some mouthed the most awful of obscenities, in front of "their" high
school, and in the privacy of the home, the backyard, the local grocery
store, the restaurant or bar. Some tried to transfer their children to parochial schools, though there were few openings. Some moved, and quickly,
to the safety, as they saw it, of so-called streetcar suburbs (the relatively
less affluent towns that hug Boston to the south and north and west). But

most of South Boston's people were too poor to move; most stayed and worried and (sometimes) took to the streets in rage and resentment—and (slowly) accepted a given legal and educational reality.

Such a time—the past decade, actually—tested not only a vulnerable people ("a marginal socioeconomic population" in the cold abstract language of sociology) but their leaders, many of whom had a hard time distinguishing themselves from their most vocally agitated followers. "Those were the years when Ray Flynn's character was really tested," a South Boston priest told me several years ago, as I was finishing up my work in his parish. He meant that Flynn deeply sympathized with the ordeal his constituents were experiencing but could not stomach the intensely mean passions generated by this worst crisis his neighborhood had ever experienced.

Flynn remembers those recent years as "tough," as "confusing." No wonder he tried a part-time return to school:

> I went to Harvard's School of Education. I got a master's degree
> there in 1981. I wanted to understand what various experts
> (the ones who teach, the ones who write books) thought about
> our urban problems, including the racial tensions we've
> been having. I learned a lot. One thing I learned was that *we've*
> been learning a lot, people like those of us who are white
> and live in South Boston or black and live in Roxbury: we've
> learned through these hard years of suspicion and conflict.
> Some of my teachers over there [at Harvard] told us that they
> learned something, too—how dangerous it is to talk about
> something going on from a distance. I know these books [in his
> office, at which he nods] are important, but it's also
> important to listen to people, and learn from them.

That is his great strength as a mayor. He was elected to the office after a surprise primary upset, in which he overcame other candidates with far more support from Boston's various social, cultural, and economic elites. Kevin White's last year or two were not his best. He had been elected to four consecutive four-year terms and by his own admission had made his fair share of mistakes, accumulated his enemies. He had been a mayor who helped change Boston's downtown business district, a mayor who enabled dozens of buildings to be built, a mayor much admired by the city's bankers and lawyers (many residents of towns a substantial distance from Boston). Meanwhile, in the city's neighborhoods, black and white alike, ordinary people had not been doing so well—men, women, and children unseen by or even unknown to the tourists who visit the posh restaurants and clothing stores of the Quincy Market, or to the businessmen who hurry from the Logan Airport to State Street, where stockbrokers and realtors and their ever-eager attorneys are to be found in abundance.

Those who have big offices on State Street and its environs obviously own wealth, wield power—but are not necessarily regarded by Boston's working people as interested, considerate friends. Ray Flynn reached out to those working people—did so with an energy, a sincerity, a compassion not seen in Boston for several generations. He went tirelessly, eagerly to neighborhood meetings. He heard just about everyone's complaints. He tried to intervene for dozens of ordinary citizens in dozens of ways. Everywhere he was familiar, accessible, concerned, ready to respond—and the result was not only his victory, but a sense among thousands of plain people living on plain streets of a city known for its symphony orchestra and educational institutions and hospitals and colonial history that somehow *their* significance had, at least, been affirmed.

In a runoff Flynn had faced the strong candidacy of Mel King, a black man and also a social worker. It was a courteous, utterly decent campaign —as if Boston's recent (and nationally known) racism had at last found itself a stranger all over the city. Flynn's strong victory was no signal for him that he settle into City Hall and behave as a big-deal bureaucrat. He has, rather, kept on being what he has always been, an attentive healer to those who are hurt, hungry, frail, needy. As one watches him on the move, always on the move, going to one neighborhood meeting after another (racial tensions, housing squabbles, the dire medical and financial emergencies of particular families, the sewage problems of a harbor, the affront to the eyes and to the health of litter, the matter of raising enough tax money to make ends meet, the struggle to trim a bloated budget and curtail patronage), an impression grows of a man seized by great moral energy, ever anxious to live up to a mix of Catholic piety and the kind of politics he acknowledges as his moral sponsor: "Franklin D. Roosevelt, John McCormack, Hubert Humphrey—they're my heroes: they tried to help average American families with all their might; they gave everything they had to that kind of politics; they were a people's kind of politician." That said, he pulls back, worries about the risk of being sentimental: "It's tough, to be in politics. I know. But what's the point, if you can't be of help to those who most need help. That's what I want to do."

94

He can drive his own loyal aides crazy (not to mention a waiting interviewer) as he breaks all the rules of the orderly (at all cost) impersonal bureaucracy. He sees someone on the street who has gotten hurt, whose car has broken down, who is getting rough treatment from someone else, and he stops, and looks, and listens, and soon enough, tries to do what he can: make a phone call, help push the car, get an ambulance or the police over, fast. In a novel titled *The Case Worker*, published here in 1974, the Hungarian writer George Konrád evokes a particular bureaucrat's struggle with himself, with the organization of which he is part, with others he meets in the course of his life—the children he sees as a welfare worker, as a person who mediates between troubled people and the institutions that ought (and often do not) serve them. It was a powerful story, brilliantly rendered in lean, suggestive prose. Out of all the wretchedness and frailty portrayed, out of all the hypocrisy and betrayal and deceit given representation, a strange, unpretentious, surprising dignity emerges, that of the case worker, actually, who does not pretend to any special virtue other than that of a willing endurance, propelled (the reader begins to realize) by a good heart, a stoic one, too.

Ray Flynn is now Boston's "case worker" at large, it seems, and as for his purposes, not to mention his purported limitations, he is quite direct and instructive—a reminder that some people do not write articles or books, yet manage, quite blessedly, not only to say what matters morally, but much harder, to live according to their espoused tenets:

When I started this job, I began to read, after a few weeks, that I was grandstanding. I was riding on snow plows or ambulances or fire trucks for TV coverage. . . . Look, if I spent all my time over there [his head moves in the direction of Boston's big banks and law firms], sitting holding hands with those people, or over there [his head moves in the direction of the well-known universities], would I *then* get lectures on how I'm spending my time, or how I should be spending my time? I'll bet not! I'll bet I'd be called a real responsible mayor, who does what he should—takes his orders and advice from the right people. . . .

The first thing I did was make *anyone* welcome to this office. I want to do all I can to keep this place open. Access is important—for everyone in the city, not just the people who are called "big" and "important." I remember when I was a kid

95

liking Harry Truman. He had a common touch when he got into
that office in Washington, and he never lost it. This city
has its troubles, all cities do. All people do, and all families do.
But in families you stick together, for the good of all, and
that's what a mayor has to try to help bring to a city, people in
there pitching in together.

There is in this man an essential modesty that uncannily mixes with a
fierce, energetic, knowing determination to forge a strong bond between a
particular city's political authority and its various ethnic, social, cultural,
racial groups—to bring a New England "family" of sorts together. Raymond Flynn has never made any great effort to put his past behind him,
to move on and up, as many avowedly ambitious and successful people do
and are urged to do in this consumerist society: get away from one's
earlier neighborhood, break one's ethnic ties, go to the "best" schools,
where one blends into a composite America, an America where one is
known by a whole range of secular, if not commercial, labels—someone
who is, say, a lawyer or an advertising man, a doctor or a businessman,
and someone who lives in a town where the houses sell at x figure, the
average family income is y figure, and someone who has gone to Harvard
or Yale or Columbia or the University of Michigan or the University of
California, and someone who takes cues about how to eat and dress and
otherwise spend money from advertisements in the newspaper or any
number of magazines.

We have been hearing of late that America is newly conservative. Raymond Flynn knows better. America has always been profoundly conservative in certain respects: the long-standing Puritan tradition, not completely
extinct, energized by wave after wave of Catholics, Lutherans, Presbyte-
rians, deeply pious Jews, members of the Greek Orthodox church—and
simple peasants or artisans who may not have looked to God, but who
wanted not only material success but a strongly disciplined personal life
for themselves and their kin. To be sure, there have been increasingly
numerous departures from such a conservatism—a social ideology (to
repeat: long hours of labor, thrift, sacrifice for the next generation, a
strong family life) often buttressed by religious convictions. But we often
note digressions, rebellions, transformations, outright reversals—and forget those millions who are less apt to march in the street, who have no
interest in writing letters to newspapers, never mind articles or polemical
announcements, who do not talk to reporters or appear on television

96

programs, but who do, occasionally, vote and sometimes surprise observers by a logic that is there, quite there, even if not comprehended by some of us because *we* have blind spots, perhaps, and have failed to see that such people have examined rather insistently what exactly they believe and want to see happen in their city, state, nation.

As Mayor Flynn has observed, there are many inconsistencies and contradictions in us, and many paradoxes to this life. This political leader —like others now emerging, Mario Cuomo, Barbara Mikulski, Tom Harkin—has reminded us, yet again, that voters can elude the clever categorizations of those who observe and poll them, or try to cater to their various worries and fears. I have heard Ray Flynn described as a "reverse Tom Watson," able to move away from what is sometimes called the "narrowness" of urban politics, or the "selfishness" of people whose home has become a castle in the exclusionary sense, with wide moats desired on all sides, and cannon everywhere. Words such as "parochial" or "prejudiced" are quickly attached to a South Boston. There is, needless to say, absolutely no evidence of smug parochialism, no sign of craven egoism in, say, Harvard Square or among those who live in Manhattan's Upper East Side, or Washington's Georgetown district.

Without question, Flynn would describe himself as having "grown" in the past decade or more—as having moved out of particular neighborhoods into much broader ones. Even within those original constituencies, however, one hears not only a social conservatism but many strongly egalitarian sentiments—and a clear recognition that any number of big shots get very good deals out of various levels of government, while the ordinary working person is strictly on his or her own: "Socialism for the rich, free enterprise for the poor," as one factory worker put it a couple of years ago to me as he contemplated the tax laws, the tax shelters, the bailouts in the forms of loans and subsidies, the oil-depletion allowances. All along Flynn has known of this side to his neighbors and friends. Maybe it is some of us so-called intellectuals who have some growing to do—some broader and deeper knowledge of others to acquire, a release from our solipsistic susceptibilities. Anyway, one has to keep remembering that many of us who write about social and political matters have nice deals going for ourselves, can afford the protections and immunities offered by particular neighborhoods, and are rarely tested in the way Mayor Flynn's South Boston is—in the heart and the gut, not by the measurement of one's signature on a petition or an article or one's publicly revealed contribution to a cause.

As for those almighty pollsters, some of them Rasputin-like in manner, Flynn certainly showed them up as strawmen. Who *are* these pollsters and media consultants—and what, if anything, do they really have to teach Ray Flynn, whose instincts, honed from his life, seem exactly right again and again? One shudders at the thought of Lincoln, Roosevelt, or Truman consulting pollsters before their important decisions—an effort, say, to find out whether the Gettysburg Address would "sell" in Pennsylvania, or what the exit polls showed about the fate of someone who supported New Deal or Fair Deal legislation. The one president who, God save us, took a pollster into the White House did not turn out to be our strongest, most decisive leader.

Does one need a pollster or a pundit to figure out what the political emergence of a Ray Flynn has to tell us about America today? "Maybe the time has come to vote for the neighbor you know, who has done a little better than you but not turned his back on you, and run away to play love games with the fat cats," I heard last fall from a man who repairs television sets in a Boston neighborhood of working people. He saw me phrasing my next question (what else to do?) and decided to make his point as terse as possible: "A lot of people, they don't want anymore to vote 'up.' That's the way we used to vote, but not now."

I pushed a lot of inquiring words at him, and he would not go any further—and in fact gave me every indication that he had had enough of me for the day, and maybe the longer run of things. Then, on my way back home, I suddenly realized that the three great reformers and/or heroes of this century's Democratic Party were Woodrow Wilson, who went to Princeton, and Franklin D. Roosevelt and John F. Kennedy, who went to Harvard. Harry Truman and Lyndon Johnson would never on their own have been nominated by their party; they came to power through the death of a president. Adlai Stevenson, twice nominated in the 1950s, also went to Princeton. The man I had just been interviewing—oh, hell, sitting beside, having a cup of coffee at a cafeteria—may not have had such historical facts at his disposal, but perhaps he knew something in his bones about what may have started happening in this country in the last decade or so. Not that, in any way, he has stopped admiring Roosevelt or Kennedy, or forgotten what they tried to mean to people like him. The point is that today's government (federal, state, local) is asking people to change their lives, their ways of getting along with one another, and such a demand is hard for someone to make from afar. The old tradition of *noblesse oblige* (in the nonpejorative sense of the expression) no

98

longer works, when the issues are those being put to the people of South Boston and Queens—even as blacks have also grown tired of that (white) tradition.

What Ray Flynn has not forgotten, after all these years, is the family principles, the religious lessons of his early childhood. He jogs with pleasure, and one suspects, comes morally clean with himself as he runs along. Certainly Ray Flynn can be running along, then see someone in distress, or someone doing quite commendable work—and stop to help or sing a person's praises. Whether walking or running, or yes, running for office, he is not only sure who he is but is quite clearly known to others—hence his credibility, his ability to take controversial stands without losing traditional supporters. "Flynn has said and done things since he's become mayor that I don't agree with," one of his strong South Boston supporters told me—but then he added, "Hell, I know the guy. He's one of us. He's entitled to his opinion, and me to mine. I'll give him the benefit of the doubt—of two or three doubts!" Some of us card-carrying liberals or neoliberals (and maybe for good reason) would not be so lucky were we to need that man's tolerance.

The same man, pushed a bit by me on the subject of Boston's mayor, gave me this terse analysis: "He's a Good Samaritan." Stupidly, I could not let the matter drop there. I asked him what he meant. He was silent. I said, "You mean, he helps those in need." He gently but firmly corrected me: "Well, I'd put it this way: he goes out of his way to notice the other guy; he puts himself in other people's shoes, and then he works like a dog to give them a hand." He had captured the essence of a certain kind of practical goodness at work in Raymond Flynn—a reminder that America's long involvement with a politics of decency and compassion, with a working people's politics, is by no means over, no matter what we now see prevailing in our capital city.

Six

Robert N. Bellah

POPULISM AND INDIVIDUALISM

There is a close and deep relationship between American individualism and American populism. This relationship poses both opportunities and dangers for those who would espouse a new populist politics.

Individualism means many things, and this is not the place to describe the varieties.[1] But whatever else it means, it implies a sense of respect for the integrity and dignity of the individual person and a belief in the efficacy of the individual's action. Thus individualism implies the capacity of the individual to act in the world, to make a difference, not only to join a movement but to start a movement. From Rosa Parks, who refused to move back in the bus, to the founder of MADD, we have many examples, even in our recent history, of individuals who have had a significant political impact on our society. Indeed, the model of the individual with a concern who then reaches out and finds other individuals who share the concern so that together they can make some change in the world is close

100

to the heart of politics as empowerment as exemplified in the self-help and quality-of-life movements. The vigor of these movements as evidenced by many of the chapters in this book shows that the long-standing American tradition of voluntarism is still very much alive.

The proclivity of Americans to join voluntary associations noted by Alexis de Tocqueville 150 years ago continues, according to recent research, even today to be stronger than in most other advanced industrial societies.[2] But the strength of our voluntarism (perhaps just another name for populism) seems to be correlated with the weakness of our political parties, for in many other industrial societies with less involvement in voluntary associations there is a concomitantly higher participation in political parties on the part of ordinary citizens. We could interpret this fact as an indication of the flexibility and openness of American politics compared with societies where established political parties dominate. But it might be more useful to take it as a basis for some self-critical reflections about the limitations of our individualistic, voluntarist, populist politics. Populist politics, in good part because of its individualistic component, tends to be discontinuous, oriented to single issues, opportunistic, and therefore easily coopted, local, and anti-institutional. As a result it is difficult to sustain pressure over time for the attainment of principled political ends.

Populist politics suffers from the general problem of American voluntarism, namely, that it depends on the moment-to-moment feelings of individuals to make it go. As a New Mexico activist expressing his political motivation said to Robert Coles, "I am in the struggle because it means a lot to me. It's where I'm at."[3] Such personal motivation may bring excitement and vitality to politics but it is also fragile and volatile. A new enthusiasm may lead the activist to espouse an oriental religion, or even to decide that making money is really more exciting than politics. What is missing is commitment to principles in a social context where one can count on others to be similarly committed so that together it will be possible to sustain long-term political engagement.

When an individual is propelled into political action on the basis of some immediate impulse, it is likely that political concern will not extend beyond the single issue that has aroused the impulse. Often the impulse arises from some interest. The pursuit of interest is a legitimate aspect of democratic politics. But narrow interests must be tempered and balanced against the interests of others before the common good is served. Tocqueville believed that the very process of participation in public life tended to educate people beyond their narrow interests. When citizens take part in public affairs, he said, they "must turn from the private interests and occasionally take a look at something other than themselves. . . . At first it is of necessity that men attend to the public interest, afterward by choice. What had been calculation becomes instinct. By dint of working for the good of his fellow citizens, he in the end acquires a habit and taste for serving them."[4] But often this does not occur. Where the reason for entering politics is too narrowly focused, involvement may be quickly extinguished before the educational process has had a chance to begin, and this can be the result of success as much as of failure. The parents who are incensed because their child must cross a dangerous intersection on the way to school lose interest in civic politics when they and their neighbors succeed in pressuring the city to put in a traffic light. Or they lose interest because they do *not* succeed—"You can't fight city hall."

Sometimes the narrowness of single-interest politics is not due to self-interest at all. Rather, it may arise from the personalization of an issue about which an individual feels strongly. For example, sympathy with whales or with unborn fetuses may so dominate the political motivation of individuals that they simply do not see other issues or the place of the issue that most concerns them in some larger whole. Single-interest politics lends itself to opportunism and cooptation, whether deriving from self-interest or sympathy. The person concerned with a single issue tends to give his or her support to the politician who does something actual, or perhaps only symbolic, in favor of the issue in question even though the politician might not on some larger political view deserve support at all.

Where political involvement derives largely from an immediate impulse of interest or sympathy, it is likely to remain local in scope. It is a problem that is visible in one's neighborhood or locality that galvanizes to action. Often this is seen as "getting involved" for the good of the community rather than as politics at all. One wants to "make a difference" in the life of one's community, and usually in a quite tangible way. So one works with the YMCA in helping to raise money to provide new recreational facilities for needy Mexican-American children. Or one helps the Kiwanis Club in its effort to provide a free optometry clinic for senior citizens. Or one joins the PTA in order to try to improve the local school. Activities of this sort involve face-to-face cooperation with people one knows and understands. Conflicts may develop but they are seldom irreconcilable. But if "outside interests" are involved, local politics can become rancorous. Developers seek to preempt the last remaining open space in a community. The city proposes to locate a new housing project nearby that would bring in people whose class or racial background are seen as posing a threat to the neighborhood. The state is planning to put a freeway right through the middle of a residential area. Under these circumstances "concerned citizens" can become involved in quite bitter political battles. Yet they are likely to see themselves as resisting "politics" more than engaging in politics, for they see politics as the quasi-illegitimate things that professional politicians do in governmental bodies, often representing "special interests."

Localism is the strength of individualistic populist politics: people are participating in the processes that directly affect them. But localism also has serious weaknesses. Few significant problems in modern society can really be solved at the local level. Decisions of large corporations, national and international market forces, actions of federal and state governments can seldom be controlled at the local level. Yet it is very difficult for people who have "gotten involved" at the local level to see themselves as political actors in these larger arenas. Indeed, they actively resist such involvement. Their suspicion of "politics" is one of the reasons they got involved. They tend to be resolutely anti-institutional, but it is large institutions that must be confronted and altered if political change is to be effected.

A degree of anti-institutionalism, in the sense of dissatisfaction with the way existing institutions are operating, may be effective in mobilizing people for political action. But where anti-institutionalism becomes a pervasive orientation, as it does in the ideology of American individualism, it hinders the development of the counterinstitutions that are the only vehicles for substantive change. Indeed, no politics beyond the level of spontaneous protests can exist without some degree of institutionalization. Let us therefore look at the relationship of individualistic populist politics and institutions in America.

It could be argued that the social movement is the form Americans have characteristically used to reconcile their anti-institutionalism with the necessary degree of institutionalization. The social movement is an ad hoc response to a social issue. It is flexible and spontaneous in its organization. It lasts as long as the issue that brought it about, and then it fades away. Sometimes its successes are major: for example, the civil rights movement or the movement against the Vietnam War. One could argue that the very volatility of the social movement gives a spasmodic quality to reform politics. With each new issue we start almost from scratch and have to reinvent politics, as it were. Yet the point I would like to make is somewhat different. American politics, even the politics of the social movement, is never as anti-institutional as our ideology would lead us to believe. Indeed, for good sociological reasons, it could not be.

Let us take the civil rights movement as an example. It may have been the individual action of Rosa Parks that ignited the fire, but there would have been nothing to ignite if there had not been a long history of institutional preparation. Decades of careful legal work by the National Association for the Advancement of Colored People (NAACP) were an essential precondition. The existence of the black church, the largest institutional complex under autonomous black control, was even more indispensable. Out of these churches came a number of well-organized associations such as the Southern Christian Leadership Conference (SCLC). White churches and synagogues provided the allies without whom the movement could not have succeeded. Other long-standing organizations such as the American Civil Liberties Union (ACLU) also made significant contributions. It is interesting to note that the movement against the Vietnam War was indebted to the civil rights movement in that it drew not only from the enthusiasm and organization of that movement itself but also from its institutional basis, especially the churches.

I have developed these examples of recent populist movements to show how they to a degree transcended the limitations of radically individualist populism. I would argue that it was their institutional basis that allowed them to overcome, to the degree that they did so, the volatility, opportunism, and localism that often plague populist politics. What the institutions provided were principles and the loyalty of others committed to those principles. Principles make it possible to test the emotions that prompt individuals to engage in political action. In the white churches, for example, there was a real struggle over whether segregation was in consonance with Christian belief. Many whites who had accepted segregation came to see that their views were mistaken. (We should not forget, of course, that some white churches provided support to those who opposed the civil rights movement.) Principles also help to overcome the single-issue myopia that has often characterized the social movement as well as local populist politics. Martin Luther King, Jr., because his Christian principles extended beyond his loyalty to his own racial group, could not speak out against injustice at home and at the same time keep silent about the horrors of a war in Vietnam, even though some of his political advisors thought the linkage unwise. Institutions, civic organizations, and

104

especially churches provide the continuity that populist politics otherwise lacks. It is institutions that provide the principles that make for sensitivity to issues and the loyalty of ongoing membership that again and again are the indispensable resources for successful social movements.

It is interesting that in our discussion of the institutional basis of populist politics we have not mentioned political parties. In the examples we have used political parties were not absent but they were not central either, until late in the day. It is true that the Democratic Party had a civil rights plank in its platform since its 1948 convention, but it neither led the movement nor, despite legislative majorities, did it make significant changes in the laws until the movement itself had gained enormous popular success. Some Democratic politicians began to oppose the Vietnam War early on, but it was not until 1972 that the party in principle opposed the war, by which time public opinion was overwhelmingly against it.

Why do American political parties so often come in on the coattails of successful popular movements rather than leading them? I think it is because they are primarily parties of sentiment rather than principle, and because they are not membership organizations that sustain the loyalty of their members. Aside from rather vague orientations of sentiment—the Republicans are the party of things-are-all-right-as-they-are and the Democrats are the party of things-could-be-better-than-they-are—our political parties are as volatile and opportunistic as our most individualistic local politics. Indeed, for the most part our parties *are* local, the local followings of local officeholders or office-seekers, more concerned with election or reelection than with any consistent principle. Our national parties are congeries of local leaders and their followers rather than organizations composed of active members dedicated to principles and loyal to each other as supporters of those principles. Party politics then suffers from the same individualism that populist politics does, though it takes somewhat different form. Party politics is particularly vulnerable to the cult of personality. This has always been important in America but has become even more so in the era of television.

When one thinks about third parties, the situation is not much different. Most third parties have arisen from temporary emotional issues and have evaporated as fast as they have appeared. One would have to go back to the period before World War I to the Populist and Socialist parties to find significant American third parties that sustained continuity, devotion to principle, and the loyalty of active membership. We have not had for many decades in America anything like a Labor Party or a Social

Democratic Party or a Christian Democratic Party that could provide sustained leadership toward well-understood ends. Such parties are not without their difficulties in the world today,[5] but we are without their virtues. It is really just because the political parties have not provided the institutional basis for a principled politics that the churches and their associated religious organizations have been so consistently central. Though the churches, too, have been seriously penetrated by our individualistic ideology,[6] they are among the few places where that ideology is effectively resisted.

My argument has been that though individualism provides much of the vibrancy of populist politics, it can cause serious problems unless tempered by the resources that only ongoing institutions can provide, particularly ethical principles and loyalty. In *Habits of the Heart* we give examples of individuals whom we could call heroes and heroines of everyday life, who are dedicated to the common good and joyful in their dedication. Most of them have found an institutional context that sustains them when things do not go well. Some of them had parents or grandparents who, through their religious or political dedication, serve as exemplars. Many of them have a sense of larger relationships and longer time spans than American politics usually encourages. They work in organizations like the Campaign for Economic Democracy or the Institute for the Study of Civic Values or through committees of their local congregation or parish.

We learned that people who had found a vital institutional context were stronger individuals, not weaker ones. For example, Mary Taylor, a member of the California Coastal Commission with whom we talked, found in her family and the network of people concerned with environmental issues the strength to deal with sustained political commitment under sometimes trying conditions: "Of course I feel lonely. I would be lying if I said I didn't. People who are willing to love are always going to be lonely—that's what you are going to have to cope with. I'm lonely all the time. It goes with the territory."[7] But Mary Taylor has no interest in being a martyr. What keeps her going is the sense that she is contributing to making our society better for the long haul, and the loyalty and support of those who share her concerns.

Populist politics, then, if it is to resist the diffusion that radical individualism imposes on it, must find the principles and institutions that can sustain continuity and coherence. Only strong civic and religious organizations create the possibility for the emergence of social movements that will address the great questions before us.

Notes

1. On some of the forms of American individualism, see chaps. 2 and 6 of Robert N. Bellah, Richard Madsen, William M. Sullivan, Ann Swidler, and Steven M. Tipton, *Habits of the Heart: Individualism and Commitment in American Life* (Berkeley: University of California Press, 1985). This essay depends heavily on research more fully reported in *Habits of the Heart*.

2. See, among many studies, Sidney Verba, Norman H. Nie, and Jae-on Kim, *Participation and Political Equality: A Seven Nation Comparison* (Cambridge: Cambridge University Press, 1978).

3. Robert Coles, "Civility and Psychology," *Daedalus* 109 (Summer 1980): 140.

4. Alexis de Tocqueville, *Democracy in America*, trans. George Lawrence (New York: Doubleday, Anchor Books, 1969), pp. 510, 512.

5. See, for example, Steven Lukes's analysis of the British Labor Party in "The Future of British Socialism?" *Dissent* (Spring 1985).

6. See chap. 9 of Bellah et al., *Habits of the Heart*.

7. Ibid., p. 194.

Four

GRASSROOTS POPULISM

Seven

Studs Terkel

WHY I AM A POPULIST

An Interview by Harry C. Boyte

Studs and I talk the day after he got the Pulitzer Prize. His picture is on the front page of the two Chicago dailies. Well-wishers are calling from around the world. A banner stretches across the elegant studios of the radio station, WFMT, on which he does his talk show: "Congratulations, Studs." Studs's office looks the same as ever—books scattered everywhere, coffee cups, cigar butts, a half-finished bottle of Scotch from the celebration the night before. So does Studs—cigar stub in the corner of his mouth, red checkered shirt. He leans over and growls. It's overrated, you know. They're overdoing it. But as we escape to a restaurant, he buys a paper to show an old friend working in a beauty parlor downstairs. Did you see this? What do you think? he asks her.

What is a democratic populism? The question is at the heart of Studs's stories.

I call myself a populist. It avoids the goddamn liberal label. Radical means get to the root of things. Conservative means to conserve. The Bill of Rights, the Constitution. So I call myself a radical conservative. I want to get to the roots of things. I want to preserve clean air, whatever sanity there is. Populism is the movement in which a great many people participate. It's participatory democracy, the words the kids used at Port Huron [in The Port Huron Statement, *a manifesto of the 1960s student movement.*] That was sixties populism. The town meetings in New England were populist. People got up. They talked. They participated. They said their piece. They voted after saying their piece. They took part in their community. Populism is taking part in your community. *Vox Populi.* Populism is in the best interest of a great many people, if they can determine what their best interests are. It's someone joining a union, because he has a better chance dealing with this behemoth.

If your day is no good. Your life is not very good. You come home. You got six kids. Your wife may fuss at you. There's got to be somebody less, lower down, to make it bearable. Damn nigger. Damn commie. Why does a guy join the Klan?

I interviewed this guy, Clayborne P. Ellis, who became the head of the Klan in Durham, North Carolina. It's an incredible tale.

He's a poor white. His father was a Klansman. He never questioned. His life was rotten and lousy. He thinks these goddamn black guys are stealing his money. They're getting everything. One day he joins the Klan.

He says, "You've got no idea, that thrill, Studs."

I say, "What's that?"

"For somebody who's nobody, me." It's like a reversal of Jesse Jackson saying, "I am somebody."

He said, "I was somebody. You walk down that goddamn room. There're four hundred people in the semidarkness. With a cross up there. I'm in that silky robe. I say to myself, 'I'm somebody.' "

So Clayborne joins the Klan. He becomes a hotshot in it. But he starts questioning a little bit when he gets this call from the mayor or some big shot. "You broke up that meeting of that goddamn civil rights. You're good. Clayborne, you're great." Next day he's walking down the street and the same guy walks across the road not to be seen with him. So he wonders, "Am I being used?"

Next thing you know, there's a grant from the government for discussions about the schools. This black fellow calls him and says, "You got a kid in school. We're inviting everybody to talk. The White Citizens Council, the NAACP, Ku Klux Klan, the Southern Conference on Human Welfare. Everybody."

So Clayborne says, "I'm going to go. It's my money. I've got a kid." So he goes and it's a mixed group. Hostile to one another. Somebody gets up and calls the Klan racist. Clayborne says, "I got a right. I'm poor. You people are making it rough for me. You're racist."

Then this black guy says, "You know, I like this guy, C. P. Ellis." Clayborne thinks, "What's he doing to me? He's getting me all confused."

Next thing, he goes to another meeting. There's one person he hates more than anyone. Her name is Ann Atwater. A big, heavy black woman, who's always leading this picket line against department stores to hire black clerks. He hates her. She hates him. Man, they can't stand each other. At the same meeting, they're looking daggers at each other. Somebody gets up, and says, "I nominate Ann Atwater as chairman." Then this same black says, "We don't have to have one chairman. How about two chairs? How about Ann Atwater and C. P. Ellis?" Ellis thinks, "What the hell is going on here?"

So he says to himself, "Goddamn, am I going to let her get away with this? I'm going to meet with her." So they meet. They say, "I don't like you. I don't like you either. But on this one thing, can we have a truce? Okay." He meets with her regularly. As he's telling me this story, his voice starts to break. He starts to choke up now. Clayborne says, "That that woman, that gal. Ann Atwater. I love that woman."

I say, "You do?"

He says, "Yea, I do. I don't mean sex love. I mean I love that woman." He says, "One day she walks in crying. I ask her, 'Ann, what you crying about?' She says, 'Clayborne, my girl came home crying from school, because the little black kids are mocking her. They're saying her mother is going around with a Klansman.'" Now, he's gotten just about to the point where he's going to quit the Klan. But he's still a member. He tells her, " 'A funny thing happened, my kid came home crying too. My boy. It was the kids in school, saying his father is going around with one of these black agitating women, you know.'" They both start crying. And they hold each other. That was the key moment.

So he quits the Klan, and these guys start to threaten him. They are confused. Some of them are vicious. "C. P., we're going to kill you." "But goddamn," he tells me, "I'm starting to feel a little better about myself. But I still got it rough." He's working as a janitor at Duke University.

He says, "So I join the union. It's 80% black. Black women. Custodial workers." He says to himself, "I'm going to run for business agent. My opponent's a black man. I ain't got a chance." He says, "But I'm going to run anyway." He makes a speech. He says, "You know who I am. I was once a member of the Klan. You know that, because the company sent out circulars, a picture of me in white robes. But I'm not now. You know what I am. I want you to vote for me. You may not want to." They shouted him down, "We don't want to hear any more. We want to vote now." He tells me, "I was elected, four to one."

Then he starts crying. He says, "You know, when Martin Luther King died, I cheered they got that son of a bitch. And now I hear these records. I got these records, I hear his speeches. I say 'Boy it's the truth.' Now I'm looking for some kid, a black kid, to be my assistant."

Studs shakes his cigar.

So that's Clayborne Ellis's story. What did it? Values and needs. One need transcends another. It's opening a window.

Populism can go both ways. It's not always good. It can also be racist. Populism based on fears and bigotry and meanness. Tom Watson [*the Georgia Populist leader of the 1880s and 1890s*] became a racist. Richard Viguerie [*the fundraiser for the new right*] uses the word. That can be populist too.

The Bible's a good example. I knew this guy in the south named Claude Williams, a friend of Clifford and Virginia Durr. Claude would use all the Bible as a working man's book. He organized unions in North Carolina. This woman he worked with helped him, and would talk like a preacher. He would tell me, "She could soar, once she was talking cadence." The Bible is a working man's book. Populist preachers always use the Bible.

But the preacher Gerald K. Smith was a populist, too. Against the New Deal. Against civil rights. He had this statue down in Arkansas called Christ of the Ozarks, blessing all four states at once. We were having some chicken at his house. Old Gerald K. was telling me about "those goddamn civil rights marchers." He didn't like the preachers wearing their collar and letting people know they were ministers. "Namby pambies," he said. "I told them to take your collar off and face the town like goddamn men." The next thing, he tells me a story when he met a whole mob of these New Dealers. He hopped on a rock and said, "Who dare attacks me attacks a man of God." Smith was a right-wing populist. So was the Townsend movement.

114

[*Today*] a whole new generation has come up, working with machines, computers, technology. So, Reagan has said, "It's okay to be a racist, to have disdain and contempt for those up against it, because you're not. It's okay to be a bully with smaller countries. You make it no matter what." Years ago Ford said, "History is bunk." He was laughed at. Today, Ford's goofy credo is the credo of the day. Images. That's all we've been taught. You've got to make it no matter what.

This is the heart of the problem that makes for Reagan as president. Liberals always say Reagan is terrible. Of course he's terrible. But how did he get to be president? What is it with the American people at this moment? What are their sources? What news do they get? The liberal media. That's a joke—it's not liberal. They're scared. They've got a pass for years. The banality is so much part of it. And the listening and the watching. It works two ways, you know. TV can serve a purpose. Like during the civil rights movement, strangely. At a certain moment in our history, during the civil rights movement in the South. People saw on TV Sheriff Jim Clark and the hoses and the kids. I know people who got roused. They were not problack or antiblack. There it served.

But generally speaking, the role of TV is horrible. It gives us facts, or misfacts, and we're spectators. Then you have the banality. You have a mother and you have a fire, and the mother's carrying a dead kid out. Then they cut from that to a sweet-faced actress talking about a detergent. So the detergent becomes as important as life or death. Or the other way, life or death becomes as insignificant as the detergent. That flattens things out. There you have it. Then you have your sources of information. You have a TV interviewer ask me, "In thirty seconds, what's your view of the world?" In thirty seconds! How often do you hear that? That must do something to the community.

Our own history. Our past. I say, we're the richest country in the world and the poorest in memory. The poorest in the sense of the past. I'll tell you a funny story. It applies to every aspect of our lives, even pop culture. I'm on a bus. We're passing an old-time ball room up in Uptown, called the Aragon. Aragon years ago was a waltz palace. In fact, my brother met his wife there, years and years ago. Now they have rock bands, or now and then a prize fight. There was a rock concert that night. There were half a dozen kids on the bus. I say, "Where you going?" They say, "We're going to hear Chicago." That's a rock group. I say, "Whatever became of Bob Dylan?" "Bob who?" Black kids don't remember the blues. Paul Robeson, of course not, that has no meaning.

What the hell do the kids know about the CIO being organized? About minimum wage? They think it came from the goodness of the employer. General Motors gave them a big raise. They don't know a god-damn thing. It's not their fault. They haven't been told. You pick up a paper, what have you got? You don't have a labor section. You have a business section. What do you see on the air? All these financial shows on PBS, yet. They've become more sexy than sex.

It brings us to Reagan. Deep down, people know he's not right. Deep down they know that. The emperor has not a goddamn stitch of clothing. Banality. The idea that Reagan is the Great Communicator. But we're so used to bullshit. To mediocrity. So, our standards have become so low. Our language has become perverted. People say Ted Kennedy is a leftist. There was an indigenous American left pre–World War One. Oklahoma was part of it. But we have no left today, so we call the center "left."

Studs acts it out, standing straight, then leaning right.

If you're on the floor you're ultraconservative. Our thoughts become perverted. The very way we talk.

The people I look for when I interview are ordinary people. Most people I've interviewed, they've never heard of me. Even if they do know me, they forget who I am when they start talking. They think about their story. People are storytellers. I don't mean quote, unquote, somebody. But the people themselves. Ordinary, whatever that may mean.

I'll never forget this one guy I asked to begin at the beginning and tell me what his day was like. He's a southern white guy. Works at an auto plant outside Hammond, Indiana. He lives in a trailer park with his wife. A big old Bible is in their trailer. He's an umpire in the Little League with his kid.

He says, "First thing I do, I open one eye and I look at that clock radio. 'Sheese,' I say. And I get up and I kiss my wife—that's routine! Then I go to the bathroom and I comb my one hair. Then I come out. I get a cup of coffee. But you know, sir, sometimes it might be half a cup. Then I get in the car. But before I get in, I kiss my wife again. That's routine! And then I gotta get to that plant on time, 'cause if you're one minute late, you're docked for an hour. They're a lot of railroad crossings. If there's a freight train going by with a hundred cars, it's a fifteen minute wait." As

116

he describes this, it's dramatic, it's funny, but there's suspense. It's an adventure getting to the plant.

I always prefer ordinary people to academicians. Take a musty academician. He teaches Philosophy One at one of these colleges. He tells me, "I get to my morning class and it's Aristotle's ethics." That's it. You contrast the two. I look for storytelling. They forget about me. That's never been a problem.

You know what a community organizer does? Saul Alinsky, Heather Booth? It seems to me the organizer asks, "How do you get those people in the community to do it themselves?" In other words, an organizer offers a kind of scenario, there are certain things that gotta be done. But they've got to do it.

An organizer opens windows. There's a musty room in this society. It's musty, cramped. The organizer opens the window. There's a breath of fresh air. "Hey, that's a pretty good breath of fresh air!" So you really open a window [*when you interview people, too*]. But the people really open their own window in talking. When they tell about their life story.

I remember once this woman, a white woman with six kids. She lived in a project. She was poor. She said, "The kids want to hear their mothers voice on the tape recorder. What's it sound like?" So I play it back. "Oh my God." She listens with her hand over her face. But she likes it. And then she looks up. She says, "My God, I never knew I felt that way before!" That's a revelatory moment, for her and for me. That's a high moment. Everybody's different. It's somebody on that block. Let's say it's a housewife. She's called by her first name. They know her. She's lived there thirty years. She's part of their group, their ethnic group, their economic group, their church group. But she's also a little different than the others. She's one they can look to at times. She is able to say what the others may feel but can't say. It's inchoate in them. She becomes the spokesman. Like Peggy Terry, the Appalachian woman I know. There's a natural eloquence about her. She went to fifth grade and that's all. From Kentucky. She traveled in the Depression days. A fifteen-year-old wife, pregnant with a baby, with a sixteen-year-old husband. In every community you'll find somebody like that. Maybe somebody who's considered slightly a kook. Slightly flaky. And yet they like her very much.

Look at Mary Lou Wolff. She was a housewife with nine kids. Her husband worked for the city. She's Italian-American. Then she goes to a meeting. They're talking about which home is going to be demolished for the expressway. Someone—not Mary Lou—gets up and asks an impertinent question. "Who needs the expressway to begin with? The hell with the expressway! Do we need it so that the goddamn automobiles can go through faster?" That began the struggle. She takes part. She begins to speak. Suddenly she realizes, "Hey, you're pretty good!" She was saying things that were in her. Next thing you know she was the speaker at the convention of the Citizen Action Program [*a large coalition of Chicago neighborhoods in the early 1970s*]. She's a leader.

Or Jesse Della Cruz, in Fresno, California. Jesse is Hispanic. She's Mexican. Cesar Chavez is organizing the farm workers. Women didn't speak. But her husband is a quiet guy. So Cesar Chavez is talking, and she gets up and says something. Her husband didn't want her to. But she starts talking. Cesar says, "Wow, you're the kind of person we're looking for." Jesse's a leader in Fresno.

The right wing takes the symbols and phrases. Right to life. The Flag. They take everything. We've got to take them back. You've got to start from scratch. Begin with self-interest. Good organizers know that. What is it on that block? The kids are huffing and puffing because of the factory, so they have a campaign. So there's a big turnout to do something about that goddamn factory in their neighborhood. Goddamn Commonwealth Edison utility rates. Once people start that, they begin to make the connection. The same kind of people who are doing this are the same as in the Pentagon.

Eight

Ernesto Cortes

EDUCATION
FOR CITIZENSHIP:
A PROFILE

An Interview by Harry C. Boyte

Ernesto Cortes, the community organizer from San Antonio, Texas, has become a legendary figure in the world of citizen activism over the past decade. He was first organizer for the group that transformed politics in the city, Communities Organized for Public Service, or COPS. COPS pioneered new techniques of citizen participation and grew to be the largest community organization in the nation. Later Cortes worked in Los Angeles, helping to build United Neighborhood Organizations. Then in the 1980s he returned to Texas, where he has overseen development of a network of groups like COPS in El Paso, the Rio Grande Valley, Houston, Austin, and elsewhere that has had major impact on state politics.

Cortes is a large man who fires a rapid stream of abrupt questions at those around him. He is often intimidating, demanding precision and extraordinary commitment from those he works with. And he is known for getting directly to the point. The only thing really lacking in the Latino community is some-

119

body to teach us about power, *Cortes told one Los Angeles* Times *reporter. We have our baseball* players, our businessmen, and many people who do good works. But until Latinos learn about political power in this country and how it really operates, the Decade of the Hispanic will be just so many beer commercials.

Under the surface gruffness Cortes is also a rare democrat. He radiates what is best called a "populist" sensibility, most striking when he reflects on the role of organizer. No organizer should be so arrogant as to pretend he's going to organize the organization, *said Cortes.* I didn't organize COPS. The leadership organized COPS. I taught them. I trained them. I identified them. I challenged them and I worked with them on a one-to-one basis. But they did the organizing. *Cortes stresses the importance of forcing community organizers themselves into situations where they can* rekindle energy and passion *from the inspiration of ordinary people.* If you're a lead organizer for a group like Communities Organized for Public Service or any powerful organization, *he explains,* you're into heady arenas. *The challenge is to* see new possibilities in people . . . to see them in a different way.

For Cortes, drawing inspiration from ordinary people is not an easy or superficial process. Cortes is an indefatigable reader who communicates an intense intellectuality. He regularly carries around a briefcase overflowing with the books he is currently studying. Conversations with him range widely from theology to ancient history or political philosophy. What he means by drawing inspiration is to create new ways for people to learn to express themselves in the whole of their personalities—their values, traditions, aspirations for the future.

Ernie Cortes learned much about organizing in the late 1960s and early 1970s as he worked first with Cesar Chavez and the United Farm Workers and then with the dean of American community organization, Saul Alinsky, and his associates like Ed Chambers. But his deeper motivations grew from the experiences of the Mexican community in San Antonio itself, its feeling of invisibility and powerlessness that reached back through many generations, and its growing determination to do something about it. Such experiences also taught him insights into the dynamics that motivate people which were to impact dramatically back upon the traditions of organizing itself.

San Antonio, Texas, *is known in much of the country for "Tex-Mex" music, Spanish architecture, and the flower-lined river that winds through downtown. For Americans of Mexican ancestry, San Antonio, the only large city with a majority Mexican population, was long a symbolic capital of sorts* *and simultaneously the symbol of their exclusion from significant power. Immediately after the Texas Republic secured its independence from Mexico, in 1837, forty out of forty-one political candidates in city elections were Mexican. Ten years later the number had dropped to five. By the early 1970s Mexicans had virtually no representation in city offices. And the effects were stark, indeed. Flooding from rains regularly affected more than 100,000 in the barrios of the city's west and south sides. The city had had plans for drainage since 1945 and had even approved a bond issue—yet no money had been spent. Roads were unpaved. Schools were deteriorating. Few city services reached the community. And, perhaps most crippling, there was a widespread sense of despair. "Our children were leaving for the North Side, those who could afford it," remembers Helen Ayala, a leader in COPS. "There were not jobs or good housing. It was very sad."*

Cortes, too, remembers decay in the community's spirit. The struggle was to become American, *he explains.* If someone called you a Mexican you were supposed to beat them up. *But Cortes came from a family that had long imagined a different future. His father's brother had started the first Mexican-owned television station in the city and had been deeply involved in politics. Similarly, his mother's side was close to Henry Gonzales, the crusading Mexican congressman.* Politics was something that all my relatives talked about a lot, *Cortes recalls.* When the first major news story came out about COPS, people were jubilant. My father said, "we always thought something like this was going to happen someday."

In the 1960s Cortes went to the University of Texas at Austin and earned a degree with a dissertation exploring different approaches to "dealing with poverty." War on poverty approaches. Educational approaches. Fiscal approaches. None seemed convincing. But the statistics he learned about the phenomenal rates of poverty, school drop outs and other problems in San Antonio brought home on an aggregate level what I had known personally growing up. *Cortes decided to try a different approach.*

He worked with the United Farm Workers, the migrant union headed by Cesar Chavez. Then, returning to San Antonio in the late 1960s, he devised an economic development strategy for the Mexican American Unity Council. But none of it spoke directly to his perception that the problem was a lack of power. Whatever the plans, there was not the clout to get them accomplished. So Cortes decided to spend some time with the Industrial Areas Foundation (IAF) in Chicago, the training school for organizers started in 1969 by Alinsky.

Alinsky had always had disdain for those he called "do-gooders" out to help the poor. The goal in his view should be to assist the poor to organize

121

themselves through building what he called "mass power organizations" that would gain them a new voice on a continuing basis. Only through such groups, he believed, could people who were accustomed to humiliation and defeat all their lives experience power, gain new self-respect, and feel some hope.

Alinsky's insights into the self-respect and sense of empowerment at the heart of democratic organizing were to prove enduring, vital legacies that since have been enormously influential. But in many ways his organizing also mirrored the world in which he operated. Like trade union leaders, for instance, he was driven by the desire to see poor and marginal people get more from the system in the terms of the system itself. "Organizing for power," as interpreted by many of Alinsky's subsequent disciples, was often described as an end in itself, with little or no reflection about how power might be used or for what purposes. And Alinsky himself often used a wry, cynical language that reinforced such tendencies. "In the world-as-it-is, what you call morality is to a significant degree a rationalization of the position which you are occupying," he wrote. "The right things are done only for the wrong reasons and vice versa."

Cortes learned many practical skills of organization at the IAF. Perhaps his most important lesson, in his view, was insight into his personality. I had a tendency to jump down people's throats, which could intimidate people, he reflects. But in Chicago, he believes, he learned not to allow my anger to get so vociferous, to get more focused. He also no longer felt compelled to dominate the discussion. I learned the value of listening. He also brought to IAF his own thoughts on organizing, just at the moment that others, like Ed Chambers, were also asking new questions about the tradition.

Ernie Cortes had once considered becoming a minister and had a deep interest in theology. I thought a lot about a conversation I'd had once with Cesar Chavez, he recalls, that every organization needs an ideology if it is to continue. The United Farm Workers' was Christianity. For the Mexican community in San Antonio, it was hard to imagine effective organizing that did not draw powerfully on the religious languages, stories, and institutions at the heart of the culture. Cortes saw church as the center of strength in the community. And he found that priests, while strongly interested in issues like the financial health and physical survival of their parishes, had often a deep engagement in questions of values and broader ideas. They questioned the ministry, their faith; they challenged you and themselves. That's what gave them energy, made them interested and interesting. If you took Alinsky literally, you'd never probe below the surface.

Thus Cortes helped the IAF broaden its understanding of people's motivations. It continued to stress the importance of self-interest, that organizing poor and working people required working on questions of immediate, visible, and pressing concern. But it began to distinguish between self-interest and selfishness. It argued that people's basic concerns are with what might be called "hometown values" like their families, communities, faith, the dignity of work, the future of their children—and that through organizing that empowered people, their visions could extend far more broadly as well.

In 1973 Father Edmundo Rodriguez invited Cortes and the IAF to help the Mexican community in San Antonio try to get itself together. Cortes brought back with him the skills he had learned. And he returned with a passionate determination to see his own people gain power and dignity. He knew there were traditions of struggle and community to draw upon. But his initial approach was simply to listen. I began to interview pastors and from them got the names of lay leaders in the parishes, he remembers. I kept records and tapes of each conversation. In the first year, Cortes talked to perhaps a thousand people. And he sought out leaders different than the traditional "activists." "One of the remarkable things about COPS," explains Sister Christine Stephens, a later organizer for the group, "is that it builds around the moderates. Not the activists on the Left or the conservatives on the Right. It didn't begin with people who were the politicos or who were in public life who wheeled and dealed. It grew from the people who run the church festivals, who lead the PTAs, whose lives have been wrapped up in their parishes and their jobs and their children. What COPS has been able to do is give them a public life, the tools whereby they can participate."

COPS's approach has combined detailed reflection upon the basic values of the Judeo-Christian faiths and the American democratic tradition with a detailed process of what leaders call "citizenship education." It trains thousands of ordinary citizens in the techniques of holding meetings, doing research, analyzing public policy positions, confronting city officials, registering people to vote, and the like—all with the purpose of giving values "clout" in the real world. Such an approach has now been adopted throughout the IAF network and, more broadly, influences democratic organizing across the United States.

"There is a war being waged on television and in taverns, in local stores and massive shopping centers, in corporations and congregations, over who will shape the values of our society," reads the basic training manual of the IAF. "It is about this fundamental question: Who will parent our children? Who will teach them, train them, nurture them? In isolation, families and congregations have no chance. With the citizens' organization as a context and as an instrument, families and congregations can move with dignity and confidence into the arena of institutional power." In San Antonio, COPS has won

123

more than $500 million in community development projects in the Mexican and poor sections of town, mounting an extraordinary challenge to political and economic elites in the process. Each year, for more than a decade now, five, six, or seven thousand delegates come to the COPS annual convention. Henry Cisneros—the mayor of San Antonio who owes his career largely to his championing of COPS issues—acknowledges that the organization probably speaks directly for 150,000 families.

But for all the physical signs of improvement and the numbers, the most profound changes wrought by COPS are more elusive. Leaders speak about the "cultural changes" they have seen, as people have come to value the broader community good and ask what areas are most in need of aid. Young people increasingly remain, rather than fleeing for the northern areas of town. Women have taken on unprecedented leadership roles, including the last several presidencies of the organization. Individual congregations involved in COPS— which includes institutions like churches and neighborhood groups as a central part of its structure—have seen often wide-ranging democratization of their internal life, with lay leaders emerging in every aspect. This sort of activity, in turn, begins to repair bonds that have been gravely weakened by mass culture and economic pressure.

Such changes, in turn, come in Cortes's view from an authentic public life. Indeed, the heart of organizing, in his opinion, is a new public life—unlike "public" and "politics" in the world as it is but recalling earlier American notions of citizenship as a continuing obligation and community vocation. Groups like COPS are ultimately like universities where people go to school to learn about public policy, public discourse, public life. And the process of such learning is itself transformative, what Cortes calls metanoia, a Greek word meaning the change from one state to another. Organization means hope for people, Cortes argues. Real hope, not just fantasy. Getting in touch with themselves, with the center of their feelings, their own anger, their own joy, their own sense of who they are. It means building the kind of relationships they never had. It means making their institutions relevant. But most important, organizing means the ability to move on issues. An opportunity to do something about things they've been frustrated about all their lives. Organization means power.

Finally, for all their successes, organizations like COPS, according to Cortes, only begin again a discussion of democracy that has long atrophied in America. They create the framework for what he calls "neopopulism." What is democracy? How does it operate in a technological culture? There has to come out a vision which is relevant to this culture, this situation, that is decentralist and pluralist, not statist. I don't necessarily subscribe to a socialist vision. America is never going to adopt a vision which is not decentralist and pluralistic. But I would agree with Pope John Paul II that there needs to be a vision of work, of labor as dignified and meaningful. Where people gain the fruits of their work—all kinds of people who work, scientists, laborers, housewives.

These organizations don't have the answers. What we have is the beginnings of a process. *His immediate objective is to see the creation of networks of dozens of substantial and deeply grounded citizen groups throughout the Southwest and perhaps extending into northern Mexico, as well. In turn, such organizations will be part of a broader dialogue.* There has to be a re-creation of an agenda for the United States that draws on all the rich seeds that have been planted over the years by a lot of people. How do you cultivate those seeds? How do you draw on our traditions and reframe them where it's appropriate? How do you make connections? Those are the critical questions—that have been lost by a politics of electioneering and campaigns and media events. What will be exciting will be to see a new agenda put together, with everybody participating.

Nine
Cora Tucker

BORN A REBEL:
A PROFILE

An Interview by Harry C. Boyte

    Southern Virginia is famous mostly for textile mills and rolling farmland that grows brightleaf tobacco. Roads sometimes trace the path of the old trails, created by rolling hogsheads of tobacco through the forests and grasslands to markets, a hundred or more years ago. At intervals widely separated, those who worked the mills and farms suddenly rose to public visibility—the Knights of Labor and the Populist movements of the 1880s and 1890s; union campaigns in textile mills during the Great Depression; a civil rights march led by Dr. Martin Luther King, Jr., in Danville. But despite such moments of democratic protest, Prince Edward County, where all public schools had been closed to prevent integration, was the more prominent symbol of the region. Indeed, nearby Halifax County, along the border with North Carolina, was the home of Governor William M. Tuck, leader of the state's "massive resistance movement" which fought integration with intransigence that matched or surpassed that of states like Alabama and Mississippi. Schools in Halifax County were

126

not integrated until 1969, under court order. Even in the 1970s some restaurants refused to serve blacks. And blacks were barred from virtually all middle-class and white collar positions: as bank tellers, clerks in downtown stores, sales people in car dealerships, high school principals, and the like.

Southside Virginia—and Halifax County, in particular—has been an area of apparent social tranquility through most of its history. To keep it that way, its white power structure has commonly reacted to "uppity" protestors with swift and fierce reprisal. But Halifax County is also the home of Cora Tucker. And Tucker has in recent years, in the name of another vision of America, turned the area's mores and social patterns upside down.

I was born a rebel, *says Tucker, laughing.* I've always been outspoken. A story from decades ago makes the point.

In the 1950s Tucker's high school assignment to write an essay on "What America means to me" brought to mind the pain and humiliations of her years growing up in southside Virginia. Having to go in the backdoor of white peoples' houses. Reading from books in her school that had been discarded by the white school across town. Worst of all, getting dressed for school and having the white man my family sharecropped with tell me, "No, you can't go to school today. You've got to stay and do housework." Her impassioned essay won the contest for the best in the entire state. With her family, Cora traveled to Richmond to receive the award from the governor himself, then Lindsay Almond. On stage in an auditorium filled with 3,000 people she started to read her piece—and found it had been changed to remove references to segregation. They wanted me to sound like a happy little person, *she remembers. On the spot, she refused the award.* Lord it created a stir. My mama cried like a baby. White folks told her, "You'd better do something with that little girl or she's going to cause you pain. She's too uppish." Parents wouldn't let their kids talk to me. But it wasn't right. They weren't giving me a prize for what I wrote. They were giving me a prize for what they wanted me to say.

Tucker's indomitable anger, however, was not disillusion. She has always been an authentic populist, whose deep sense of roots lead her not to acquiescence but to outrage and action against what she sees as the violations of the true American spirit. Tucker sees herself in the tradition of Martin Luther King, Jr., or Henry Howell, her first political hero, a self-described populist politician who championed alliance between the state's poor whites and blacks even in the age of massive resistance. (I heard them lambast him for a whole week on radio in 1954, *Tucker recalls.* He had got up and said, "the time has come when a white elite can no longer speak for black people. Black people can speak for themselves." I fell in love with him right then. He had principles.)

Today, as one of four cochairs of Citizen Action, the national organization that describes itself as democratic populist, she is a position to help fight for her vision of America. We have to take back the American dream and redefine it. It's not what we've been hearing, where big quails eat up little ones, where people are expendable. The founding fathers may not have seen everything. They had some blind spots. But they sure had a different vision than Ronald Reagan. We've lost what we were supposed to be. It's really sacri-religious. *Her vision is national. But its origins lie in the rural folkways and small towns of her native Halifax, and the strength of a people who had endured for centuries.*

My father's side of the family were very proud people. My grandmother used to say, "Only you can make yourself a second-class citizen." They owned a farm, about five miles away from where I live. They didn't have much money. But they taught school and worked for the railroads. My Daddy worked on the railroads. But he died when I was three, and left my mother with nine children.

Tucker's childhood brings back harsh memories. I never figured out how my mother could take care of all those kids. She plowed, sharecropped, did everything a hand could do. She'd come home at six or seven, make supper, then go to some white people's house where she'd clean and scrub floors until nine or ten at night. Then she'd get up at four A. M. She did that for fifteen or twenty years. I just couldn't see how she survived. In the beginning, I was angry that she worked so hard. Later, when I was older, I realized somebody had to do this, 'cause we had to eat.

But Tucker also remembers celebration, community, and strength. There were times when food was really slim and my mama would sit there at the table with us and tell stories or sing songs. You were starving to death when you set down, but she would sing songs or pray and all of a sudden you really weren't hungry.

Church was a pillar of strength for all of us. There were days when you thought, I cannot take this another day. But we always had scripture that would say, "you can go one more day." You grow up not hating people. You hate some of the things they've done, but I thank God for my mama. She taught us how not to hate. *Tucker's mother also conveyed a message of resistance.* One day my brother and I saw this oak tree and cut it

128

down for wood. The white man found out we cut the tree down, and mama whooped us, 'cause blacks weren't allowed to cut down no trees.

But afterwards she told me, "I don't agree with you cutting down that tree. But next time you go further in the bushes so they won't find out." And she told me that if you took ashes and put it on a stump, it dried it out faster and made it look like a tree had been cut down a long time, so when the man walked through he didn't pay attention.

Tucker had other moments of self-assertion as a young woman. In the late 1950s, when she was sixteen, she refused to go to the back of the Trailways bus she rode to South Boston—which created a stir as well. But during her senior year she dropped out of high school to get married. For fifteen years she raised a family, joined an occasional march, read black history. Then in 1975 she went back to get her high school diploma. And when she traveled to Washington to visit a cousin, she heard Rep. Barbara Jordan speak. Cora Tucker was inspired to speak out herself.

We were going backwards in Halifax then, *Tucker remembers.* The County Board of Supervisors commissioners said, "We've got enough integration already." *When it decided to refuse a $500,000 grant to build a recreational facility—because it would be integrated—a group of young people Cora had been working with formed into an organization of black and white youth, named Citizens for a Better America (CBA). With help also from several other adults—Estell Poindexter, Viola Poindexter, William Venable, Harvey Baldwin, Judy Hendrick, Baily Hendrick, and others—CBA spent a couple of years registering blacks to vote and doing a survey on black employment in the county.* We found out that only 7 percent of government jobs were black, though blacks were 43 percent of the county. Only two blacks in the whole county made over $10,000 a year.

The name, "Citizens for a Better America," was important. We knew what we wanted, *Tucker explained.* We were citizens. One of my cousins, way back, went underground and taught people to read so they could register to vote. And we weren't just youth. If we said citizens, we could get anybody. And we wanted a Better America. *When the group was barred from holding demonstrations without a permit—and the county refused a permit—Tucker sent out letters to all the churches saying CBA planned "A Citizenship Day of Prayer." The intent was simple.* We planned to pray for a better America. We wanted to pray about there not being recreation for the young people, about blacks not having jobs, about places not being integrated. Nobody could stop us from praying. *The site, as well as the name of the day, was natural.* The courthouse is where everything happens to black folks, *Tucker elaborated.* I wanted people to get so they felt like the courthouse is ours. We can sing, pray, do anything. *Much of the power structure was not impressed. Jerry Falwell in nearby Lynchburg got one of the letters.* He preached for a whole week about us being like the publicans in the Bible, *Tucker laughs.* But now we've had nine Citizenship Days of Prayer. It's become a great annual event.

Tucker and other leaders in CBA experienced more dangerous forms of harassment and intimidation, yet. In 1978 a car slowly drove past where one of Cora's daughters was playing with other children, turned around, passed again—and then suddenly turned off the road and hit her. The child, hospitalized for more than two months, nearly lost her leg. Bomb scares became common occurrences. Anonymous callers threatened Tucker's husband and children. Her church, Crystal Hill, was vandalized, and city officials warned that if Tucker continued "agitating" it would be subject to taxes. Once, the brake lines in her car were cut when she was inside a bus station in South Boston. But throughout it all, the organization gained strength and recruits.

Sympathetic young whites as well as blacks in the county joined—by 1981 CBA had chapters in five cities. In 1976 Tucker was cochair of the Carter for President organization in Halifax—and the county went for the Democratic candidate in the election. In 1977 CBA registered 1,400 people during Henry Howell's nearly successful campaign for governor—all but 12 of whom actually went to the polls. Outside speakers at the Citizenship Days of Prayer like Congressman Parren Mitchell, long a friend and ally of Tucker's, gave the group's efforts visibility and prestige. And hard-hitting, effective, and imaginative tactics gave it clout.

In 1979 the organization completed another survey of area businesses and began a boycott against local merchants, which proved a considerable success. It sued the school system and other government agencies for discrimination. The federal Office of Revenue Sharing ruled "there is evidence" that discrimination in fact existed and ordered the county to correct discriminatory practices or lose $300,000 in funds.

CBA further charged that the governing committee of the Halifax Democratic Party shut out many blacks, women, and the young and that it needed new blood. The committee dismissed the charges. Shortly afterward, the local paper, the News and Record, *broke an embarrassing story. "Democrats Reelected Dead Committeeman," the paper headlined. "I have no other comment other than none of us is perfect," commented the county party chair, lamely.*

In 1981 CBA joined with groups from across the state to form the statewide citizens organization called Virginia Action, and Tucker soon became the new group's president. When I went to the meeting of the first sponsoring committee for Virginia Action, I said, "this is great," *Tucker recounts.* We'd been working with young whites and blacks, but not with whites of all ages. But here were people of all ages saying something has to be done in this commonwealth. *("Commonwealth?" I ask.)* You know, Virginia was called a commonwealth. The elite people say commonwealth. So we take it over. It's our word.

There were white people there from southwest Virginia who had never had any dealings with blacks before, churches, the Firefighters Union, tenants, people from all over the state. For two days we set and wrote down all the reasons why a coalition won't work, thousands of things. Then we had another list saying why it might work. Something has got to be done in the commonwealth. *Virginia Action also joined with other state citizen efforts in the new national organization, Citizen Action.*

Virginia Action soon proved its usefulness.

Mining companies were planning exploratory diggins in southside Virginia for open-pit excavations of uranium. Children played there. Scientists warned that contamination might get into the streams and water table, damaging the farming and textile manufacturing.

The campaign produced moving testimony. "Where I live, I see lots of animals drinking from the river and fish swimming in the water," testified Cindi Cunningham, age ten, at hearings in the state capitol in Richmond. "If radioactive waste leaked into the Banister River, it would harm or kill the fish and the animals that drink from it. The contaminated river could even take human life." The fight also showed considerable political muscle. The coalition protesting the mining contacted more than 50,000 families. Boards of supervisors from six counties and organizations as diverse as the Virginia Farm Bureau Federation, the Orange County Chamber of Commerce, and the Virginia State Dairymen's Association joined the effort. The state house and senate voted a moratorium on any mining operations.

For Tucker, the story was another confirmation of the central lesson she believes she has learned from her years of struggle. As she told the convention of Virginia Action, So many black and white people have not worked together before and it is going to take some time for us to realize what is going on within us. But there is one fundamental goal we have that is a whole lot bigger than any other problem we may face. The ultimate goal is for us to organize little people to have a voice in the destiny of their lives. Everything else is secondary.

131

Ten

Mike Miller

POPULIST PROMISES
AND PROBLEMS

Democratic Populism's Themes

Democratic populism points us in several important directions: (1) Wealth and power are concentrated in the hands of too few people, particularly those at the helm of major business and governmental institutions. (2) The capacity of average people to define their own problems and to come up with solutions to them should be understood as central to a vision of a democratic future in America, as well as to an understanding of its revolutionary past. (3) If we are to successfully challenge concentrated wealth and power, we need to begin by building and strengthening autonomous organizations and institutions that are deeply rooted in the experiences and values of people in local communities.

To reclaim our democratic heritage is simple but not easy. This is another of the pointers of democratic populism. In an age that emphasizes

132

complexity and the need for experts to solve all problems, populism is a proper antidote. It can take us beyond policy debates that are indeed complex and complicated and point us toward the need to organize. It suggests that to engage in policy debate without the power to be a player at the decision-making table is either the stuff of cruel illusion or coffee-house chatter. It further reminds us that when the noncredentialed have had the power to determine solutions to social and economic problems, there was a rich inventiveness in their programs. It suggests to intellectuals and activists that they must develop a connectedness to the struggles of local people and organizing if they want to find an opportunity to connect policy and program with people. As a friend of mine puts it, you've got to earn the right to meddle. Leadership is earned, not claimed.

Some Populist Problems

The new interest in populism is not without its problems. It is, after all, a slogan that has been adopted by a very strange assortment of bedfellows: many of the participants in this anthology—and Richard Viguerie and Ronald Reagan. Those who breathe a 1980s content into the slogan will, with exceptions to be noted below, be those with the power to do so —namely, those who define the news media's presentation of reality and those who now are centrally situated in positions of power in America.

As a slogan for our times, democratic populism *may* make enemies it does not want and exclude allies it needs. Racial and ethnic minorities are, at least in my experience, relatively suspicious of the new populism. So, too, are many involved in the labor, women's, and environmental movements. The problem is not solved by calling everything we think is good and appropriate for our times "populist." The fact is that ideas are both formers and expressions of movements and organizations. If those expressing the idea today are largely Anglo, college-educated whites, then instead of being something that unifies a new majority, "democratic populism" will go the way of "participatory democracy," a once vital idea that never got beyond the social base of its exponents.

Populist rhetoric today appears to be limited to an electoral arena. With the exception of those places where the historic memory of the Populist movement still lives, local members and leaders of powerful organizations that might do something about the inequities of our time

133

simply do not call themselves populists. The idea is not organically connected to the richness of hundreds of serious local and regional organizing efforts that are taking place both around work and in neighborhoods.

Last, though the list could continue, the idea could go the way of any number of new slogans debated in journals and magazines ranging from the center to the left: the search for the "real" populism will assume that some metaphysical populism exists. The discussion and debate over it will miss one of its historic points—that powerful ideas need to be rooted in powerful movements and organizations.

Where to Find Today's Populist Spirit

The populist impulse should make us look at what kinds of organizations and institutions are appropriate for our time to enable us to resist the continuing encroachment on our freedoms by the mega-institutions. We should be looking at the labor movement and what is going on there; we should be looking at broadly based community organizations and what is happening within them; we should be looking in the religious institutions of America to see how they are doing as a source of resistance and articulation of differing visions from those exemplified by J. R. Ewing and other advocates of greed.

We should be encouraged by the fact that Lane Kirkland and the Executive Council of the AFL-CIO have recently published a self-critical analysis with the idea that there are new things that the labor movement should consider if it is to renew itself. Similarly, we should be encouraged by such developments as the recent Machinists Union contract in which union members are now doing work that previously was done by a layer of supervisory personnel, by the Toledo Teacher's Union agreement with their school district in which teacher union representatives will participate with management in quality of teaching review, by the takeover of inner-city food stores in Philadelphia by the United Food and Commercial Workers Union local there.

Note that in any of these cases it is not only what is being done but also who is doing it that is important. Unions are the only vehicle that workers now have to defend and advance their interests across the board in the American economy. With the exception of a few unions in which you might take your life in your hands to mount an opposition to the

134

incumbent's campaign, the unions are responsive and democratic institutions. Innovative managers are doing many of the things that are involved in the Teacher Union and Machinists examples. There are many examples of worker ownership as well. Neither of these, however, offers the promise of making a significant impact on the power relations of the country. Things that change how the labor union defines itself will.

A populist orientation at the workplace would have unionists increasing their challenge of management prerogatives, demanding more involvement of workers in issues having to do with the appropriateness, quality, effectiveness, and efficiency of what is produced or served. It would have workers, through their elected representatives, having a say in investment decisions, relocation decisions, and other areas now considered the sole prerogative of management. The focus, then, is not primarily on getting an international president to be the sole dissenting voice on the board of directors of a corporation or, for that matter, on the formality of "co-determination." Where neither changes the real relations of power, little results. This is precisely what is the matter with many of the employees' stock ownership plan, or ESOP, buy-outs: workers formally own, but there is no real change in who controls.

The orientation toward the building of counterinstitutions and power gives us a new way of understanding worker ownership and producer and consumer co-ops as well. That these can be built and that they can work is only partially the point. David Thompson, director of international relations of the Cooperative League of the USA, puts it well: "Cooperative housing is strongest where development has been centralized and projects decentralized. Norway, Sweden and Germany have successfully created over a million units of cooperative housing through their central cooperative housing organizations. For us (in the U.S.), every cooperative housing development is almost always an independent, single entity destined to play no future role in helping others, or in building a housing cooperative movement." The result is interesting "models" but no general impact.

In religious congregations across the land a renewal of the concern of the Judeo-Christian tradition for social and economic justice is taking place. Important for our point here is that this concern manifests itself in a pastoral way as well as a prophetic one. That is, it is based on concern for the people of the congregation in their own lives as well as a call on the people of the congregation to reach out to others. This linking of vision and self-interest, of broad values and immediate concerns, is at the heart of what is happening in these religious settings. The phenomenon is one

135

qualitatively different from that of middle class religious activists being involved in a range of issues that make up the "progressive" or "liberal" agenda.

Congregations led by those looking at people, power, politics and values are now contesting the new right for leadership on issues that were snubbed by liberal cosmopolitanism: crime, neighborhood safety, pornography. At the same time, these congregations are dealing with issues of employment, quality of education, affordable housing, toxic wastes and so on.

The Broadly Based Community Organization

The context for much that is hopeful in America today is the broadly based, multi-issue, multiconstituency, democratic community organization. Such organizations now exist in too few communities—and the organizers who can build them are relatively small in number. But both organizations and organizers are a growing phenomenon, and the results of these organizations' efforts are gaining increasing attention. The characteristics of these organizations may be summarized as follows:

□ The organization is rooted in local tradition, leadership, and people.

□ The organization's practice is guided by the values of the democratic tradition.

□ The organization recognizes the importance of self-interest as a source of energy and motivation for its participants.

□ The program of the organization arises out of the local people themselves.

□ The organization has the support of the majority of the people of the constituency for which it claims or seeks to speak.

□ The organization involves a substantial degree of individual participation. It is characterized by a constant day-to-day flow of volunteer activities and the daily functioning of numerous local committees charged with specific short-term functions.

□ The organization emphasizes the functional relationship between problems and therefore its program is multi-issue, and it seeks to relate to others similarly situated in other communities.

□ The organization avoids circumscribed and segmental approaches to the solution of the problems of the community.

136

◻ The organization recognizes that a democratic society is one that responds to popular pressures, and therefore realistically operates on the basis of pressure. For the same reason, it does not shy away from involvement in matters of controversy.

◻ The organization concentrates on the utilization of indigenous individuals who, if not leaders at the beginning, can be developed into leaders.

◻ The organization gives priority to the significance of two major sources of human motivation: deeply felt values and self-interest. The organization proceeds on the idea of channeling the many diverse forces of self-interest within the community into a common direction for the common good. It emphasizes the values of the democratic tradition and the particular culture of various groups of people as guideposts for settling disputes among the people. By values we mean: liberty, equality, community, love, mutual respect, dignity, and so forth.

◻ The organization recognizes and respects the autonomy and diversity of individuals and organizations.

◻ The organization is or becomes self-financed through direct dues and membership participation in fundraising activities. This testifies to its representative character in that the local community supports its organization financially, ensures to the membership the accountability of its paid staff, and guarantees the financial independence of the organization.

Much of this summary is adapted from a statement written by Saul Alinsky in July 1955.

Activities of Broadly Based or Mass Organizations

The activities of these broadly based community organizations include:

◻ winning and enforcing victories on particular issues;

◻ encouraging and strengthening voluntary associations and mutual aid activities;

◻ bringing together on a basis of mutual respect diverse groups that have historically been antagonists—victims of their own parochialism as well as tactics of divide and conquer used against them;

◻ providing opportunities for leadership training and development;

□ deepening an appreciation of the values of the democratic and Judeo-Christian traditions by combining action with reflection;

□ educating themselves (meaning their members and constituents) about the problems and issues of our time.

In a number of places these organizations have participated in the electoral process. They have understood such participation as a tactic—one of the means by which to build the kind of popular organization necessary to defend and advance the interests and values of their members within the broader framework of democratic and religious values that underlie our nation. Even the most powerful of these organizations are wary of becoming the tail on a candidate's kite.

The Heart of Populism

Note, then, that what may be called a "populist" organization and program emerges from patiently constructed, from-the-bottom-up organizations. Note also that to look at specific issue "accomplishments" or specific programmatic ideas is to focus on only one part of the picture. The entire picture is one of building the counterinstitutions and organizations that can enable us to deal powerfully with those who now wield power. In our century the CIO, the Non-Partisan League, and the Montgomery Improvement Association probably provide us with the best historic examples of this possibility.

The Battle of Democratic Versus Elitist Ideas

An important role to be played in the recovery of America's democratic past is that of challenging opinion shapers and makers about their ideas. The major antidemocratic impulses in American life can be traced to two ideas: (1) The protection of individual and minority rights is more assured if power is in the hands of elites—the more educated and sophisticated. (2) The people "at the top," those who "run things," know better than most of us how to make our society more effective and efficient. They are more qualified to make decisions than are most people.

Most of our dominant institutions are organized to protect and enhance these ideas.

For democratic populism to become a reality we need historians who will write more about what average people did and less about what elites did, journalists to find out more about what's going on in neighborhoods and less of what politicians are saying, political philosophers who will ask more about what Jefferson had in mind when he talked about the importance of the yeoman farmer and less about how Jeffersonian ideals do not fit in high-tech, urban America, schoolteachers who will more often point out how local residents organizing to fight toxic-waste dumps are like the American revolutionaries and who are less tied to the bland civics of most texts, labor educators who will more often celebrate working-class history and culture and less often present labor history to workers as simply the story of an alternative set of "great men."

An Emerging Movement in America Today

A powerful new movement to reclaim democracy is emerging today in America. It is built on the basic values of liberty, justice, equality, and community. It also claims the traditional values of family, religion, neighborhood, work, and national pride. It needs a richer language to distinguish itself from dominant cultural themes of material success, "me-first" and America first, private (corporate) enterprise as the guarantor of economic progress. Whether democratic populism can provide that language is the challenge facing its proponents.

The organizing task for populist intellectuals (people of ideas) is to bring a different language and perspective to bear in their professional organizations as well as in America's major cultural institutions. Pacific News Service has been pioneering this method of news reporting. Teacher union locals could be testifying before school district curriculum committees for supplemental texts. Media unions could publicly criticize the Archie Bunker images of working people. Historians, political scientists, psychologists, sociologists, and others could challenge "great men" theories of history. Theologians and clergy can emphasize the missionary and evangelist in each member of a congregation. Labor educators and writers can help workers tell the story of today's workplace—perhaps not the dungeon of yesterday's mine, but a place with its own degradations of the human mind and spirit.

My first organizing experience was in an anti-urban renewal fight in San Francisco. While most city planners, urban sociologists, and architects argued before political bodies, wrote policy papers for commissions and candidates, debated ideas in professional and learned journals, there were a few who met with the resident leaders of our anti-urban renewal coalition and patiently described how they could have a voice in the renewal of their own neighborhood. Not only did they offer their skills to people who were not sure that what they were doing was possible, they also offered ideas that added a clarity to what the people wanted. "Downtown" was portraying the local group as "selfishly" interested—and not looking out for the good of the city as a whole. The planners, politicians, and editorial pundits counterposed their own concern for "the city as a whole" to the "narrow interests" of local residents. What our little band of intellectual allies provided was both technical expertise and moral justification for the popular struggle. Residents, local business people, and local institutional leaders (congregations, fraternal and civic associations, the elderly, and other groups) discovered that their concerns could be articulated as a vision of the good city. They also discovered that those who were their adversaries just might have been serving the interests of the developers and downtown money and that their vision of the city was probably the more selfish one.

The creation of this kind of public self-confidence on the part of the vast majority of Americans is one of the most important tasks of our time. It is something to which the new populism may make a great contribution.

Five

ECONOMIC AND PROGRAMMATIC ISSUES

DEMOCRATIC POPULISM

In the last years "populism" has again emerged as a political label and as a political stance. Increasingly, on the right and on the left, political groups fly the banner of populism over their work for political change. They have been meeting with increasing success.

The most public attention has been given to the political activists and organizations of the new right. The shrewdest Republican strategists from Kevin Phillips to Paul Weyrich to Jack Kemp have grasped the utility of a populist politics in contemporary, changing America. The left has been somewhat slower to embrace the populist label and fashion a progressive populist philosophy. In recent years, however, largely because of the work of Harry Boyte and others, a growing set of organizers and activists at work in communities across the country have come to recognize their work and their general approach in the description of "democratic populist organizing."

One of the greatest contributions of the articulators of a progressive populism has been to slowly get organizations and leaders who had self-consciously eschewed ideology and labels to accept that their work, insights, values flowed from and into a coherent if developing American political philosophy. Reacting to the dogmatism, sterile ideologies, and overblown rhetoric of the late 1960s, many of the most talented political organizers set out to find ways to organize new, broader political constituencies in the 1970s. The result has been a significant growth in grassroots citizen organizations. They are firmly determined to resist any labels, to be energetically eclectic, experimental, and pragmatic. More than ten years of organizing "ordinary" Americans has produced a network of progressive organizations, a body of experiences, and an emerging political stance and philosophy that most easily recognizes itself in the word "populist."

We have several purposes in this chapter. The first is to praise what we see as the major contributions of democratic populism and of Harry Boyte in particular. The second is to raise some issues that significantly challenge supporters of a progressive democratic populism and by all of us who want to build a coherent, effective, and popular progressive politics. We want to avoid a long, historical, or academic discussion of American populism. Instead, we focus on the emerging democratic populism of contemporary citizen organizing. We discuss populism interchangeably as an emerging ideology, political philosophy, strategy, and organizing approach.

Praise

In a very real way democratic populism provides a way of understanding what is actually happening in a major section of progressive organizing in the United States. It names our practice. It begins to make us aware of the underlying themes and the realities of our work. By naming and expanding on what we are doing, it begins to suggest future directions. At the same time it gives us a language to describe our work and our values, not just to ourselves but also to a broad cross-section of our fellow citizens who will recognize our values and impulses as their own.

144

Democratic populism stresses the issues of popular control, popular participation, and grassroots realities. The practitioners and theorists of democratic populism stress how issues affect people in their everyday lives. They are ardently democratic. At the heart of the progressive populist vision is the value of grassroots organization, participation, and democracy.

Thus the new progressive populism in both theory and practice offers an alternative both to overly centralized socialist forms and to the over-reliance on the state of most recent liberalism. For populists, the goal is not an ever-expanding government bureaucracy or the creation of an ever-increasing dependency on government. But there is a clarity that government must be activist and does constantly intervene. For the democratic populists, the issue is not more or less government but who government works for and how it works. The new populists stress that government must work for the vast majority, that democracy is not an empty form. To live up to its promise, democracy requires forms for participation, new grassroots social organization, and an organized, aroused, and conscious citizenry.

This perspective departs from the increased statism of many modern progressive visions. For the populist, progress is not equatable simply with increased planning or nationalization of industry that leaves power in the hands of bureaucrats and politicians. The new democratic populists are beginning to Americanize radicalism by connecting to an American past, American roots, and American values based upon popular organization.

This vision of democratic populism clarifies the meaning of progressive "politics." Democratic populism asks what happens to the lives of ordinary people, demands that we not see politics as simply the changing of leaders, the pursuit of power, reactions to inevitable economic collapses. Implicit in democratic populist practice and philosophy is the belief that progressive politics must be about transforming social relationships, developing popular consciousness, enhancing people and their everyday lives.

Thus populism provides a new way to look at our reform efforts. By stressing what people learn, what creates popular organization, what creates new democratic forms, the new populism suggests ways that our reform campaigns can prefigure the democratic society that is our goal at the same time that they build progressive political power.

The new populism stresses a politics of the majority. It is based on the belief that a common, public interest can unite a population as disparate

145

as America's. That commonality does not now exist in any functional manner. Politically such a public interest must be created, fought for, brought into being through political struggle. Populism sees that struggle as between the interests of the vast majority of ordinary Americans and the greed of remote special interests. Thus populism believes that policies that derive from the needs of the vast majority will be progressive. Populism rejects the implicit elitism of recent liberalism that all too often barely veiled a conviction that many less sophisticated Americans were part of the problem. It glorifies as unbounded the *potentially* deep wellsprings of democratic decency to be found in the average American.

Building on this belief in the potential of the ordinary person, the new democratic populism, especially as articulated by Harry Boyte, makes a very important contribution to progressive political positioning. It demands that progressives connect to traditional American values and argues that tradition, mainstream institutions, and social customs are important to developing a progressive politics and culture. Not only Boyte's writings but the very prosaic realities of most of the grassroots organizations fly in the face of the last twenty years or more of progressive political culture.

Over the years progressives developed a political culture that stressed cosmopolitanism, that rejected traditional values, that glorified riding on the cutting edge of change. By the 1960s, many who rode this trend claimed an alienation from all mainstream culture. Only intellectually "advanced," avant garde, and "liberated" activities were accepted in the progressive political culture. Modernism was carried to an extreme. Only those who were most alienated from our society's norms and culture were considered capable of being progressive agents of change.

The new populism asserts a dramatically different understanding: first, not all that is new is good, not all that is old is bad. The new populism suggests that critical wellsprings of progressive politics can be found in traditional values and culture. Much of the new progressive populist politics is a defense of traditional values, positions, neighborhoods, economic status, and institutions from the onslaught of atomizing, depersonalizing, homogenizing, modernizing economic and political forces. Is it progressive to "urban renew" once stable, socially rich blue-collar neighborhoods? Is it progress when neighborhoods are gentrified? Is it conservative to fight for the family farm?

The populist answer is clear. The populist constituencies are those, both young and old, who seek to preserve roots, defend community,

146

resisting the mania for the new at the expense of everything traditional. The populist ideology and practice suggest that only those not totally alienated from a society can lead it toward badly needed changes. The populist experience suggests that some of the most important motivating forces leading people to progressive political activity are traditional values and a desire to preserve the best of the promise of the past.

This reaction to alienated cosmopolitanism connects to some very deep impulses in the particular constituencies involved in the recent citizen organizing. It is a sharp challenge to the dominant progressive assumptions of at least the last twenty-five years.

The new populism usefully stresses the importance of community, both as an arena of action and as a critical building block in the democratic vision. Particularly as Boyte unfolds populism, community takes the theme of empowerment and gives it a place, a concrete location. Further, it links the democratic impulses of the 1960s with the history and traditions of mainstream and particularly blue-collar culture.

Finally, the new populism dramatically shows that even in a period of conservative triumph there are numerous openings and spaces for progressive organizing if it will connect with the real problems of people's everyday lives. We are not caught in a one-dimensional society. Even as atomizing and undemocratic political and economic forces roll forward, they create new possibilities of change in our personal lives and political practices.

These are major, substantial contributions. We are strong supporters of the work, both the theoretical and practical work, being carried forward by the organizers and advocates of democratic populism. By raising questions about the road to a populist ideology, we do not demean its possibilities. Rather, we seek to raise issues that inescapably face the new democratic populism.

Issues

The recent articulations of progressive populism stand out because so little else has been happening on the left in recent years. Along with the nuclear freeze movement, it has been one of the few new, positive trends to emerge in the current period. History is not a Chinese restaurant menu: we do not get to choose one movement from Group A and another from

147

Group B. Instead, we must pay attention to what is actually going on in a society, what is emerging that is significant. We must examine carefully what progressive movements are possible and understand clearly their social basis.

The new trends that we must look for and understand do not follow some unalterable trajectory. The new trends enter the historical stew, and what finally develops is different from the various ingredients added to the stew. The new ingredients do not necessarily dominate. Rather, the new often serves as a *kuche laffel*, a cooking spoon, that stirs the pot.

It is our sense that the new populism, both as ideology and as organizing approach, has and will stir the pot. But what will emerge is a democratic populism that will differ in its historical character and role from what it is currently and from what many may now believe its future will be.

As it evolves, democratic populism faces a set of challenges that it must address if it is to become a viable progressive political philosophy and a powerful political force. It must confront its own contradictory tendencies as well as its economics, politics, and social psychology.

The Dark Side of Populism

Populism reveres traditionalism and localism, especially blue-collar, ethnic traditionalism and working-class localism. Yet traditionalism and localism have a spotted history. The association of localism, traditionalism, and populism with a dark side of racism and demagogy is historical reality. Appreciation of the deep wellsprings of democratic decency and common sense in Americans should not obscure the continuing traditions and threat of racism, anti-intellectualism, and chauvinism that are deeply imbedded in the political culture in general and in that of ethnic blue-collar Americans in particular. To say local and populist is not necessarily to say democratic, open, unbiased.

Many of our populist friends dismiss this danger as a historical problem of which they are well aware and have surmounted. That is too easy. Any examination of Alinsky's organizing in white ethnic neighborhoods such as the Back of the Yards raises it again. The experiences of the South West Parish Federation of Chicago in the 1970s highlights the duality of populist political culture and practice.

148

Populism as ideology and as political approach must face squarely the problems of social issues. Most of the current populist base is found among blue- and white-collar residents of older cities and among small farmers. In general these are groups whose experience of the last fifteen years has made them increasingly angry and restless. By and large, they have played by all the rules, done everything that society has asked them, and, having jumped through all the hoops, they feel shortchanged. In the early 1970s, after thirty years of a general rising standard of living, they suffered a period of prolonged stagnation and decline. Constituencies that had seen themselves as the heart of our society feel increasingly marginalized, their entire way of life threatened by rapid economic and social change.

This experience has produced a populist anger: the people are being betrayed by the greed of special interests, manipulated by remote elites. The anger and searching are impelled by great changes, ranging from the shift in the economy to service and high technology to the declining U.S. global position. Political culture is dialectical: very strongly conflicting currents are at work within people and within the new populist consciousness.

The Republicans have perceived this tension quite skillfully. They have seen that an appeal to community, to family, to tradition, to populist anger can quite easily be joined to a new nationalism, foreign-policy belligerence, unsubtle racism, and a reaction against feminism. It is insufficient simply to dismiss their efforts as slick demagogy, given the historical antecedents.

The last fifteen years have seen a new rise in populist anger but it has been primarily channeled into conservative directions: the antibusing movements, the conservative tax revolts, the right-to-life efforts, the anti-obscenity and antipornography campaigns. It is disingenuous of progressive populists not to recognize the populist impulse of the new right campaigns. Over and over again in recent years, the populism of blue-collar ethnics has been effectively counterposed to progressive social positions to the benefit of conservative causes.

The very same constituencies may exhibit great support for a progressive populism on economic issues. As populism is advanced as a serious political philosophy, as a major part of a progressive strategy for national electoral power, progressive populists must address the social issues head on. The challenge is difficult. They must argue that accepted progressive formulations on social issues are deeply flawed and should be changed to new ones more acceptable to potential populist supporters, or they must formulate new progressive populist positions on the social issues that effectively counter right-wing appeals.

There are similar problems with the populist glorification of the concept of community. We have pointed out its positive features. The reality is, however, that America is a very mobile and transitory society. Fewer and fewer geographical and social sites can accurately be described as engendering a high degree of commitment and a sense of community among the residents. All too often, community becomes defined by its struggles, creating uncertain boundaries, uncertain citizens, and dismayed outsiders and bystanders.

Despite the convenient and articulate definitions used by organizers, very often community is as much associated with exclusion as with inclusion. There is a dialectic in the creation of a sense of community, inclusion creating exclusion. A community is often created momentarily in struggling against a common threat.

An important part of a progressive consciousness is an enlarging identification with broad groupings of people who are not homogenous, who are not alike in appearance, race, nationality, heritage, but who share common needs, who share a common humanity. Often intense personal involvement in citizen organizations that stressed community has created that larger identification and consciousness for only a very limited number of people. We have not seen many examples of that widened identification occurring among the far greater numbers of the less involved supporters.

The stress on community and decentralism must also be accompanied by a populist perspective on national political structure and even local political structures. So far there has been a lack of such a perspective. In fact, the absence of much attention to the issue is a striking hole in new progressive populist writings. Further, the organizational realities of many populist citizen organizations cannot be seen as successful models for solutions to the problems of large-scale decision making, service delivery, and the making of public policy. While there has been much rhetorical attention paid to process, there has been little substantive thought to how governmental decisions should be made, services should be delivered, participation formalized, bureaucracy transcended.

In truth the internal life of many of even the very best citizens' organizations over the last two decades does not produce great optimism about quickly transferring the populist organizing approach to governmental realities. All too often, small cliques have dominated. Democratic voting is often less important than it appears. When large amounts of governmental money were poured into community groups in the 1960s and 1970s, it was not unusual for corruption to appear, rivals to be intimidated, narrow ethnic or political groups to become increasingly competitive in pursuit of resources.

Empowerment does not unfold a magical process that immediately wipes away all human frailties, organizational weaknesses, social conflicts. There has to be a political process that makes empowerment a democratic, a contentful, positive experience. To say "empowerment," "local," or "decentralized" is not necessarily to say "democratic" or "effective."

Populist citizen organizations need a clearer political structure that shows that they are capable of including democratically the participation of very large numbers of people. All too often there is a core of very committed people who are devoted to the organization and then a very large group of supporters who are not heavily involved at all. Many of the larger citizens' organizations have come to understand the tyranny of structurelessness and have developed much clearer internal structures. But even these still display great confusions over the role of leaders.

For populism to become a powerful political force it will need sustained, consistent, skilled leaders capable of articulating a vision and of leading people, not simply reflecting their current understandings. That will require the nurturing and supporting of a leadership that in turn is tied democratically and structurally to a base, a leadership that can articulate a political direction based upon populist values, and a structure or set of structures that allows large numbers of people to participate democratically. In both theory and practice, democratic populist citizens' organizations are not very clear on these issues, especially when expanded to a national stage and applied to the problems of achieving national political power and making the national governmental structures work democratically and efficiently.

On the level of theory, populists need to articulate a clear vision about the role of government and how to make it work to serve the great majority of people rather than the special interests. How will that happen when there has not been dramatic redistribution of economic power? How will populists deal with the problem of bureaucracy? What are the new democratic forms that will apply to the national level?

On the level of strategy, it remains unclear what is the strategy that builds from the local level into a successful challenge for national political power. Few people now argue, as some did in the early 1970s, that localism will be the salvation of America. It is evident that the national economy, national policies, national politics determine what can and cannot happen at the local level. For progressive populists to be a force, they have to be able to contend for national political power. There is increasing agreement about that.

What is the strategic connection between local work and national strategy? Many groups that do very solid local organizing simply retreat into the excuse of "taking a long-term view." We are for taking a long-term view—we would like to hear one articulated that actually makes the case for how national political power will be built from loosely connected organizations in two dozen cities, or even fifty cities. We are for taking a realistically long-term view, but what is needed now is an articulated strategy that clearly connects local actions to national effectiveness.

Many populist and citizen organizers who articulate national political strategies sometimes seem to be simply overlaying local work with electoral campaigns and campaign apparatus. The connections among them are not always obvious.

The lack of clarity about the strategic relationship of the local base building and a necessary national political goal is troubling. Ideally, the work of the groups at the local level is critically building a base and transforming consciousness. For this work to be effective, it must directly connect with the national political struggles that will have to be waged. It is not clear that it does. The idea that we will take local power, build a political movement at the local level that will surround Washington, seems muddled at best.

Yet to think that we will succeed in national politics without building a base, transforming consciousness, connecting to people's everyday lives, building new forms of mass democratic participation, seems as muddled. Populist theorists and strategists need to work more on this crucial linkage of their local work and national strategy.

Consciousness

Linking local work and national strategy becomes even more important when we examine the practice of the citizens' organizations. In the Boyte model, local empowerment work is almost mystically transforming people, their relationships, their sense of the possible, their sense of themselves. Such a process seems highly desirable. And we are confident that it does occur for those who are heavily involved in the activist organizations. We know personally scores of activists in populist organizations whose new experiences allowed them to reevaluate their life experiences. The results are impressive: dramatic flowering of potential, a new political consciousness, great commitment.

But in reality the cost is high: in general this transformation occurred in people who were willing to devote great hours every week to the organization, who were at its core. The numbers are rather small.

While progressive populists ask people for heavy participation, risk taking, and commitment, right-wing populists frequently ask for much less: some money, a vote, reading something. Progressive populists rely primarily on individual contact and communication. The right relies on the printed word, mail, radio, and television. Progressive populists seek to transform people. The right seeks only to define people's understanding of the political issues, drawing on what are prevalent themes in the political culture. The right relies on leadership and communication. Progressive populists have yet to prove they can either transform people in massive numbers or develop leadership and communication systems to shape people's political definitions.

Many citizens' organizations try to avoid this problem by not seeking to have tens of thousands of citizens understand fully the goals of the organization. Instead, the organizations define a few issues that virtually everyone agrees with and develop communication efforts about them, for example, promote identification of the organization with opposing rate hikes. But for democratic populism to compete as a national political force, this is not enough. Populist politics must become a value-based and value-articulating politics.

What Are Our Values?

Populists must be able to articulate positions on a range of issues that they have often avoided. To do that well, the populist movement needs to develop a body of leaders at both the national and local levels who can articulate those positions, values, visions, and are not afraid to take the risk of being divisive on occasion.

We have raised the problem of a populist position on social issues. It is equally true that the populists need to address the issues of foreign

153

policy, international economics, underdevelopment, the arms race, and intervention. It is not difficult to imagine the beginnings of a populist foreign policy that is anti-interventionist. But in the long run we will need more than that: we will need a positive vision about the U.S. global role.

One of the two dominant political facts underlying the growth of both the right wing and progressive populism of the 1970s was the stagnation and decline in the standard of living for blue-collar Americans; the other crucial experience was the obvious decline in the U.S. world position. The question of national security in a changing world is a central one for this political period. Either populists will provide a convincing vision of what constitutes a serious program for national security, for relations with the U.S.S.R., for dealing with hunger and underdevelopment, or populism will be swept aside by a continued reactionary nationalist politics that does speak to these issues, however demogogically.

The Future

Democratic populism faces a major intellectual as well as political organizing job. Its importance is accentuated because of the absence of any overall progressive movement and of political vehicles and because of the disarray of many traditional liberal and progressive forces.

One of the key unaddressed questions about democratic populism is its relationship to a larger progressive strategy. Is democratic populism the overarching progressive politics of the 1990s? So far, there is little indication of that. Instead, it appears to be the political approach of very specific, important, and narrowly delineated constituencies. If this remains so, populism will appear to be another name for "special interests" only concerned about their particular economic needs.

One of the weaknesses of populist analysis is that it tends to lump everybody together as "the people." The new theorists of a progressive populism are guilty of taking this even further. For Harry Boyte and others, anything that is decentralized, self-organized, folksy, self-reliant, and good can now be described as populist. This leads to obscuring simplifications. The blue-collar populists of the citizen action organizations probably feel that they have more in common with right-wing causes than they do with the feminist collective that produced the book *Our Bodies, Ourselves*. Important ethnic, racial, class, and cultural differences divide "the people." And they are expressed in different progressive political efforts as well.

The new populism of the community organizations has not developed either an intellectual breadth or a strategic clarity that would create conditions for a broader appeal to the constituencies that are at the heart of the women's, peace, and environmental movements. There are increasing points of convergence between these, but enormous gulfs in styles, values, and vision remain. The new democratic populism will have to address many of the issues we briefly raise above either before it can become the embracing politics for a new progressive movement uniting these disparate elements or even before it can figure out its relationship to a larger progressive strategy.

Twelve

Charlene Spretnak

POSTMODERN POPULISM:
THE GREENING OF
TECHNOCRATIC SOCIETY

The word "populism" commonly connotes a political impulse based in nostalgia for a simpler time when community bonds were stronger. The Populist movement of the late nineteenth century was, however, far more than merely an expression of community in our agrarian past. The Populists addressed the most pressing issue of their day: whether the federal government would return to the gold standard after the Civil War or adopt "greenbacks, the people's currency." The Populist movement arose because neither of the two major political parties was willing to challenge the bankers and financiers who held government bonds from the war. The only way ordinary citizens could even frame an alternative in the national debate was to do it outside of the two-party system.

One could draw parallels, then, between the Populist movement and various citizen movements today that draw members from both the Democratic and Republican camps. The crucial issue of our time, however, is

156

nothing as simple as the monetary system. Rather, it is the interrelatedness of all the crucial issues: the web of cause and effect created by a global economic system based on open-ended growth; a hair-trigger system of nuclear warheads mounted to defend the competitors in that economic system; an ignorance of and disregard for the carrying capacity of the natural world; the enthusiastic acceptance of patriarchal values, which establish a hierarchical ordering of white men's desires over those of women and people of color; and an uneasy faith in "modern progress" based on the mechanistic worldview.

If the new "populism" is to take shape in the United States and address that web of complexities effectively, it must have a strong head as well as an alluring heart. The heartfelt longing for community bonding as an escape from contemporary alienation and loneliness is a well-documented aspect of the new populism. For its head component, I nominate the postliberal, postsocialist, post–finance-capitalist body of ideas for our era called Green politics. It combines global responsibility and the values of decentralist, Jeffersonian democracy with the ecological wisdom of a sustainable, steady-state economy, one based on maximum private ownership by the maximum number of citizens.

Green politics is currently taking root in nearly all industrialized nations and in many Third World countries as well. It begins primarily among the educated middle class who challenge their technocratic governments on behalf of *all* citizens—because all people suffer from the poisoning of air, water, and soil; from the disintegration of community; from the powerlessness of white- *and* blue-collar workers that results when human existence is shaped to serve unqualified industrial growth at all costs. Green politics is about the values in everyday life and the empowerment of ordinary people in order to safeguard and evolve those values.

This new politics is the political arm of a profound cultural revisioning. It is an ecological, holistic, and feminist movement that transcends the old political framework of left versus right. It emphasizes the interconnectedness and interdependence of all phenomena, as well as the embeddedness of individuals and societies in the processes of nature. It addresses the unjust and destructive dynamics of patriarchy. It calls for social responsibility and a sound, sustainable (steady-state) economic system, one that is ecological, decentralized to a great extent, equitable, and composed of flexible institutions, one in which people have significant control over their lives. In advocating a cooperative world order,

Green politics rejects all forms of exploitation—of nature, individuals, social groups, and countries. It is committed to nonviolence at all levels. It encourages a rich cultural life that respects the pluralism within a society, and it honors the inner growth that leads to wisdom.

The phenomenon of Green politics is primarily a grassroots citizens' movement, which in some countries has won seats in the parliamentary government. Greens see the major political parties, both liberal and conservative, as dangerously enmeshed in the destructive dynamics of a global economy based on mindless growth that is oblivious to our dependency on the natural world and is immoral with regard to our responsibility to less affluent members of our planetary community and to future generations. Those dynamics are furthered by the growth of centralized, control-oriented governments that protect the interest of the military-industrial complex in our nuclearized nation-states.

More than a reaction against reckless economic development and nuclearism, Green politics is a deeply rooted cultural response to the dominant social paradigm, modernity. Modern society is guided by mechanistic analysis and control of human systems and of nature, rootless cosmopolitanism, nationalistic chauvinism, patriarchal anxieties, sterile secularism, and monoculture shaped by mass media. An enthusiast of modernity has little use for the traditional institutions that further human bonding—the family, the church, community groups, ethnic associations—championing instead an "individualistic-liberationist" stance, as it has been labeled by Harry Boyte and Sara Evans.

Such an escape from one's roots and the fabric of community allows one to re-form the self as a free-wheeling player in technocratic society and to accumulate enticing material rewards for productive behavior—as long as one does not ask the obvious questions about the consequences of a system that operates as if there were no tomorrow. Modernity—powerful, sleek, and frenetic—requires only that one become a stranger in the natural world, a force alien to one's neighbors in the global village, a master of guardedly shallow relationships, and an uncanny apologist for greed and cool detachment. It is a Faustian agreement we entered into when we turned our attention away from the subtle, intangible dimensions of life, which are spiritual. The only demonic force at work is our own willful ignorance.

The values of modernity inform both socialist and capitalist nation-states. It is not surprising that citizens' resistance networks in socialist countries often find a home in the churches and that both liberal and conservative churches in capitalist countries are rethinking religion's contemporary role as an inconsequential observer who is to make accommodations to the modern world and not interfere with "progress."

One of the most serious questions in that rethinking is whether institutional religions will be radical enough to reclaim the wisdom of their mystical traditions, which have been denied for some three hundred years. Christians, for instance, might cultivate inner development and a new relationship to the natural world if they took seriously the words of Hildegard of Bingen, Mechtild of Magdeburg, Meister Eckhart, Francis of Assisi, Teresa of Avila, Julian of Norwich, and others. Their teachings, which are part of a theology known as "creation spirituality," leads directly to a Green worldview, not toward "dominion" over natural "resources" in a zombie-like march to the tune of mindless industrial growth. Equally important is a new cosmology that locates humans *as a species* in the unfolding story of the Earth and the universe. If we do not comprehend our role, our position, our potential, how can humans act wisely in a context that spans national boundaries and countless generations hence?[1]

Whatever the particulars of postmodern culture, it will not signify an uncritical return to the values of the medieval world that immediately preceded the Enlightenment or those of the Gilded Age preceding World War I and the aggressive burst of modernism that followed it. The pioneers of modernity were right to reject certain conventions and restrictions that were stultifying to the human spirit. But, with the impulses of a rebellious adolescent, they destroyed too much and embraced a radical disregard for limits, especially concerning the natural world. What we need now is the maturity to value freedom *and* tradition, the individual *and* the community, technology *and* nature, men *and* women.

The European Greens usually speak openly about taking their inspiration from citizens' movements in the United States: the civil rights movement, especially its nonviolent tactics; the ecology movement; the feminist movement; and the consumer-protection movement. When various European Green parties, especially the one in West Germany, captured the attention of American journalists in the early 1980s by winning seats in local, state, and national elections, primarily on environmental and antimissile issues, efforts were revived to build a movement of the new politics in this country.

The largest Green political organization in the United States today is the Committees of Correspondence (P.O. Box 30208, Kansas City, Missouri 64112), which takes its name from the grassroots networks that flourished during the American Revolution. It is a regionally based, national organization that was founded in August 1984 at a meeting in St. Paul, Minnesota, of theorists and activists who had been involved for many years in Greenish work.

Out of that weekend gathering came *Ten Key Values*, a constellation of questions for discussion among grassroots groups. Its preface states, "We feel the issues we have raised below are not being addressed adequately by the political left or right. We invite you to join with us in refining our values, sharpening our questions—and translating our perspective into practical and effective political actions." A draft of a partial platform suggesting Green approaches on several issues central to American politics today was circulated within the Committees of Correspondence for discussion in 1986, but I have reproduced *Ten Key Values* below because it is a concise presentation of the core concepts in American Green politics. Their correspondence with populist impulses, I believe, is quite evident.

1. *Ecological Wisdom*—How can we operate human societies with the understanding that we are part of nature, not on top of it? How can we live within the ecological and resource limits of the planet, applying our technological knowledge to the challenge of an energy-efficient economy? How can we build a better relationship between cities and countryside? How can we guarantee the rights of nonhuman species? How can we promote sustainable agriculture and respect for self-regulating natural systems? How can we further biocentric wisdom in all spheres of life?

2. *Grassroots Democracy*—How can we develop systems that allow and encourage us to control the decisions that affect our lives? How can we ensure that representatives will be fully accountable to the people who elected them? How can we encourage and assist the "mediating institutions"—family, neighborhood organization, church group, voluntary association, ethnic club—recover some of the functions now performed by the government? How can we relearn the best insights from American traditions of civic vitality, voluntary action, and community responsibility?

160

3. *Personal and Social Responsibility*—How can we respond to human suffering in ways that promote dignity? How can we encourage people to commit themselves to lifestyles that promote their own health? How can we have a community-controlled education system that effectively teaches our children academic skills, ecological wisdom, social responsibility, and personal growth? How can we resolve interpersonal and intergroup conflicts without just turning them over to lawyers and judges? How can we take responsibility for reducing the crime rate in our neighborhoods? How can we encourage such values as simplicity and moderation?

4. *Nonviolence*—How can we, as a society, develop effective alternatives to our current patterns of violence, at all levels, from the family and the street to nations and the world? How can we eliminate nuclear weapons from the face of the Earth without being naive about the intentions of other governments? How can we most constructively use non-violent methods to oppose practices and policies with which we disagree and in the process reduce the atmosphere of polarization and selfishness that is itself a source of violence?

5. *Decentralization*—How can we restore power and responsibility to individuals, institutions, communities, and regions? How can we encourage the flourishing of regionally-based culture, rather than a dominant monoculture? How can we have a decentralized, democratic society with our political, economic, and social institutions locating power on the smallest scale (closest to home) that is efficient and practical? How can we redesign our institutions so that fewer decisions and less regulation over money are granted as one moves from the community toward the national level? How can we reconcile the need for community and regional self-determination with the need for appropriate centralized regulation in certain matters?

6. *Community-based Economics*—How can we redesign our work structures to encourage employee ownership and workplace democracy? How can we develop new economic activities and institutions that will allow us to use our new technologies in ways that are humane, freeing, ecological, and accountable and responsive to communities? How can we establish some form of basic economic security, open to all? How can we move beyond the narrow "job ethic" to new definitions of "work," "jobs," and

161

"income" that reflect the changing economy? How can we restructure our patterns of income distribution to reflect the wealth created by those outside the formal, monetary economy: those who take responsibility for parenting, housekeeping, home gardens, community volunteer work, etc.? How can we restrict the size and concentrated power of corporations without discouraging superior efficiency or technological innovation?

7. *Postpatriarchal Values*—How can we replace the cultural ethics of dominance and control with more cooperative ways of interacting? How can we encourage people to care about persons outside their own group? How can we promote the building of respectful, positive, and responsible relationships across the lines of gender and other divisions? How can we encourage a rich, diverse political culture that respects feelings as well as rationalist approaches? How can we proceed with as much respect for the means as the end (the process as much as the products of our efforts)? How can we learn to respect the contemplative, inner part of life as much as the outer activities?

8. *Respect for Diversity*—How can we honor cultural, ethnic, racial, sexual, religious, and spiritual diversity within the context of individual responsibility to all beings? How can we reclaim our country's finest shared ideals: the dignity of the individual, democratic participation, and liberty and justice for all?

9. *Global Responsibility*—How can we be of genuine assistance to grassroots groups in the Third World? What can we learn from such groups? How can we help other countries make the transition to self-sufficiency in food and other basic necessities? How can we cut our defense budget while maintaining an adequate defense? How can we promote these ten Green values in the reshaping of our global order? How can we reshape world order without creating just another enormous nation-state?

10. *Future Focus*—How can we induce people and institutions to think in terms of the long-range future, and not just in terms of their short-range selfish interest? How can we encourage people to develop their own visions of the future and move more effectively toward them? How can we judge whether new technologies are socially useful and use those judgments to shape our society? How can we induce our government and other institutions to practice

162

fiscal responsibility? How can we make the quality of life, rather than open-ended economic growth, the focus of future thinking?

The values of Green politics locate this movement squarely in the American radical tradition of self-government of manageable scale and of distrust of centralized power. Mark Satin, editor of *New Options* newsletter in Washington, D.C., characterizes American Green politics as the combination of populism and futurism. Perhaps. We certainly encourage the kind of future-thinking that will result in sustainable solutions to our problems rather than high-tech, macho quick fixes that are ignorant of systemic realities. But I hope that Green will mean something deeper: love, grounded in knowledge, for the natural world, especially for the particular bioregion we call home.[2] I hope it will mean a sense of kinship with all sentient beings, a sense that our being is diminished because 40,000 children in the global village starve to death every day. I hope it will include a spiritual awareness—which need not mean compulsory participation in organized religion—of the subtle processes that constitute life and of our profound interconnectedness.

At very least, any one of the clusters of questions in *Ten Key Values* demonstrates the difference between Green values and those of either the left or the right. In my partisan view, Green concepts are the closest to the expressions that have surfaced so far as the new populism, but that interpretation would be hotly disputed by my colleagues on the left and the right. Frankly, my stomach feels queasy whenever I hear certain "progressives" who are still firmly rooted in left-wing modes of operation speak of knowing how to *use* the new populism or a right-wing tactician speak of the *potential* there. Both of those camps bring somewhat hidden agendas and fixed ideologies: much of the left operates on the assumption of the empty values of modernity, and much of the right on the rigid values of patriarchy and nationalism. Green politics is embryonic in this country and sincerely invites participation from all relevant quarters in our development; we are not pushing a finished package at the new populists.

Suppose that the new populism does become a coherent political force, adopts postmodern, Green politics, and advances it with intelligence and vitality. To be effective, Green populists would have to leap two formidable hurdles identified in Lawrence Goodwyn's introduction to his book *The Populist Movement*. First, he notes, "People do not believe they can do much 'in politics' to affect substantively either their own daily lives or the inherited patterns of power and privilege within their society." Clearly a broadening of the meaning of "politics" is necessary in order for successful efforts at democratic participation and empowerment to take root. But that broadening is thwarted by the second hurdle Goodwyn identifies: the disappearance of a sense of commonweal and a visible public ethic. This disappearance, he observes, "has been the subject of hand-wringing editorials in publications as diverse as the Chicago *Tribune* in the United States and *Izvestia* in the Soviet Union."

The problem is indeed collective, but is also personal: we do not know how to *be* in the healthier, sustainable world toward which our ideas are drawing us. Goodwyn maintains that the generating force of a new mass mode of behavior may be described simply as "a new way of looking at things." But is that enough to save us from the worsening crises of the modern world? In spite of our new vision and analyses, we slip into old, destructive modes of communicating and interacting when trying to develop the new politics. In spite of the genuine enthusiasm I have witnessed in Green audiences when Harry Boyte presents his ideas on community-building, the demographic swell that is the Baby Boom generation is probably the most individualistic in history and does not know how to be otherwise. In spite of the religious awakening many cultural analysts have noted in this country in recent years, few clergy are trained to be spiritual guides of the sort who could encourage the inner work that generates equanimity, insight, and a sense of our species' role in the cosmos. The changes we need to effect are located in our own body-minds as much as in our economic and political systems. Our politics must deepen as they broaden. Let wisdom and compassion be our guides.

Notes

1. See *Original Blessing* and *The Illuminations of Hildegard of Bingen* by Matthew Fox, plus the *Meditations with* series. Also see *The Universe Is a Green Dragon* by Brian Swimme on the new physics and the cosmology of Thomas Berry, a theologian-turned-geologian. All are published by Bear and Company, P.O. Drawer 2860, Santa Fe, NM 87504.

2. See *Dwellers in the Land: The Bioregional Vision* by Kirkpatrick Sale (San Francisco: Sierra Club Books, 1985).

Thirteen
Gar Alperovitz

TOWARD A
TOUGH-MINDED POPULISM

The United States is the wealthiest nation in the history of the world: Were we to divide today's gross national product equally among families of four, each would have roughly $65,000. Self-evidently, a much more equitable distribution of resources than our present one is technically possible—even allowing for the current poor functioning of the economy.

Traditional progressive theory—at least as it has operated since the New Deal—has held that a set of liberal ideas and ideals could, through the force of political action, press the overarching corporate economy to achieve goals in the "public interest." The power of the corporation, it was urged, could be limited through regulation and/or breakup via anti-trust activity, and the worst features of the economic system ameliorated through tax policy, social expenditures, minimum-wage legislation, the

This chapter appears with slight revisions in *Dissent* (Spring 1986). Reprinted by permission.

165

organization (and recognition) of trade unions, and through various health, safety, and environmental requirements.

While important gains have been achieved following this broad approach, it is now clearly facing major difficulties: the corporation and its economic allies have demonstrated their enormous "countervailing" power on virtually every front. Traditional liberal theory occasionally supported alterations in the underlying structure of economic power (for instance, it believed in helping establish co-ops). However, it has had very little to say about fundamental changes in the role of the large corporation.

Populist Ideas have the potential of transcending the limitations of traditional progressive thought in general and liberalism in particular. A considerably expanded conception of populism will, however, be required if there is to be a meaningful new politics—for, despite the popularity of the word, there are major obstacles standing in the way of a populist strategy.

In the first instance, populism is very easily focused in "antigovernment" ways—at a time when it is increasingly clear that unless a powerful strategy of government economic management is adopted, ever larger number of Americans will be left out of the economic process. Furthermore, on its own terms, populism does not necessarily offer an answer to the deep structural challenge at the corporate core of the political economy.

We have had eight recessions since World War II; the last reached a record depth of 10.7 percent unemployment. Each decade the average level of unemployment has increased—from 4.5 percent on average during the 1950s to 4.8 percent during the 1960s, to 6.2 percent during the 1970s, to 8 percent on average so far in the 1980s. The figures are roughly double for blacks and more than double again for black teenagers. Looking beyond the current "recovery," we see that the longer trend is clearly ominous.

Much economic thought these days centers around "industrial policies" to help selected firms and sectors become more competitive. But the likelihood of even the most fully developed industrial policies reversing the trends in our economy is very slim. We are dealing with the fundamental fact that the postwar boom and the conditions that produced it are over.

No longer is the United States dominant in a world economy devastated by the conflicts of 1939–45. No longer is there an internal domestic boost of investment from the pent-up demand (and savings) of that war. No longer are the major additional boosts of economic energy from the Korean and Vietnam wars able to generate jobs and growth.

It is possible that the U.S. economy will maintain sporadic upward movement; but it is doubtful that this will be achieved in more than marginal ways by the kinds of public policies now being considered. The policy most commonly urged by both parties—reducing the deficit—is also likely to reduce growth; the real question is *when*, not if, the next recession will hit. A major military buildup could do the job, of course, but even here there are difficulties: The $4 trillion economy is so large that it takes a gigantic and absolute military buildup to make a significant dent. Ronald Reagan is right to point out that even his big defense budget is a smaller percentage of the GNP than that of many Democratic presidents—and this means less relative economic stimulus.

Only a full-scale and coordinated economic plan can put the economy into sustained high gear—and only one that has a dramatic new source of public support can overcome the political deadlocks that now stymie progress. As a retired working woman in the Midwest recently put it: "We know that when the politicians want to put everyone to work in time of war they can do it easily. What will it take to do it in time of peace?"

Historically, populism has stressed a sharp division between the haves and have-nots; and it has attacked elites and centralized power. It has been opposed to "big government." It is conceivable—and necessary, I believe —that a new progressive politics will accentuate major themes and programs that would shift resources and power away from the top, but this alone does not answer the fundamental question. Indeed, on its own, such an attack on bigness can easily play into the hands of extreme conservatives and reactionaries; Ronald Reagan has dressed his own new tax package in "populist" garb; and people like Richard Viguerie have offered fullblown political theories of conservative populism based on such themes.

The central question a serious progressive populism must answer is how it will deal with the overall problem of economic management and structure. Else it will end up as just one more effort to change the subject without facing the main question.

If planning is required to manage the modern economy—and I believe that it is, certainly if the trend toward leaving out increasing numbers of blue-collar workers and minorities is to be reversed—then populism must offer a longer-term vision that combines its historic themes of decentralization, anti-elitism, and antibigness with a model of economic planning designed to achieve its goals and values.

The first requirement is a structure that encourages—and is based upon —increasing participation for all. We have garnered enough experience with co-ops, community development corporations, worker-management, worker-owned firms, and so on, to know that *if there were a real program aimed at developing and extending this experience*, it could offer both greater economic productivity and more democracy. However, consider that hundreds of community-based economic experiments have been wiped away by larger economic forces in the last decade: high interest rates, deep recession, declining markets, and failing local economies have all generated their casualties. Even so-called economic improvements have often been costly—especially when rising real estate values have forced residents to move and thus eliminated the base of some local housing and various co-ops.

Without an overall plan supportive of decentralized, community-based enterprise, even the best experiments are likely to falter and then disappear. Or they will be left to stand as isolated models representing an interesting "moment" in history—of significance to a few activists, but (except as a conversation piece) not to their 238 million fellow citizens. We have almost no experience in this area; nor are we likely to develop a supportive planning approach without self-conscious awareness of the need to transcend our current limited posture. If participation is to be meaningful, there must also be citizen involvement in framing the economic strategy or plan for the community in which a firm exists and for the larger regional and national economy in which both live and die.

This brings us to a further difficulty, one also not easily wished away: the United States is not France, not West Germany, not Japan, and certainly not Sweden, Norway, Denmark, or Austria. We have neither the social-democratic tradition of those countries nor the cohesiveness of an island culture relatively recent in its departure from Oriental feudalism. *We are, above all, a continent.* How, really, can there be participation in overall economic planning in a nation so big? Really? We are talking about 3,000 miles and a population that will be moving toward the 250 million and then the 275 million mark.

There is a bullet that needs biting: historian William Appleman Williams and advocacy-planner Robert Goodman have put forward the challenging argument that ultimately we need to reconceptualize the nation as a commonwealth of semiautonomous regions. Both because the idea is important in its own right and because there is no alternative, demagogic right-wing politics has an open field: if the "big government" issue has been exploited in part because government *really* is too big, then either we will continue to hack away at it in reactionary fashion—trying to cut down the services it offers and taxes it extracts. Or we will have to make "big government" smaller. Literally. That unit of scale smaller than a nation yet bigger than a state and sufficiently large to deal with overarching economic matters is a "region."

If this is so, then a serious populism—one that cares about both progressive and humane values and participation—had better begin to develop a truly regional long-term vision. I am not talking about "bioregionalism," though that idea certainly has a role to play; nor about regional decentralization of the existing federal government, though that too might be a way station on the road to a new economic structure. I am suggesting that the only answer to the conundrum—it will not go away—is a long-term vision of how, specifically and concretely, this great nation might begin to be restructured into semiautonomous regional units capable of managing, under democratic control, the separate regional economies.

The easiest way to think about this initially is to expand a vision of what the existing regional-scale states might do if there were an appropriate strategy: California, Texas, Alaska, New York, all are large enough to be conceived as regional units capable of substantial self-management. In the heart of Central Europe, Austria (population roughly 7.5 million) suggests what can be done by a much smaller "regional"-scale unit of economic governance and planning: its record on jobs, inflation, social programs, economic justice, and environmental balance is remarkable—even though it floats within the ups and downs of a larger, capitalist European market.

It is relatively easily to develop models for community participation, planning, and cooperation within the framework of a larger regionalism. We have useful local experience and a reasonable intellectual tradition to draw upon. (Paul and Percival Goodman's *Communitas* is still one of the best guides.) But the regional problem has merely been broached. A first requirement for those who are serious about a progressive alternative to "big government" is therefore some basic intellectual homework in this area.

There is a second requirement that takes us beyond the traditional populist themes of equity, antielitism, and participation: the United States is
the only advanced industrial nation in which the working class is fundamentally, not marginally, divided along racial lines. There are other nations
with small immigrant colored populations, but they are nothing like the
United States. This has consequences.

We have recently seen how neoconservative politics turns to subtle
or not-so-subtle racism when in trouble: the Helms-Hunt Senate race
in North Carolina was ugly; and this, in my view, is only the beginning.
The most important reason we call 7 percent unemployment a "recovery"
is that, for white people, it is. For blacks it is not. But blacks are not
well organized; nor is there a serious political alliance between blacks and
whites.

We are just about at the end, I believe, of the "soft-gloves" liberalism
of the last decade—the political strategy that muffled militancy in the
name of a moderate appeal to the middle. Despite the Democratic party's
current attempt to look the other way when challenged on social and
racial issues, it is clearly a losing politics for the long run. Walter Mondale's decision—after the forceful liberal speeches of Cuomo and Jackson
at the 1984 nominating convention—to cut back the Democratic tradition in the name of a "new realism" was instructive. As was his fate. To
build the kind of fire in the belly that is needed to break loose from the
politics of decay will ultimately require a different, powerful thematic. *A*
thematic capable of uniting the races against common enemies—one that is
capable of withstanding the forthcoming intensification of racism as a strategy
to divide and conquer when conservative politicians begin to get into trouble.

This means drawing a much sharper line between the interests of the
vast majority, black and white, and the upper elites, corporations, and the
military establishment. Without a clear line, mushy confusion can too
easily be exploited by the opposition—and it will be exploited! Several
issues are obvious and traditional: tax policy, military spending, corporate
control. An aggressive "populist" approach to each could be dramatized,
were there a will to do so—as a matter not only of social justice but of
necessary politics. Beyond this, a serious long-term populism would begin
to introduce the ideal of full equality—not merely "equity"—as appropriate to the challenges of the coming century.

Another area, however, is not so obvious but nonetheless crucial: inflation
is the issue right-wing politics and governments have historically used to
beat down labor, attack social programs, and justify throwing millions of

people out of work. Progressives have had no serious answer to inflation, yet it is of central concern to millions of people. You can't beat somebody with nobody. Nor will the conservative tight-money, cut-the-budget answer to inflation do.

The Reagan recession and temporary grain and oil gluts have moderated recent inflation, but the present situation is not stable. During the last fifteen years the major sources of rising costs in America have been military spending, oil-price and grain-price explosions, housing-price and medical-cost escalations. To deal with each of these problems over the coming decade will require a tough plan, including: military cutbacks, energy conservation and controls, grain reserves and export management, health-cost controls and alternative health-care delivery systems (preferably under community control), and an expansion of the supply of low- and moderate-income housing. But to implement such plans requires a politics willing to take on the military contractors, the oil companies, the grain exporters, banks and insurance firms and developers, and the hospital-industrial complex.

The control of inflation in sectors of fundamental importance to the average family is a principle that underscores a particular populist emphasis on what is important to produce, and what is important to keep within economic reach of the vast majority. It is also a strategy aimed at avoiding the use of planned recession as the way to control inflation. Finally, it involves a politics designed to deprive the opposition of one of its most important issues: the crude linkage of inflation with social spending, especially for blacks.

At the same time such a strategy could begin to develop a new theme centered on the priority of production for necessity use. It offers a challenge to those institutions and corporations that stand in the way of such a program. *And in so doing, finally, it defines goals and targets, politically, that inherently can help unite black and white in a common struggle.*

If there is neither an alternative economic strategy to deal with inflation nor an alternative, common political target for the anger that is building up among blue-collar and black Americans—when the next burst of price hikes hits, the right-wing attack on the poor, on labor, and on overall higher levels of economic functioning will intensify. And make no mistake about it: the issue is when, not if, current relative price stability explodes.

Within a planning framework organized around regional semi-autonomy, and based upon participation, community involvement, and con-

171

trol of inflation in the necessities of life, the overarching themes and directions of economic management becomes self-evident: they are *to manage economic affairs to put people to work to meet these priorities —and, one might add, to do so in ecologically sane ways. Production of mass-transit systems and solar collectors rather than nuclear reactors and gas guzzlers, for instance, is a logical planning outcome of such criteria.*

This brings us back to the role of the large corporation: we need to go beyond traditional ideas of regulation and antitrust. The central question is whether the values of the overall vision are met. We are talking about a longer-term goal of rebuilding the structures needed to sustain, enhance, and encourage both successful economic management and a renewed experience of community. At one point in American history a grass-roots populist conception of how to manage large economic enterprises on a regional basis was put forward—in the very early days of the TVA. This was quickly abandoned or, rather, overridden.

Nonetheless, it is still a useful precedent and concept—for if the large for-profit corporation cannot or will not participate in the building of a new economy, then there must be an alternative to it. Accordingly, the idea of regional public enterprise must be offered—for, again, it is no longer possible, I believe, merely to criticize the major corporations—and the model of regulation and antitrust does not speak to the larger requirements of planning.

Ultimately, there cannot be a new direction without a political breakthrough. Nor can a new progressive program be achieved without new political energies. We live at a dark moment of American political history: traditional liberalism is stymied; but so, too, in many ways is traditional conservatism in the closing days of the Reagan administration. We shall surely see many empty "thematic" approaches to politics—to a politics of surface and rhetoric rather than substance and power. The word "populist" will be degraded by both liberals and conservatives, and emptied of all content.

But even if such a politics succeeds in winning an election, it cannot offer solutions to the problems that beset us—economic, social, moral, military. Hence, ultimately it must fail and the need for a new direction grow. Now is the time to begin a dialogue about what a new populism would

172

entail—one that is serious about values, but also hardheaded about what it takes to manage an advanced industrial economy.

The issue transcends the economy, however, and it also transcends politics as usually conceived. If the final decade of the twentieth century promises to be a difficult one, if there is a limit to the pain that people will endure, than we are likely to see violence. And with violence, repression. If the dangerous thrust of American foreign policy is toward intervention, particularly in Latin America, then we are likely to see death and protest, also followed by repression. And there is, finally, the failure of our present politics to deal with the expanding threat of nuclear war.

Traditional politics does not offer answers to any of these challenges —or what answers it offers are usually too little, too late. What is needed is truly a moral equivalent of war, and of the usual response to domestic violence that is war by another name. Without a new source of inspiration, vision, and commitment, the prospects for regaining a progressive initiative are dim.

The development of a tough-minded populism based on a recognition of what it will take to realize and enhance fundamental values is a necessity in its own right. It also may well be that such a vision and strategy is the only way in the coming period to develop enough political energy to transcend our current stalemates, and their sad, dangerous, and ultimately foolhardy domestic and international consequences.

Only a bold alternative has the chance of generating sufficient emotional power to achieve this goal. Several years ago conservatives realized this at a time of set-back in their own politics: difficult as it was (and as high as the short-term costs were) they broke with mushy attempts to adjust politics to early compromise and cautious interest-group brokering. Such a course has the central advantage of maintaining principles—and thereby offering an appeal based both on moral clarity and a tough-minded assessment of what it will take to achieve basic goals.

Various groups, particularly among the religiously oriented, are beginning to understand the importance of such integrity, and are organizing themselves accordingly. Though it is not a strategy for the fainthearted who can only function in the easier environment of "instant-gratification politics," it is the only approach likely to get us beyond the impasse presented by a dying liberalism and neoliberalism that are nuzzling ever closer to conservative ideas in the name of politics as usual.

173

Fourteen

Colin Greer and Barry Goldberg

POPULISM, ETHNICITY, AND PUBLIC POLICY:
AN HISTORICAL PERSPECTIVE

Populism is a compelling progressive clarion because it seems to summarize (if not resolve) serious contradictions in fifty years of social reform. Ann Bastian, in a report to the New World Foundation, frames those contradictions in this way:

> Without ongoing struggles, recognizing that conflict is intensified rather than diminished with every victory, reforms are readily set aside, eroded or coopted into new tools of domination. The NLRB, which once represented an impressive extension of labor's democratic rights, becomes a mechanism for entrapping unions in self-defeating legalism. Welfare entitlements, once the hard-won expression of government's responsibility for social inequity, becomes another way to regulate the poor and ensure a dependent cheap labor reserve. These outcomes are not inevitable, but reflect the

174

weakness of movements that have come to rely on the state
rather than on their political capacities to fight in the state arena, as
well as in economic and social battlegrounds.

Populism, as a set of social values, is quite ambiguous, and so its capacity
to generate a unifying program is by no means as certain as its adherents
often claim.

The populist response to the state is frequently in danger of forgetting that government is not an autonomous institution to be praised or
condemned for its functions. Rather, the state is the battleground for
power waged by deeply conflicted interests. However, as corporate interests dominate the state, the popular sense of betrayal becomes anti-statist
and is ready to support the dismantling of these areas of government
built on public service. Clearly, anti-statist strains in populism need to be
recognized and confronted. By not embracing the state as a decisive area
for altering power relations, the new populists echo the strains and contradictions among the new ethnics of a few years ago.

The ethnic revival of the 1970s has proven a significant, if shortlived
and sometimes shallow, episode that helped shape the contemporary
populist vision of democratic empowerment. Like its nineteenth-century
agrarian namesake, today's call for a renewal of participatory democratic
politics envisions the mobilization of grassroots community organizations
in order to reclaim government as an instrument of popular sovereignty.
While not unaware of the specific features of domination characteristic of
late capitalist society, populism rejects the Marxian language of politics
and proposes a radicalism drawn from the American heritage: an up-
dated Jeffersonianism shorn of its agrarian bias. But unlike its celebrated
nineteenth-century counterpart, it is not a democratic precursor of the
liberal interventionist state. Contemporary populism is a response to the
antidemocratic corporate tendencies of the "progressive" state. Populism
proposes an alternative to the corporate state, liberal reform, and socialism. As such, its challenge to the alleged suppression of nineteenth-century
populism's democratic promise verges on an overly simplified identification of government per se as the source of domination. This hostility
toward government bears a striking resemblance to the white ethnic revival's condemnation of state intervention as a means of redressing racial
injustice. In addition, while populism appeals to democratic aspirations of
an American political tradition that can be traced back to the American
Revolution, its "Americanism" rejects the nativist and racist sentiments

175

that have been associated, perhaps mistakenly, with nineteenth-century agrarian radicalism and its twentieth-century variants. Rather than pitting the "people" against the interests, contemporary populism envisions a pluralist struggle of many "peoples" against the forces that not only drive farmers from their homes, but undermine the vitality of urban ethnic neighborhoods. Thus if populism derives its name and much of its ideology from the democratic promise embodied in white Anglo-Saxon Protestant agrarian protest, its vision of a genuinely democratic nation is also rooted in the diversity of American communities celebrated by the new ethnicity. But whether the new populism will prove any more successful than the new ethnicity in wedding democratic empowerment to ethnic diversity remains to be seen.

Populism is an effort to retain a unifying vision for integrating progressive politics. In the 1980s populism can provide new links to a unified national vision of social change in place of the diverse pluralism that dominated social vision in the 1970s. Following the unifying social visions of the New Deal and Great Society eras (spurred as they were by movements —respectively, labor in the 1940s, civil rights, student, and women's liberation in the 1960s) came the reassertion of the illusion of pluralism as a unifying vision through the ethnic revivalism of both the 1950s and 1970s. The diverse history of both these periods of categorical interest-group competition makes the populist vision of an integrated "commonwealth" deeply attractive.

Indeed, the ethnic revivalism of the 1970s can be seen as a precursor to contemporary rejection of the struggle for public over corporate ownership of the state. The assertion of populism can, in turn, be seen as a reclamation of the state as ground for struggle. But ethnic revivalism, since World War II, has had that state-oriented component too. The strength of its challenge to private corporate interests was diluted by its integration into a larger pluralism, public ethnicity, which put the image of heroic individualist immigrants at the heart of its narrative structure. Public ethnicity, in this usage, refers to the broad persuasion that America is an "ethnic" nation in which it is no longer necessary to live in actively ethnic enclaves or directly associate with a country of origin to be ethnic. Ethnic particularity existed, but it was the general integration of ethnic particularities in a national ethnic identity that gave ethnic revival its force. A closer look at it might be a useful reminder as we approach the problems and attractions of populism.

The widespread popular and scholarly rediscovery of ethnicity that surfaced a decade ago revitalized America's self-image as a nation of immigrants. This dramatic revival of ethnic consciousness compelled us to pay attention, once again, to the cultural mosaic that emerged from the historic peopling of America. This vision of America as a "nation of nations," as Walt Whitman puts it, was not new. After the imposition of restrictive quotas on immigration in the 1920s, gradually Americans began to celebrate the varied roots of the national family tree. By the 1950s American popular culture and scholarship celebrated our diverse origins. But coming as the alleged demand of aggrieved descendants of white immigrants in the aftermath of over a decade of black protest and "new," primarily Asian and Hispanic, immigration, the new ethnicity promulgated a highly politicized understanding of American experience predicated on an emphasis on the significance of immigrant origins. Ethnicity expressed the continuing hold of a people's immigrant roots. Appropriately echoing the ambivalent ties of new ethnics with an interventionist government, the crowning symbolic political achievement of this ethnic consciousness was the Ethnic Heritage Act of 1974.

Predictably, the advertising industry captured the new ethnic pluralism. Birds Eye Foods, for example, launched a television campaign for its line of foreign-style foods using American families, with both foreign and English-speaking members gathered around an authentic homeland meal prepared by Birds Eye. "We make it here," the advertisement claimed, "but it tastes like there." A wide range of foreign-origin elements in the American population were represented in the succession of those advertisements, expressing something crucial to American ethnicity: both the wide diversity of cultural origins in the nation and the prideful ideal that the elements of that diversity, while still visible, were a product of life in America. You could taste diversity in the freezer of your supermarket as well as in the Chinatowns, Little Italys, and kosher delicatessens of America. Similarly, an airline offered to fly Americans back to their ancestral homelands. For the price of a round trip ticket, you could fulfill an allegedly archetypical American odyssey as the prosperous citizen of industrial America.

The identification with "primordial" pre-American roots had found its place in the imagery and economy of cosmopolitan consumer culture as a commercialized return of the descendants of the uprooted to their lands or origin. Ethnicity had become a cultural commodity. The public

177

images and commodities of twentieth-century capitalism promised to re-establish a symbolic connection to the very cultural worlds it had supplanted. You could go to Broadway and be entertained by singing shtetl dwellers, or buy spaghetti at your supermarket confident that it retained the "flavor" of Italian South Boston. As an American you could participate in an eclectic consumption of ethnicity—yours and others.

The Harvard *Encyclopedia of American Ethnic Groups*, the result of years of academic attention to American ethnic character, was a scholarly testament to the new mood. With the bulk of the volume composed of individual ethnic histories, the structure of the *Encyclopedia* affirmed the growing climate of ethnic awareness and acceptance. Including Copts as well as Croatians, it implicitly defined the American community through the presence of these groups. Whereas in the past there was a core culture largely defined by WASP identity to which the offspring of immigrants had to adapt, now all groups occupied the mainstream of a smorgasbord national identity.

Ethnicity increasingly has been taken as a baseline definition of Americanness that seems to merge the assimilationist motif of the melting pot which early in the century pioneered a belief in the practicality of erasing foreign identities with the more recent beyond-the-melting pot pluralist belief that differences might and ought to prevail in the interest of American strength and ingenuity. The product has been an ideology of the assimilation of difference based on their continuing distinct presence in the society.

However, this very triumph with its focus on immigrant origins and cultural identity as the central factor in ethnic experience has limited our understanding of the general phenomenon of national acceptance of ethnicity as a key aspect of American life. Ethnicity, this essay will argue, cannot be understood solely by reference to immigrant origins and cultural persistence; it must be recognized as what we call public ethnicity, a public definition of group identity that emerged in the context of public policies that regulate immigration and, particularly since the New Deal, establish the framework for labor-capital relations and maintain a social wage.

Ethnicity is a form of group and national identity peculiarly appropriate to and characteristic of the relations with government necessary in the post–New Deal economy. Indeed, it is noteworthy that the recent withdrawal of government as the major operational and promissary actor on this scene has coincided with the more recent fading of white ethnic particularity in national consciousness. *Public ethnicity's growth paralleled the rise of government public policy as a significant actor in the social contract negotiated through and developed after the New Deal.* The emergence of public policy and public ethnicity as prominent components of national life after World War II had a twofold character. In public policy discourse two kinds of policy initiatives were pursued. One focused on amelioration of social conditions through the input of professional planners and providers. The second focused on the "maximum feasible participation" of those to be helped in the control of the ways and means of social improvement. In local communities threatened as well as promised by the aid brought through urban renewal, school reform, and the like, ethnic identity became a clarion for citizen participation and for recognition that the U.S. prosperity had yet to be visited on large numbers of the children of immigrants. Thus, in a quest for pride and economic benefits, ethnicity could legitimate demands upon the state.

But while the social chances and consciousness of ethnics developed in the context of an interventionist state, conventional accounts of the immigrant odyssey told a different story. Ethnicity served to celebrate the success of previous immigrants and on that basis to emphasize the future prospects of newer immigrants and internal migrants—Asians, Hispanics, blacks—who had yet to reap the benefits of urban and government growth. The demands of these groups for affirmative policy initiatives in education, jobs, and housing were portrayed as a radical rupture from a mythic memory of allegedly self-reliant immigrant forebears who grasped the opportunities of American life without the helping hand of public policy.

Thus, an understanding of ethnicity in America requires an analysis of the mythic association ethnics and the society maintain with the immigrant past. It also entails an analysis of the politicized structure of opportunity and well-being confronting immigrants and ethnics. Furthermore, the continuing U.S. experience with immigration following successive restrictive acts must not be forgotten, since it is on the basis of that kind of amnesia that the conventional fabric of public ethnicity weaves immigrants and ethnics as one.

To be sure, the wide and obvious demographic reality is that most Americans are either immigrant or ethnic. Since this is clearly a nation formed by immigration, most Americans are the offspring of immigrants. It is another matter to explain ethnic experience simply as a function of

179

ancestral immigration. The ethnic character of American society must be derived from more than immigrant origins alone. If the immigrant origins of Americans were without ongoing political and economic significance, it would be unlikely that those origins would retain the power to define inclusion and exclusion in the political economy, as they have for generations. Variables that must be considered include the continuing supply of cheap labor through immigration, the identification of new immigrants as distinct and less desirable than earlier immigrants and their offspring (mostly their offspring), the style of participation in a political economy that seemed to have produced lively group categorization and coherence. Yet, for the most part, scholarship has been fixed on the immigrant origin and immigrant cultural roots as the core of ethnic meaning. The made-in-America component on the basis of which ethnic history still needs to be written is largely uninformed except to the extent that there is a presumption of general mobility.

Significantly, that gap has been addressed by so-called neoconservatives. Out of dissatisfaction with recent consequences of racial and ethnic politics, they are attuned to the implications of the post–New Deal state that sustain ethnic consciousness. While expanding the net of ethnicity to include international tribal tendencies, Nathan Glazer and Daniel Patrick Moynihan's anthology, *Ethnicity*, offers important considerations of the U.S. experience. According to Glazer and Moynihan, it is interest-group politics, not the power of the primordial tribe, that makes ethnic organization a "practical," even inevitable, vehicle for political participation. When government is a source of "entitlements" and perceived as a guarantor of social mobility and economic security, ethnic cohesion makes sense. In that same collection Daniel Bell advances the political character of ethnic identification further. In the period since the last "ethnic revival" in the 1950s, according to Bell, there has been a fusion of status order with political power in U.S. political economy that has followed the growth of the state's role in the economic life of the nation. The rise of ethnicity coincides with the rise of the state's post–New Deal centrality in the nation's economic life.

Bell has gone furthest in clarifying the nature of the society in which ethnic identity is intrinsic to national identity. For Bell, such a society is one that has been increasingly politically determined: "generally, we find a subtle but pervasive change, namely, that the revolution of rising expectations . . . has become a sustained demand for entitlements." As skill and education have grown in importance, so credentials and certification have become central for individuals striving to get ahead: "for our purposes the essential point is that as the mechanisms for occupational advancement become increasingly specialized and formalized, the political route becomes almost the only major means available for individuals and groups without specific technical skills to 'upgrade' themselves in society."

The resulting demand is for "social rights" (jobs, unemployment insurance, adequate health care, and a minimum, decent standard of living) to be delivered via political rather than economic processes. He sees the upsurge of ethnicity to be directly related to national political life. It is both that "in the competition for the values of the society to be realized politically, ethnicity can become a means of claiming place of advantage. And it is a means for disadvantaged groups to claim a set of rights and privileges which the existing power structures have denied them."

It would be a mistake to take this line of reasoning to suggest that ethnic is simply synonymous with group mobilization for government support by either the disadvantaged or relatively privileged. It is accurate, however, to argue that ethnicity has developed within the framework of government-based definition of options for action.

Some studies have shown that native-born American groups have discovered ethnic organization in response to the character of requirements for federal and state government resources. Just as, in the past, some immigrant groups discovered their national-origins identity in the United States, so the offspring of immigrants have often found the molding force for ethnic organization from the political character of the economy as it has been constructed since World War II. The creation of the ethnic variable as a vehicle of a politicized economy is a major aspect of *public ethnicity*. Antidefamation and antidiscrimination were the earliest sources of this cohesion. Since then, the direction has had far wider application. Public institutions, most especially public schools, were the channels for the negotiations and struggles for and among ethnics. From the late 1940s local parent groups sought to influence the ethnic composition of the teaching staff in their schools, the content of the curriculum, and the observation of ethnic celebration days. These efforts reached their zenith in the 1970s when ethnic identification had become so integrated in the polity as a basic mechanism of its pluralist operations that "ethnic" desks were created in the National Endowment for the Humanities and the Department of Housing and Urban Development. The national culture was to be encouraged to reflect the diverse origins of the nation, and local ethnic groupings were to be encouraged as vehicles of community renewal.

Public Policy and Ethnicity

Since World War II, government funds served to accelerate income and status mobility among white ethnics at least as much as it did for blacks. It was during this period that education, public schooling from grade school to college, emerged as the authorized route to meritocratic opportunity. As schools and college programs opened up for those previously denied entry, it was white ethnics who crowded the first several years of such efforts from the G.I. Bill of Rights to the programs of the Great Society. During this same time ethnics of southern and eastern European origin won a new dignity in the removal of all national quotas in the immigration legislation of 1965 which, alongside the Civil Rights Acts, confirmed the centrality of government in the agency of an apparently workable pluralism.

The increasing reliance on government intervention in support of both protectionist barriers to foreign labor and foreign products as well as government guarantees of improved conditions for an "aristocracy" of labor, defined as such by their now valued immigrant origins and "primary" role in a segmented labor market, established the context for the rise of public ethnicity as a central legitimating ideology. As the state has become central to maintaining the economic order, so the issues of economic well-being and class relations have become increasingly political. Ethnicity, as we have known it in recent years, is a critical variable in the complex ideology and power in which U.S. workers grappled with the historic romance that attaches to the nation's immigration history and from which they seem to benefit, and its continuing reliance on immigrant labor.

But it is crucial to remember that this politicization of class relations and ethnic awareness was not a radical rupture with the past. The existing conditions and future prospects of ethnic Americans have long been inextricably bound to government action through immigration restriction, domestic labor policy, and social reform. The post–New Deal expansion of government policy proved so successful in fostering and celebrating

182

ethnic participation in American life that the memory of its role in structuring the opportunities and conditions of immigrants and ethnics faded and was replaced by the romance of immigrant origins.

Indeed, immigration restriction efforts are an early example of ethnic workers' demands upon government. In a succession of restriction initiatives beginning in the nineteenth century, coalitions including native-born and newly settled workers sought protection and confirmation from government on the basis of a pattern of exclusion of new immigrants. This inclusion/exclusion nexus has been intrinsic to the fusion of status order with political order that Bell describes. Indeed, according to Alexander Saxton, anti-Chinese hysteria proved "indispensable" to the growth of unionism and class organization in nineteenth-century California. But, simultaneously, it weakened labor solidarity and integrated labor into an interclass anti-Chinese political system. The ethnocentric stance of organized labor is also demonstrated very clearly in the work on nativism spearheaded by John Higham, and more recently realized in Mark Riesler's work on Mexican immigration in the twentieth century. Even when labor leaders were themselves immigrants they were, as in the case of Samuel Gompers and John L. Lewis, not part of what in their time was a "new" immigration. The trades-union hierarchy has retained this flavor ever since. And those third-and-fourth-generation Americans so frequently tied with organized labor in anti-immigration, nativist coalitions were indeed early signs of the paranoid class expression of ethnicity.

The pluralist optimism that has informed the most popular scholarly views of ethnic diversity assumes America's immigrant character is an historic one—ongoing immigration is rarely seen as a cherished part of a cherished heritage. Indeed, the historic character of that distinction between historic immigrants and today's immigrants is not sufficiently recognized as a major reason for the continuing significance of ethnicity for describing Americans. If immigration was not the continuing base of American labor force composition as well as the source of its historic formation, then the imperative for ethnic identification would probably be far less powerful.

The parameters of government influence have been far wider than immigration restriction. While restrictionists sought legislation to control immigration, turn-of-the-century progressive antirestriction looked to the service role of government to protect the nation from the dangers of immigration through Americanization and social reform while delivering the workers seen as essential for the enrichment of the economy and of the culture. Progressives who worked hard at the local and national levels to win protections for immigrant workers and their families must be included with restrictionists among those who put government at the center of relations between employers and employees.

John Buenker has given us an important perspective on the "machine politics" roots in the progressive era of much of what became, at the federal level, the social interventionist style of national government in response to and directed against the representation of group interests. In many major cities with heavy newcomer populations another face of ethnicity was visible as "old" immigrant politicians (and trades-union officials too) gained the support of "new" immigrants by defending them against discrimination, and restriction, with progressive legislation and public schools acculturation programs in their behalf. Urban liberalism was at once a route to political power and an alternative to immigration restriction. Welsh, Irish, and German machine politicians had helped create a governmental social responsibility that presaged, and sometimes outdistanced, the New Deal on the state level. As a result, the decades of nativist reaction at the turn of the century were also decades that saw great advances in welfare legislation.

Local disquiet about the federal government's growing role became common in the years before and after the New Deal. In towns and cities throughout the country the struggle for local control of the institutions of the state (e.g., public schools) picked up steam immediately after World War II. As the state role expanded, so too did these struggles. Organizers (e.g., Alinsky, National Welfare Rights Organization, ACORN) sought to bring people's unrest to bear on state as well as corporate agencies. The outcome in national policy was maximum feasible participation. In education and housing legislation, for example, citizen participation became a central theme, reaching for but rarely achieving local citizen control of public institutions. Through local popular control might come challenges to local and national interests that had typically run roughshod over local needs, expectations, and possibilities. Through the vehicle of government policy over which they might demand inclusion, fragments of local resistance gained a formal role. Ethnicity was a major part of this framework. In this perspective, ethnicity was a demarcation of people under threat of mindless "progress" and people who had for some time been used to represent, but had not yet engaged, the fruits of the American Dream. As Geno Beroni, at HUD's Office of Ethnic Affairs, put it, "ethnicity is anti-

184

establishment." Resistance to urban renewal was ethnic, as was resistance to and activity for desegregation and decentralization in New York City and Boston in the 1960s and 1970s.

Out of this view of things came a somewhat different consciousness of ethnicity—different but nevertheless feeding the general ethos that served to cloud its meaning. Local ethnics, working-class Americans feeling threatened by the onslaught of new immigrants, urban renewal, desegregation possessed a strong sense of a promise unfulfilled and the enduring patterns of their own insecurity. They often resented new opportunities for others as a way of stating their need for such opportunities. Opposition to new immigrants was very often tantamount to challenging the employers' commitment to low pay rather than employing Americans. The data on immigrant success signaled new threat; the data on government aid to the needy signaled resources to be won for themselves too. Ethnicity here was an expression of class condition as well as a diversion from class organization.

Conclusion

History rooted in the locally given and currently present may degenerate into a nostalgic celebration of community life that merely adds a new twist to the ethos of public ethnicity as neighborhoods will become historic bench marks of the immigrant odyssey. Academic historians may lament the presentism and political agenda of such a quest for a meaningful past as impediments to "truth in history." But given the gulf between the realities of ethnic working-class life and the power of a romanticized immigrant odyssey, the immediate conditions of ethnics as the descendants of immigrants may well be the best place to begin a critical history of ethnicity. With the social contract of New Deal America under attack and the reality of ongoing immigration evident, it is necessary, and seems possible, for Americans to reconsider the conventions that have limited our understanding of the relationship between immigration, ethnicity, and public policy.

Such a history must, of course, break out of narrow geographic and cultural parochialisms, enabling individuals to understand their relationship to wider structures of power and the fate of other communities, including their perceived rivals—immigrant and ethnic—for government service and social opportunities.

185

Thus far, the tenets of public ethnicity have had a powerful hold on American identity. As ethnic revival succeeded ethnic revival, immigrant origins remained the central concern of popular and scholarly conceptions of ethnicity. With increased awareness of the "ethnic" character of contemporary Americans came intensification of the focus on the reappreciation of national diversity through attention to immigrant struggle and achievement. As we have noted, the immigrant record referred to has been focused on a distant historic past, as if the story of immigration to the United States ended some time before the discovery of American ethnicity. The historic immigrants of the white ethnic consciousness have, in effect, been seen as distinct from any continuing American immigration. Cut off from ongoing immigration, historic immigrants are romanticized, cut off from the experience of contemporary ethnics and immigrants.

As "ethnic" became regarded as synonymous with "historic immigrant" in the ideology of public ethnicity, the ideal of independent, self-reliant economic achievement has obfuscated the strong government-centered collective efforts, liberal and reactionary, that characterize an important aspect of ethnic history. As a result, Americans with their ethnic consciousness awakened in response, in part at least, to unsatisfactory socioeconomic conditions (now, as in the past, frequently shorthanded into an anti-immigration mood) are blocked by the harsh impasse that results from their identification with a lionized immigrant ancestry, their own consequent private sector idealism, and the realities of private sector reliance on federal largesse.

The picture this nation presents to itself by placing historic immigration at the core of its self-image is one in which immigrants came to work hard and make it in America. The immigrant leads to the ethnic. The ethnic is, at once, the immigrant who has made it and confirmation of the process by which achievement was wrung from the opportunities at the bottom of the society. In this sense, above all, the ethnic entity created out of roseate immigrant images is a central legitimating tool. The ideal that things can get better because they have done so in the past establishes at once a comparative base against which many Americans can feel they have escaped and a degree of anxious comfort in distressed predicament for those yet to come up from behind.

An understanding of immigration and ethnicity as interrelated but distinct historical and contemporary experiences shaped by state action is essential if we are to break through the ideological impasse of public ethnicity's powerful, if sometimes subtle, inclusion of some Americans by

186

serial exclusion of others. The illusion of community contained therein is a repressive and regressive force that denies the possibility of a popular critical history rooted in the circumstances of immigrant and ethnic life.

Ethnicity per se, an awareness of immigrant roots, is neither progressive nor reactionary. The interpenetration of class and ethnic experience is complex. Ethnicity has served both as an expression and repression of class realities in a working-class population reshaped by continued immigration. Class struggles have also been ethnic experiences. In presenting a vision both of a community beyond and contesting established power, ethnicity, like populism, has been a ground for renewed popular memory and cultures of resistance and re-formation. But it is a dangerous illusion that posits a realized community of national interest in which both established power is legitimated and the historic strength of the popular struggle for the public interest in and through government is delegitimated by merely debunking the imperfect systems won, in part, by emergent popular forces since the 1930s.

Just as this illusion of community in the national acceptance of public ethnicity must be challenged not merely because it is inaccurate but because its mythology encourages powerlessness, so the assumption of community in populism must be challenged. If community as the essential organizing principle means circumventing all but the regulatory powers of the state, it will serve, like public ethnicity, to confound the social forces —class, race, and gender—that might only cohere around the redistributive potential of the nation-state.

As Ann Bastian notes forcefully:

> The regressive potential has been fully grasped by the Right. Reagan has become the master of the American version of "authoritarian populism." His rhetoric affirms communities of exclusion for white, middle Americans—combining the nostalgia for small town America and values of self-reliance with attacks on urban decadence, minority dependence, feminist immorality, union greed, worker indolence, government intrusion and foreign subversion.

Finally, then, the limits of categorical entitlement are confused with government and end up as a rejection of the inherent limits of public sector and government intervention. The beginning of a way out of the dilemma is through the firm distinction between government as public ownership and flawed or failed government policies. What Geno Beroni

187

called the anti-establishment heart of ethnic consciousness is the route to recognizing the struggle for the public ownership of the state. Populism has the potential for advancing that struggle. But to do so it must distinguish clearly between the rejection of government and the rejection of corporate control of government. Reclaiming the working-class ethnics' historic tie to the need for and growth of the state is an indispensable step toward a progressive populism.

Six

POPULISM AND EQUALITY

Fifteen
Elizabeth Kamarck Minnich

TOWARD A
FEMINIST POPULISM

A feminist vision of populism shares with the older versions a commitment to the rights of all people, and an insistence that those rights are not to be set aside in the interests of any power group. We, too, insist that those governments are legitimate that derive their power from the people, and that exercise that power with respect for all people. We, too, insist that significant disparities of power in society disrupt the polity, and so take our stand with those whose lack of power is not just a personal problem but a threat to the commonwealth. Populism has a mixed and sometimes troubled and confusing history; nevertheless, feminism, in its recurrence not only as a burst of outrage from people whose dignity and rights have been trampled but also as a burst of pride in the common roots of those rights and that dignity, is deeply compatible with populism.

It would be important to any feminist agenda—if there were ever to be a single one, which I am pleased to doubt—to touch some of the same

191

passions populism has touched. Most important of all, a feminist program needs to grow from the same deep, stubborn sense of personal worth the powerless of all sorts have always had to draw on when they stood up not only against their marginalization, their exploitation, their suppression, but their devaluation in the whole culture. Euro-American history is replete with examples of how those with power justify their rightness by defining all others as wrong, as lesser, as a subspecies. Feminism, like populism, takes its birth from the union of mistreatment, finally understood to *be* mistreatment, and the seed of self-respect that has been nurtured throughout not only by a stubborn individual sense of worth but by the multiple communities within which we all take sustenance. Both are movements of anger that affirm what has been violated and, in that affirmation, claim worth for what has been devalued and so open up thought about as well as action for strong, positive values.

But I, at least, do not trust populism nevertheless, no matter how strongly I may support some of the positions taken in its name, and the passions it has spoken to, and of. Almost every one of the key words I used above rings with two tones, as does "populism" itself. One tone is supposed to ring out for all of us, in all of our diversity as well as commonality. The other calls out some of the small-minded worst of the American tradition, with its fears and hatreds. We all know that about populism, but it must now be added that *both* of those tones have an undertone that those who care about humans, rather than about men disguised as Man, must listen for. A populism that speaks not just of "the people" but of "the peoples" of this land, that affirms diversity, can and has included women on its list. But women are not one more issue, one more cause, one more subject. Women are half of humankind and always have been. There is *no* issue that is not a "women's issue," and those who simply add us to their agenda as if we were one more item cannot be trusted. And, of course, when populism reverts to its bigotry in the name of "old American values," women as well as minority men are in serious danger.

Those are easy points to make. The problem is that there is yet another level, the deepest undertone of all, still to mention. The dominant meaning system of the Euro-American tradition is built on and with premises that at the very best omit half the human race, and at the worst, justify the suppression of women as lesser than man and as designed for his use, abuse, and service. Those are hard words, but they must be faced.

192

That *we* are different, that *we* mean well, is not enough to change a culture, a language, a social and political and economic system.

In short, I cannot trust *any* movement that is not feminist, out of sheer respect for the realities of history and culture—of our humanly constructed reality.

I understand that many of us wish to take "the old American values" back from the radical right, to refound ourselves on the American dream of equality given sustenance by a vision of a commonwealth. But those old American values must be carefully examined.

"The family": What is meant when we value the family? The male-headed heterosexual nuclear family that was so strongly promoted in the 1950s, when women were driven, once again, from the marketplace? The locus of resistance and rebellion for women and men otherwise deprived of their rights under slavery—and thereafter as well? The unit of society that was assumed to be appended to the singular, white, property-owning male citizen by the Founding Fathers who defined that male as the individual whose rights are to be protected by the state? The "haven in a heartless world" for men who otherwise feel free to ignore both hearts and morals, returning to women/wives at night for assurance that they are justified? The sequel to romances in which they live happily ever after, until they are divorced and she faces a job market that does not value any of her skills, now with children to support?

It may well be true that such families are endangered by a stage of capitalism in which only individuals count, individuals who can be moved about at will and who consume all the more, the more they are on their own. And it may well be true that even the small steps we had taken as a nation toward providing some support for mothers and for children have been retraced, leaving us with an ever-growing group of desperately impoverished single parents—overwhelmingly, female parents. But what are we calling for if we look to the family as any kind of a bastion against acts of an economic system, and of a government? The return of the provident male, back in power at home and more desperate than ever for a decent job because he has dependents who cannot, because of sexual discrimination, make as much as he?

I do not know how to rethink families, but I do know that I want that rethinking to start with a thorough knowledge of what they have meant to women. The picture that emerges from such study is of quite a different sort of institution than that of the privileged white male dominant culture.

In it, there are horrors aplenty, but there are also treasures of sharing, of resistance, of equality, of love, of a center for what may be quite distinct cultures whose values have long been considered trivial by the dominant culture. There are traditions in America we can affirm, but we cannot find them unless we get much, much better than we yet are at hearing the voices we have been trained, precisely, not to hear. Just as feminism can slide into universalizing white women, populism, in caring about class and—with less reliability—race issues can slide into losing the essential perspective of gender.

Some, I know, worry about the "coldness" of feminism as of the left, and turn to populism as a way of being "more positive," of going beyond, or behind, the critiques endemic to both feminism and the left. But I have some suspiciousness here as well, at the same time I agree that such movements, such transfigurations, do indeed grow from and nurture the sort of passions I first discussed, and more, and should do so.

Analyses of the "cold" individualism of Americans worry me for similar reasons. I keep hearing, behind the complaints, a yearning for some old, sorely missed experience of union, of cause, of community. I am afraid that those who have had such experiences within communities and/or causes in the past simply cannot feel the intensity of experience they miss in any other form, even if it is indeed available and real—for others. And so I am afraid that they will miss what is there and try to convince us all that something is lacking in the new world that the old really did have. The old values of community and church or synagogue, like the old values of political movements and causes, filled some people with a sense that they and others knew what it was to transcend individualism by living according to shared, overarching principles and values. But those shared, overarching principles and values of the old days *also left out women*—omitted us, trivialized us as just one more cause or issue on the list, or even justified our suppression.

Feminist scholarship has begun the fascinating process of recovering the lives and meanings of women, in all our differences, and the work has much to tell us about American "individualism." It seems to have been the plague of white men who lived and worked and fought and studied without regard to, let alone for, the real context of their lives. History used to tell us about the deeds of singular great (white) men, as if they did what they did in some sort of superb and incomprehensible isolation. Then it began to tell us about politics and policy, again characterizing the processes and products as if they were the products of the few. When we

194

finally made it to social history, the interpretive categories were already so set in the white male form that even with women and poor men present, we were interpreted from that perspective and not from our own. In every academic field today, we find that the singular white male perspective is the founding, parameter-setting, and privileged one. And that means that the knowledge we have of ourselves is downright peculiar: It gives us the few *out of any real context.*

Need we be surprised if they feel isolated, and if "individualism" seems to be to blame, rather than being just one more manifestation of a historically skewed, partial meaning system? Feminists working politically with and for women, and feminists doing the scholarship and thinking and creating that similarly shifts the focus from the isolated few to the many, do not come up with "individualism" as a problem.

Every concept, every effort we make to reclaim the peoples' values and affirm our worth—the worth of every one and of all of us—is similarly tricky. It may seem cold to keep insisting on critique, but it does not feel so. Quite the contrary. The effort to understand, to uncover and look right straight at what has been, to take on the required risk of interpretation, along with the effort to do so with a community of others equally dedicated to understanding and to change, is hardly cold, nor only negative. And any movement that searches within its people for their own meanings, as they are lived today and as they have been, not to adopt slogans but as a part of a continuing education that takes as its task centering learning in people as part of our self-reclaiming and bonding with each other, is not "only critical" or cold, either.

But will we recognize those passions, those commitments, those individual risks that both require and maintain a free community, if we ache for a lost way of life, adopt pictures and policies without such self-and-reality explorations, such education?

One more example: When we speak of equality, we raise one of the oldest and noblest of America's banners. But have we been honest about the tradition that formed and informs it still? Most of us can list, one hopes not too glibly, all the desperate inequities that persisted, and were protected, in the early days of revolutionary America. The dream has, nevertheless, gone beyond the limits set for it at first, and all of us have called on it. Populists and feminists both make of equality a prime principle as well as a goal.

What I fear in that principle now is that we will continue blurring together sameness and equality. Equality requires difference: $1 = 1$ is a

195

statement of identity, not equality. Equality is effected by something, before something. We are supposed to be equal before the law, and we are equal before death. Equality transcends difference, not by obliterating it but by marking where and in precisely what ways it is irrelevant. In that way, equality protects difference, for if we could not transcend our differences where we choose and need to, the pressures to be all the same would be even greater than they are. That is, where there is no system established to make us equal, only those who are the same as those who have power have much of a chance, leading all to aspire to be like the privileged few. And in America, despite our continuing efforts to expand the sphere of equality, we still have areas in which being like the few seems to be the goal of equality. Certainly, I have been told time and again that women who seek equality are trying "to be *like* men," and I have observed with sadness that sometimes that seems to be true. And certainly I have been told that "we all believe in equality, but you have to admit that it is impossible because we are simply born different"—as if that disproved equality as a possibility rather than simply noting that we need it because we are not all the same.

A populism, or any other movement, that tries to add women onto its agenda rather than re-forming its most basic thoughts and goals and ways of acting from the perspective of women, and of sex/gender analysis, is more than liable to think it is acting for women's equality, while, instead, it pushes toward women's sameness to men. Women are, then, to be different where it suits (the list of proper women's issues varies according to who makes it), but are to be the same as men in every other regard. It is considered ungrateful and unsporting and politically incorrect to insist that women always be considered. This is, of course, a throwback to the women's rights phase of the movement, when it was thought that getting a right or two for women would make everything all right—as it was said that giving slaves their freedom, their basic human right, would fix everything, and then that the vote would fix everything, and then that getting education would fix everything.

Letting ever more of us be like privileged white men does not strike me as a particularly moving goal, nor do I believe it is what populism intends. But it has to be said: Many who are now at least careful to acknowledge the systemic nature of racism, as they have acknowledged the systemic base of class distinctions, will not extend that understanding to sex/gender systems.

196

Such an omission throws off all class and race analyses as well as all others, of course, since women have experienced class as we have experienced race differently from men, and gender constructs are often class- and race-specific. We are not the same in a lot of different ways, in fact, and we need to understand our differences a great deal better than we do now. Unless we dwell for a while with our differences, we are always in danger of sliding back into the dominant meaning system that makes of the few, of privileged white males, the inclusive category, the category of aspiration, the norm for us all.

And that, finally, is of course the challenge to populism: Can it not only affirm diversity this time, but concentrate on difference? Can it avoid the most superficial pluralism—we can all be in this polity together because really we are all alike despite all our apparent differences—in its efforts to be inclusive? Can it affirm the passions that spring from and return to analysis of our real situation, or will it divert them in a quest for some old familiar feelings of Cause? Can it return to the past to learn afresh from the voices and stories that have not been central to the dominant tradition—really learn from them, even as they transform even some of our most basic assumptions? Can it simultaneously form itself as a movement, and watch itself with the critical eye necessary?

Remembering that women are half the human race and that you cannot understand anything without understanding it from the perspective of women as well as men—remembering what should be obvious—should help. So, too, might thinking honestly about the failures of other movements that thought women could be added onto their (then, necessarily) male agenda. No, we overturn everything. Without us, there is no People to be for. With us, there is a whole new vision of all that the people have been, are, and can be.

197

Sixteen
Manning Marable

BLACK HISTORY AND
THE VISION OF DEMOCRACY

How do oppressed people come to terms with their exploitation? This is the central theme of Afro-American political history. As slaves, we were aware of the immense contradiction between this nation's democratic ideology and its treatment of peoples of color. In the South we were legally defined as private property, and in the North we faced racial discrimination, disfranchisement, and legal segregation decades before the Civil War. The literature of black abolitionism is filled with the cries of a people who wish to participate in the democratic progress, yet find the doors of opportunity closed before them. "What to the American slave is your Fourth of July?" asked Frederick Douglass in 1852. "I answer, a day that reveals to him more than all other days of the year, the gross injustice and cruelty to which he is the constant victim. To him your celebration is a sham; your boasted liberty an unholy license; your national greatness, swelling vanity."

Morris Marable, my great-grandfather, was not Frederick Douglass, and yet he felt the same yearning to be free. My late grandmother, Fannie Marable, often told me about Morris's early life. The son of a black household worker and a white planter named Robinson, Morris was sold for $500 in Rome, Georgia, at the age of nine. I have tried, without success, to learn my great-great-grandmother's name. Family folklore reveals only that Morris's mother wept bitterly when her son was sold from her. She never saw him again. Morris became the property of a white plantation owner named Marable in 1854, and the boy was transported to the Alabama Black Belt. He worked in the fields by day and at dusk was sent to the slaves' quarters. Morris's new extended family was the field slave population on the Marable plantation. From slave Johnson Adolphus, who became his "elder brother," he learned mechanic skills. From other slaves he gained a sense of community and ritual, hope and dignity. And from the overseers Morris experienced the sting of the lash.

What did freedom mean to the slave? First, the absence of human exploitation. Blacks engaged in a variety of disruptive activities to retard the production process. Slaves added rocks inside their cotton to wreck the cotton gin; they burned crops and sabotaged farm machinery. Morris assumed the mask of the loyal slave but stole whites' food from the kitchen and distributed it to the slave quarters. Nearly every form of day-to-day resistance was attempted, but always short of open rebellion. Still, slaves constantly heard about conspiracies and even small revolts throughout Alabama. In August 1854 a slave murdered his master at Mt. Meigs and, according to white authorities, "boasted of his deed." The black man was burned alive, according to the Montgomery *Journal*, "from an imperative sense of the necessity of an example to check the growing and dangerous insubordination of the slave population." As the Civil War approached, Alabama slaves exhibited greater tendencies toward rebelliousness. In Talladega County, Alabama, a slave conspiracy was discovered in August 1860. A roving band of "maroons," runaway slaves, was captured and executed. In the same month a white man in Montgomery County was arrested for "holding improper conversations with slaves." And in December several hundred blacks in the central Black Belt were uncovered in a conspiracy with several "poor whites." The would-be rebels had called for the redistribution of "the land, mules, and money." The Montgomery *Advertiser* commented on the conspiracy on December 13, 1860: "We have found out a deep laid plan among the negroes of our neighborhood, and from what we can find out from our negroes, it is

199

general all over the country. . . . They have gone far enough in the plot to divide our estates, mules, lands, and household furniture." About twenty-five blacks and four poor whites were executed.

Alabama white planters reinforced their social controls over the black population. In 1853 the state legislature declared that any slave found with the ability to read should receive one hundred lashes. The number of night patrols was increased. These "patterrollers," as the slaves called them, rode the country lanes at night searching for secret meetings or runaway slaves. Sometime during these years Morris met and fell in love with a household slave named Judy Brooks, who lived about eight miles distant on another farm. Such relationships were difficult to maintain; neither Morris nor Judy could know whether they would be sold at any time. But over time Morris had carefully cultivated his master's trust and was permitted to close the barn and to repair broken tools after dark, Quietly, he made his way into the pine woods, circling down beyond a creek, and after running well over an hour made his way to Judy's cabin. An hour before dawn he returned to his plantation. Morris performed this feat with regularity, dodging patterrollers and their dogs. Morris was never caught, and his master and overseer never knew. But the slaves did, and they relished this small act of freedom. Perhaps they sang to themselves:

> Run nigger run de patterroller get you,
> slip over de fence
> slick as a eel
> White man catch you by de heel
> Run, nigger, run.

Morris's master permitted his slaves to hold regular religious services on Sunday afternoons, and these gatherings often lasted well into the night. The planter may have reasoned to himself that Christianity was good for labor discipline. The Negro spirituals spoke of freedom only in the afterlife, and the Bible taught servants to respect and to obey their masters. But for the slaves the religious meetings were an assertion of their cultural autonomy. Their songs of praise to the Lord revealed more than accommodation to temporal suffering.

> He delivered Daniel from de lion's den,
> Jonah from de belly ob de whale,

And de Hebrew children from de fiery furnace,
And why not every man? . . .

O blow your trumpet, Gabriel
Blow your trumpet louder;
And I want dat trumpet to blow me home
To my new Jerusalem

To the slaves the Lord was not an impersonal force. He was real, and He sympathized with them. The Bible was not viewed as a set of rigid doctrines, but as a living, creative work, a set of parables by which people could lead a moral life. Black prophetic Christianity gave spiritual freedom to the slaves, and a sense of humanity that transcended the slavery system.

The Union army did not reach central Alabama until 1864. Some slaves may have left the Marable plantation, making their way to the Union lines. Other slaves in nearby Troy, Alabama, organized a widespread conspiracy, which was discovered in December 1864. Morris, now nineteen years old, waited for his opportunity. His master, now an officer in the Confederate army, was severely wounded near West Point, Georgia. Morris was ordered to transport his master from the battle back to his home. Still trusted implicitly, he performed this service. But late one evening he gathered together his personal items, took forty dollars in gold from the house, and somehow escaped. Morris and Judy Brooks made their way into the sparsely populated hills of northeastern Alabama. This was no new Jerusalem, but freedom was theirs.

Like many other black freedmen, Morris understood that the best guarantee to freedom was land ownership. He purchased a small section of property near Wedowee, Alabama, and began to cultivate cotton. Through careful savings and backbreaking labor, Morris was able to purchase over one hundred acres of farmland in two decades. This was no mean achievement. In the 1880s the average Alabama farm was less than sixty acres, of which about thirty-five acres was cultivated. Black tenant farmers usually occupied less than one-third of that amount. Morris relied on the labor power of his thirteen children to plant and harvest the crop. When Judy Brooks Marable died in the early 1880s, Morris soon remarried. His second wife, who had the curious name Warner Clockster, was a descendant of the Creek Indians, who had lived in the region before the 1830s. Warner and Morris's sixth child was my grandfather, Manning Marable, born in 1894.

201

Morris's skills as a mechanic acquired during slavery may have been responsible for his later interest in business. Sometime during the early 1890s Morris and his best friend and neighbor, Joshua Heard, raised sufficient capital to start a cotton gin of their own. Most of the nearby towns already had gins—Lafayette and Talladega, Alabama, and West Point, Georgia—but whites owned the ginneries and warehouses. Black producers were usually dependent upon white brokers, who cheated them with regularity. Most of the farmers, black and white, purchased their supplies and farm implements on credit, and according to Roger L. Ransom and Richard Sutch, annual interest rates charged by rural merchants during the 1880s were about 60 percent. Since most farms yielded 150 pounds of cotton per acre, and cotton prices were then 8 to 9 cents a pound, an average white farmer could expect to gross $250 to $400 annually. Black sharecroppers, however, had to divide their profits with their landlords—and after paying off their debts, usually found themselves with nothing. Morris was determined to break out of the cycle of poverty and to compete against the white merchants. Black farmers soon supported Morris and his partner, and the ginning enterprise prospered.

During the 1880s many black and white farmers in Alabama joined the Alliance, a radical agrarian movement against the conservative business and planter elite. Populism, which followed in the early 1890s, drew upon the same small farmer strata. Morris was attracted to the movement perhaps because of its racial egalitarianism. Throughout Georgia and Alabama, black and white Populist Party members held joint picnics, rallies, and speeches. Populist candidate Reuben F. Kalb actually won the state's gubernatorial contest in 1894, but the conservatives used extensive voting fraud to swing the election. On the periphery of this activity, in his small rural town, Morris Marable became sheriff with the support of blacks and whites. He was intensely proud of his office and completed his duties with special dispatch. According to family legend, he even carried out two public executions—although the race of the victims is unknown. Morris carried a small Bible in one coat pocket at all times, and a revolver under his coat. In either case, he always planned to be prepared.

My great-grandfather's dream of freedom collapsed after the 1890s, with the demise of Populism and the rise of racial segregation. Between 1882 and 1927, 304 lynchings occurred in Alabama. The Sayre election law of Alabama made it illegal to assist voters in marking ballots—thus effectively disfranchising thousands of illiterate whites and blacks. Poll taxes and county levies were initiated by 1901, and the vast majority of poor and rural voters were eliminated. The total number of black voters in the state fell to 3,700 in 1908. Many white Populists turned bitterly against blacks at this time, and many rural blacks became the victims of white vigilantes. My grandmother's favorite tale about Morris concerns the harassment of one of her cousins by local whites. For some real or imaginary offense the young man was being viciously beaten in the public streets. Morris calmly walked into the mob, revolver in hand, and brought the boy home. The whites had too much respect—or perhaps fear—to stop him.

After exercising the right to vote for over thirty years, finally Morris was turned away from the ballot box. Disgusted, he became a Republican; he even named his last child Roosevelt in honor of the president in 1905. If politics could not liberate black people, economic power could. But the next blow came in 1914–15. The boll weevil, introduced into the United States in 1892, made its way into southern Alabama by 1910. In the summer of 1914 it had reached the northeastern part of the state. The fall of cotton production usually reached 50 percent in infested counties. That autumn, with the outbreak of World War I, European nations that had been the largest consumers of southern cotton were closed. Cotton prices immediately plummeted to 5 to 8 cents per pound, well below the earlier market price of 13 cents. Large white merchants and planters were able to obtain credit, and stored their cotton in warehouses.

But black entrepreneurs and small farmers were unable to cope with the crisis. As black farmers defaulted on loans, small black-owned banks and businesses collapsed. The number of black banks in Alabama fell from seven to one between 1911 and 1918; thousands of blacks lost their land and were forced to sell for only a fraction of its real value. Between 1910 and 1920 the total number of farms in Alabama declined from 110,400 to 95,000. The crisis of 1914–15 was the beginning of a long decline in black land tenure throughout the South. Black farm acreage in the South peaked at over 15 million acres in 1910; sixty years later, the amount was below 6 million acres. Morris had no choice except to sell the cotton gin, and he abandoned business entirely. At his death in 1927 Morris was still in debt, but his spirit remained unbroken.

Each successive generation of Afro-Americans has pursued the goal of freedom, the new Jerusalem, which would make the promise of democracy a reality. Manning Marable's road to freedom was the same as his father's. Manning married Fannie Heard, the soft-spoken but strong-willed daughter of Joshua Heard, in 1916. Together they raised thirteen children and in the 1930s started a small lumber company. With a little side income from my grandfather's illegal whiskey still, the lumber firm began to grow. Manning repeatedly told his children that the means of racial independence was through business: "You have to beat the southern white man at his own game." My father, James Marable, learned this lesson and ultimately became a successful entrepreneur. But always inherent in their collective activities was a moral commitment, born out of the slavery and Reconstruction experience, that united most members of the community to common goals: respect as human beings, unfettered participation within the economic and political life of this country, full civil liberties, and equal protection under the law.

Four generations removed from slavery, the vision of a just, democratic society remains. Yet the structural barriers to economic equality are more clearly discernible. In Macon County, Alabama, where most of the Marable extended family still resides, black entrepreneurs owned 234 businesses in 1977, according to the Bureau of the Census. About 76 percent of these firms, 178 in all, did not have a single paid employee. The 7 black taxicab firms averaged $12,300 annual gross receipts. The county's 94 selective services—everything from barbershops to pool halls —recorded an average $15,400 gross receipts and employed a grand total of 31 people. Out of the country's 24,000 blacks, minority-owned firms employed only 119 workers. The dream of economic self-sufficiency may have been reasonable to pursue under rural capitalist conditions in the late nineteenth century. But as a grand strategy for black group advancement in the period of monopoly capitalism, it represents a dead end.

Part of the dream of Morris Marable was realized during the civil rights movement. Black working people and the poor challenged the Jim Crow system and won. This effort, as in all significant black social movements, was rooted simultaneously in a political and moral critique of institutional racism. Just as the slaves developed a religious outlook that negated their masters' political power, civil rights activists of the 1960s led a crusade for social justice that expressed a moral dimension. The workers in the Student Nonviolent Coordinating Committee (SNCC) sang this in the Albany, Georgia, desegregation campaign of 1962:

> Ain't gonna let nobody turn me 'round
> Turn me 'round, turn me 'round,
> Ain't gonna let nobody turn me 'round

204

I'm gonna keep on walkin', keep on a-talkin'
Marching up to freedom land.

Morris Marable would have understood at once the significance of these words. Jim Crow meant inferior schools and political disfranchisement, low-paying jobs and second-class citizenship. The pursuit of democracy demanded a moral commitment of the oppressed to organize.

No more Jim Crow, No more Jim Crow
No more Jim Crow over me
And before I'll be a slave
I'll be buried in my grave
And go home to my lord and be free.

Twenty years and more have passed. The number of black elected officials in the United States increased from 104 in 1964 to 6,056 in 1985. A majority of black officials are currently in the South. However, 1,368 (22.6 percent) are only members of local school boards. Another 2,189 (36.1 percent) are members of city councils or municipal governments. Blacks make up substantial voting blocs in Alabama (23 percent of the voting-age population), Arkansas (14 percent), Florida (11 percent), Georgia (24 percent), Louisiana (27 percent), South Carolina (27 percent), and North Carolina (20 percent)—but not one black person is currently in Congress from these states.

The sting of the lash—political violence against blacks—still exists. Michael Etchinson, my wife's brother, became a police officer in Monroe, Georgia, in rural Walton County a decade ago. He made the mistake of arresting the son of an influential white leader. Thereafter, for several months, he was the target of local racists. His dog was poisoned, his wife received threatening phone calls. Michael understood that he had only days to live and put his affairs in order. In October 1977 he was assassinated by a white man with a hunting rifle. Four years later my wife's nineteen-year-old cousin was lynched several miles away. The coroner claimed it was a suicide. Black residents of Monroe claim the death occurred because the youth regularly dated a white woman. In any event, more than one dozen lynchings have taken place in Walton County since 1946.

Is the democratic vision an illusion for Afro-Americans, or a dream deferred? The struggle has not been without hardship. But the faith of a

205

people in bondage remains the moral guide for their descendants. The organic history of black Americans is a pattern of suffering and transcendence, of sacrifice and hope for the future. It has its own language, rhythms, and direction. It embraces the customs and collective experiences of those who have known slavery, Jim Crow, and now Reaganism. The moral imperatives of the slave community still find their way into the discourse and programs of a Jesse Jackson. An intimate knowledge of this history and rich cultural legacy is essential for our collective struggles for a democratic society in the future.

Sources

Aptheker, Herbert. *American Negro Slave Revolts*. New York: International Publishers, 1983.

Bureau of the Census. *1977 Survey of Minority-Owned Business Enterprises*. Washington, D.C.: Government Printing Office, 1979.

Douglass, Frederick. "What to the Slave is the Fourth of July?" *Black Scholar* 7 (July–Aug. 1976): 33–37.

Edet, Edna M. "One Hundred Years of Black Protest Music." *Black Scholar* 7 (July–Aug. 1976): 38–48.

Fite, Gilbert C. *Cotton Fields No More: Southern Agriculture, 1865–1980*. Lexington: University Press of Kentucky, 1984.

Focus 13 (March 1985): 4–5.

Levine, Lawrence W. *Black Culture and Black Consciousness: Afro-American Folk Thought from Slavery to Freedom*. Oxford: Oxford University Press, 1977.

Litwack, Leon F. *Been in the Storm So Long: The Aftermath of Slavery*. New York: Alfred A. Knopf, 1979.

Marable, Manning. *How Capitalism Underdeveloped Black America*. Boston: South End Press, 1983.

Ransom, Roger L., and Richard Sutch. *One Kind of Freedom: The Economic Consequences of Emancipation*. Cambridge: Cambridge University Press, 1977.

White, Walter. *Rope and Faggot*. New York: Arno Press, 1969.

Woodward, C. Vann. *Origins of the New South*. Baton Rouge: Louisiana State University Press, 1951.

Seventeen

Cornel West

POPULISM:
A BLACK SOCIALIST
CRITIQUE

Populism is the most indigenous form of American radicalism. Therein lie its strengths and weaknesses, its paradoxes and contradictions, its amorphous character and often vacuous content. I shall argue that the contemporary versions of populism promoted by Harry Boyte, Sara Evans, Frank Riessman, and others represent creative, gallant yet inadequate attempts to keep alive the radical tradition in America. I shall suggest that the two major ideological pillars of this country's self-definition —namely, cultural conservatism (nativism, sexism and, above all, racism) and Lockean liberalism (the sanctity of individual rights, private property, capital accumulation, and economic growth)—strongly mitigate against neopopulism's emerging as a potent radical force. This is especially so in a period of closely knit international interdependence, American national decline as a world power, and internal cultural decay. In such a period, a full-scale American populism would move much further to the right than to the left.

The strengths of populism constitute the best of the democratic tradition of a rural, preindustrial, pastoral America: local control, decentralized economic relations, small-scale political institutions, limited property ownership, and intimate, face-to-face interaction and association. This important stress on local activism, politics of everyday life of ordinary people, and discernible, credible, and visible forms of peoples' empowerment is rooted in the homespun American ideologies of Jeffersonian and Jacksonian civic republicanism. It represents an oppositional yet nostalgic form of radical plebeian humanism that is antibourgeois yet not anticapitalist. To put it crudely, populists tend to want modern liberal capitalist democracy without impersonal forms of bureaucracy, centralized modes of economic and political power, and alienating kinds of cultural practices in pluralistic urban centers.

The weaknesses of populism consist of the worst of the xenophobic and jingoistic tradition of a European settler society: racism, sexism, homophobia, inward- and backward-looking, preoccupied with preserving old ways of life, defensive, provincial, and, at times, conspiratorial. This seamy side of populism is grounded in the cultural conservatism of a deeply isolationist people, a conservatism and isolationism reinforced by geographical autonomy, economic prosperity, and cultural insularity. Yet it is this side of populism that looms large in the eyes of Afro-Americans.

A central paradox of American populism is that it invests great confidence in the goodwill of the American people. Yet, from a black perspective, it has been primarily when the federal courts and government have "imposed" populism's laws upon the American people that there has been some black progress. It is important to note that the two most important public acts associated with black progress—the Emancipation Proclamation (1863) and the *Brown vs. Board of Education* case (1954)—were far removed from the collective will of the American people. In fact, Congress would not have passed either if consulted, and both would have lost in a national referendum.

Another paradox of American populism is that its attractive theme of empowerment rarely is inclusive enough to take black interests seriously. This is not solely because of the racist sentiments of populist activists, but, more importantly, because these activists must pursue their many goals within the American political system, which forces populists to prioritize their goals and demands. Given this political context of limited options, populists (even those with the least racist sensibilities) tend to sacrifice the interests of minorities to those of the majority. The strange career of Tom Watson—from left populist to the Ku Klux Klan—is exemplary in this regard. And less dramatic examples dot the landscape of American history. I do not deny that black interests overlap with the interests of other powerless people. But I do hold that there are specifically black concerns (e.g., lynching at the turn of the century, police brutality in our own time) that are not identical with the concerns of powerless nonblacks in America.

The dominant ideology of American populism is highly contradictory. On the one hand, it is opposed to big business, big government, and big labor. This opposition is put forward in the name of decentralized control and in response to steep declines in the quality of life. On the other hand, populism is locked into the mainstream American quest for economic growth in order for more Americans to get in on the high standard of living in the country. Yet this growth presupposes the high levels of productivity and efficiency of big business, big government, and big labor. And given the deeply American character of populists, most would more than likely choose a higher standard of living with bigness and the concomitant maldistribution of wealth over a lower standard (yet possibly higher quality) of living with the decentralization they cherish. Needless to say, such a preference reveals the class affiliation of most American populists: middle class and stable working class.

The new populists intend to focus their message more and more on the minorities, the poor, women, gays and lesbians, and labor. But such culturally heterogeneous constituencies would only create even more contradictions—especially given the cultural conservatism of most American populists. As a black democratic socialist I welcome and support such a focus. Yet I believe that an honest effort in this direction will undermine the basic assumptions of populism: namely, relative cultural homogeneity and persistent economic growth of the U.S. capitalist economy. To take seriously the plight of the above constituencies means accenting and promoting, not simply acknowledging and tolerating, vast cultural differences and calling into question the conditions under which U.S. capitalist growth persists. This latter issue shifts the weight from populist concerns about consumption of goods and services to more socialist concerns about production and distribution of wealth. To question the growth of the capitalist pie is not to promote less consumption but rather to focus on how it gets baked in the first place and who more disproportionately benefits behind the mask of economic growth.

This issue of economic growth in populist ideology leads us to its major blinder: the international character of the U.S. capitalist economy. In the past American populism has supported the most vicious forms of U.S. imperialism. The new populism remains quite vague on its foreign policy pronouncements. Yet U.S. involvement in Latin America, Africa, Asia, and Europe are not simply matters of geopolitical and ideological concern. They also relate, in complex ways, to whether U.S. economic growth can be sustained.

Furthermore, the nature of these involvements shapes the perceptions of the potential populist constituencies in various ways. Examples are the impact of the Middle East conflict on Jews and Arabs in America, of Ireland on labor (especially its leadership), of Africa on black people, of the Philippines and South Korea on Asians, of Chile and Nicaragua on Hispanics. Again, the cultural conservatism—especially the uncritical nativism and naive patriotism—of most U.S. populists does not allow dealing candidly with the devastating critiques of U.S. practices past and present in much of the world. And to take seriously such critiques may result in the loss of a significant number of the original neopopulist constituencies. Yet these international issues cannot be avoided or down-played.

These potential troubles partly account for the amorphous character of U.S. populist movements. The passionate promotion of localism shuns sustained international and national considerations such as foreign policy, the role of the state, and bureaucracies. The imprecise message of decentralization tends to overlook crucial issues of productivity, efficiency, and the inescapable presence of some forms of centralization and bigness. Last, the slippery conception of democracy indeed serves as a desirable standard to criticize present societal realities, but it remains unclear what positive and constructive content it possesses.

For those of us from black America, symbolically and sometimes literally on the outside looking in, this amorphous character and often vacuous content represents the agonized conscience of the liberal white middle class and stable working class upset with their tenuous and uncertain niches in the corporate-dominated U.S. economy, an unresponsive conservative U.S. government, and a disintegrating U.S. culture. On the one hand, this agonized conscience is to be supported and encouraged, for it may lead to more fundamental issues such as organized attacks on class inequality, patriarchy (in the private and public spheres), and institutionalized racism. On the other hand, these fundamental issues that speak more directly to the needs of the black working poor and underclass would scatter the liberal white middle class and stable working class—and thereby leave the populist space to be filled by xenophobic demagogues.

This is the basic dilemma of the relation of populism to black America. And the black instincts of survival tend to lead toward deep suspicion of a movement with such negative potential. Of course, white instincts of survival tend to do the same—as seen in the white distance from the Jesse Jackson campaign, partly owing to minister Louis Farrakhan's anti-Semitic demagogy.

Given the absence of a potent leftist tradition and social presence, the black political class, for the most part, remains locked into a self-serving liberalism—a liberalism increasingly under attack from the right in both the Republican and Democratic parties. Black conservatives, be they intellectuals supported by right-wing thinktanks or preachers associated with Jerry Falwell's Moral Majority, are trying to take advantage of the vacuum created by the relative lack of organized black radicalism and the crisis of liberalism. Yet right-wing populism has little chance of broad success in black America, despite pervasive black conservative convictions regarding abortion and gay/lesbian lifestyles. This is so because right-wing populism's close association with racism is simply undeniable.

What, then, is an appropriate black attitude toward the new populism? In light of the highly limited progressive alternatives on the political scene, neopopulists should be supported in their attacks on corporate power and encouraged in their defenses of human rights of downtrodden people here and abroad. They are to be congratulated in their attempts to take culture seriously as a ground for local political activism. But the widespread cultural conservatism in the neopopulist movement must be opposed. Black progressive people should resist the sexism in American families, the racism and patriarchalism in American churches, the religiosity creeping in our schools, and the exclusivism in our neighborhoods. The political struggle over cultural ways of life should be waged under the ideals of pluralistic self-determination and self-realization through diversity. Last, black activists within and outside the neopopulist movement must highlight the age-old American problems of racism and U.S. intervention in Third World countries. No matter how tired white Americans become hearing criticisms of white and American supremacist practices here and around the world, it is the responsibility of black progressives to admonish each emerging wave of American radicalism that racism and ethnocentrism must be resisted in their old as well as new forms.

Eighteen

Adrienne Asch

WILL POPULISM
EMPOWER
DISABLED PEOPLE?

The themes of the emerging populism of the 1980s spring from deep longings to improve our lives, not just as individuals but as members of communities—whether communities of school, work, neighborhood, recreation, or worship. Only through the bonds of community, populists assert, will we transform our personal and national life. Only by working together in groups where we can all play a part to define our goals, appreciate and learn from one another, and empower ourselves through mutual aid, can we recover a sense of purpose, hope, and possibility for a change. This dream stirs us deeply because it captures our desire for a more cooperative, interdependent way of life, in which people would be recognized for their individual attributes, assisted with their individual difficulties, and valued for their uniqueness as well as for what they could contribute to a shared life.

As manifested in its main sites of struggle—neighborhood, workplace, marketplace, and environment—the populist vision and agenda for change could certainly incorporate goals fostering the participation and actualization of the nation's 36 million citizens with disabilities. To date, it has not. As blacks, Hispanics, women, gays, and senior citizens have learned for themselves, people with disabilities have come to recognize that they too have rarely been seen as valued, deserving members of the community. To change that, a disability rights movement, with its own version of populist rhetoric, has emerged.

The rise of a separate disability rights movement challenges the very notion of community as defined in the past. Slowly and painfully, Americans have been learning that social hierarchies based on biological characteristics of skin color, gender, or age will not endure without protest from those excluded or demoted for being of the wrong, less valued kind. In public discourse at least, we now assert that it is wrong to judge, classify, and exclude people on the basis of their being black, female, or old. Few, however, have found it inaccurate, intolerant, or discriminatory to categorize or characterize people on the basis of what they could or could not do because of physical, intellectual, or psychological impairments. Biological limitation itself has been seen as the problem, not the interaction of biology with a particular environment.

For instance, if a child could not hear, it was assumed that she could not participate in a public school classroom. No thought was given to whether the school environment could be altered so that speech could be supplemented by sign language to communicate with the deaf child. Instead, the deaf child received no schooling or attended a separate school. In today's society some distinctions still make sense. Within the limits of our current technology, blind people cannot drive cars. Within the limits of our current educational methods, people with profound mental retardation are not likely to edit manuscripts. Historically, upon discovering that someone could not see, hear, move, or learn as easily or as quickly or in the same way as others, or could not do some of these things at all, family, school, church, neighborhood, and employer have concluded that inability in one area equaled inability in all. The result has been to disqualify most people with disabilities from playing any social role whatever.

This is not to deny the protection and care given by families, the charity provided by religious and other philanthropic institutions, the special schools, sheltered workshops, rehabilitation programs, camps and recreational opportunities, and special government subsidies provided to disabled children and adults. It is in the words "care," "charity," and "special" that the relegation begins—relegation to a status of inferior, needy, dependent, helpless, and tolerated, if at all, only so long as people fit the helpless image.

Beginning in the 1940s and increasing substantially since early 1970s, disabled people have begun to organize themselves, seeking to redefine their problems and change their situation. They have won some important gains. Yet much remains to be done. Can the "new populism" of the 1980s incorporate the goals of the disability rights movement? Can disabled people secure full citizenship, equal opportunity, maximal self-realization, and full community participation by embracing a populist agenda?

I am skeptical. The disability rights movement and populism are not inherently opposed to one another. The disability rights movement, in fact, has its own populist flavor and shares certain beliefs with other populist struggles. Indeed, some items on the disability rights agenda would benefit the community at large. Yet I doubt that populists will broaden their agenda to press for changes that benefit people with disabilities. Even if populism worked explicitly for disability rights, problems inherent in its own agenda seem likely to prevent it from creating significant and enduring social change for disabled and nondisabled people alike. Before detailing these reservations, it is necessary to discuss the situation of disabled people today and how the disability rights movement seeks to respond to it.

Disabled People in Contemporary American Society

"The return of power to ordinary people" is a cornerstone of the populist agenda. Whether power ever actually rested with the common people may be open to debate. But clearly, people with disabilities have, by and large, been quite powerless. They seek not to regain power but to acquire it for the first time. They have not had power precisely because they have not been seen as ordinary. In a culture that defines autonomy and competence narrowly while worshiping beauty, health, and vigor, disability arouses what one writer has termed aesthetic and existential anxiety.[1] People with disabilities depart from valued aesthetic norms and remind us of human vulnerability, frailty, and death.

The battle for disability rights is first the battle to become part of the ordinary communities populists wish to build upon to create a more humane society. Although people with disabilities may have been physically present in some families (and not all families have kept disabled members in their midst), mere presence has not meant equal participation in any realm of life. Lesser value is given to the lives of disabled family members. Infants and others with disabilities are at risk of having parents or relatives withhold medical treatment because their lives are viewed as a burden to the family and of little benefit to anyone—even themselves. Their quality of life fails to meet someone else's standard of acceptability, and their very lives are threatened. Families that decide to treat their disabled members are often encouraged by medical and rehabilitation professionals to institutionalize those labeled retarded, severely disabled, or seriously emotionally disturbed. The fear is that disabled people will "burden" those around them—will take attention from more deserving "normal" people. It is as though it is not legitimate to presume that existing resources will be redistributed to incorporate the needs of the disabled member.

Persons with less serious disabilities still face problems in maintaining family relationships. When a husband and father has a heart attack or becomes paralyzed in an automobile accident, his wife and children may assume that his new physical limitations will bring changes in all family and social roles. Women and men with disabilities have been viewed as unfit mates and parents, burdens to partners and children, damaging to those around them. Disabled people are often urged to limit sexual activity, or prevented by family or professionals from marrying or from raising a child. Women with disabilities have been subjected to forced abortions and involuntary sterilization. Disabled women and men are denied child custody in divorce cases. They are also denied the rights to adopt children or to be foster parents.

The church or synagogue, often seen as a foundation for community building, has generally failed to grant full access to people with disabilities. Houses of worship are often unusable to those who cannot mount steps. Thus, millions of mobility-impaired people are excluded. Others with limitations of hearing or sight may get inside only to find that worship services are not signed as spoken and that hymnals and prayerbooks are

216

not available in large print or braille. Some disabled people have been denied the right to marry with religious sanction. Others have been refused ordination.

American neighborhoods contain millions of people whose heart condition, cancer, or epilepsy remain unknown beyond family and friends. But millions with more readily apparent disabling conditions—such as deafness, paraplegia, amputation, cerebral palsy, or mental retardation—are effectively barred from neighborhood life. Much housing is still architecturally inaccessible to people with mobility impairments and especially to wheelchair users. The lack of accessible housing and affordable minimal supports (such as attendant care) forces many people who need no ongoing medical or custodial care to live in institutions. Others who can use existing housing are routinely denied it by real estate agents and landlords. Indeed, there is no federal law prohibiting housing discrimination on the basis of disability. Group residences for people with disabilities, which can help make support services more economical, have been barred after organized opposition claimed that wheelchairs deface property or that the presence of mentally retarded persons will damage property values. This hostility has been embodied in local zoning ordinances. The community of Cleburne, Texas, for example, sought to bar a residence for moderately retarded people. Only in July 1985 did the Supreme Court strike down this ordinance, declaring it a violation of the Fourteenth Amendment. But this was, at best, a partial victory for the disability rights movement, since the Supreme Court decision failed to acknowledge that people with disabilities were being treated, in effect, as a suspect class.

Such natural sources of community as school and work are still far from routinely part of the lives of millions of disabled people. Nearly 10 percent of the nation's children are believed to have disabilities.[2] PL 94-142, passed by Congress in 1976, mandates a free, appropriate public education for all handicapped children in the least restrictive environment. In the large majority of instances, this was expected to be the public school class with nondisabled children. Yet most disabled students are still educated in separate schools or classes. Children with and without disabilities are thus deprived of the opportunity to learn together. Instead of evaluating how the ordinary school environment can be changed to better accommodate one-tenth of its pupils without segregation, schools still relegate students with disabilities to separate rooms or integrate them physically without providing the support services that will guarantee a genuine education.

217

According to 1978 Social Security Administration survey estimates, people with disabilities constitute possibly 17 percent of the working age population.[3] Unemployment is severalfold higher for this group than for any other sector of U.S. society. Disabled men are employed full-time at a rate one-third that of nondisabled men. Women with disabilities are employed full-time at one-fourth the rate of nondisabled women. Twenty-six percent of disabled people between 16 and 64 live at or below the poverty-level, compared to 10 percent of nondisabled people in the same age group.[4]

Some people's physical or mental conditions truly prevent them from working yet it is widely believed that nearly all people with impairments could be employed if our society were truly committed to upgrading their skills and education, to accommodating work environments to those with disabilities, to enforcing existing laws against employment discrimination, and to expanding Title VII of the Civil Rights Act of 1964 to forbid employment discrimination based on non-job-related disability in all employment.[5]

While populists press for lower utility rates and greater product safety, disabled people seek to have products that will ease their lives available at prices they can afford, and from other than specialized monopoly suppliers. Department stores could sell modified eating utensils, wheelchairs made from bicycle parts, and other simple devices that enable people with impairments to participate in everyday activities. Today these must be purchased from the few specialized suppliers at exorbitant prices —$700 for a child-sized wheelchair—placing them beyond the reach of those who live on earnings far below those of the nondisabled and often at the poverty level.

While environmental activists seek to preserve and purify our natural environment, disability rights activists work to reform our human-made environment so as to allow the full participation of people with disabilities. Anyone with impaired mobility is effectively barred from many public and most private buildings, from most theaters, restaurants, and other places of recreation, from much public transportation. In the past, people who used wheelchairs or who could not walk stairs because of heart or breathing problems accepted their restrictions of access or travel as inherent in their physical limitations. Now disabled people strive for changes in the architecture of buildings and transportation systems to make them available to all members of the public.

People with disabilities are denied full citizenship in several ways. Most voting places are architecturally inaccessible; most fail to provide ballots in forms non-print-readers can use. Many states still deny blind or deaf people the right to serve on juries. City and state government hearings, school board and community meetings take place in inaccessible locations or without sign language interpreters. Public documents are not produced in braille or on tape. Although Americans receive most of their political information from television, neither public nor commercial broadcasters provide captioning so that deaf people can see the words others hear, though a line is available on the screen that would easily serve this purpose. When one commercial network captioned a single news program, it was besieged by objections from distracted viewers. Not surprisingly, the network abandoned its "experiment" in opening television to the nation's deaf citizens.

In virtually all areas of life, then, many disabled people remain isolated from forms of community that are essential ingredients in the populist vision. The disability rights movement, however, has sought to create a community of people with disabilities—one united to transform an oppressive society into an inclusive society, to transform identity from one of sadness, low self-esteem, and reluctant acknowledgment of common problems to one of acceptance and self-respect.

Like populists who believe ordinary people can overcome a sense of victimization through mutual aid and collective struggle against large corporations and big government, disability rights activists contend that impairment need not be synonymous with helplessness. Indeed, disability rights activists believe that local and national institutions, not biology, victimize people with disabilities. In 1977 concerted action by disabled people throughout the country compelled the signing of regulations to implement Section 504 of the Rehabilitation Act of 1973, the major civil rights statute for disabled people.[6] Movements groups still use such tactics as picketing and demonstrations to protest the images of helplessness portrayed by television fund-raising telethons, to protest discriminatory seating policies of national airlines, or to demand access to mass transit systems.

A core movement belief, akin to the populist belief about working for neighborhood and community improvement, is that disabled people themselves—not government and private agencies, not medical and rehabilitation professionals—should decide how and where they will study,

219

work, and live. The movement's goal is full inclusion in the mainstream—in the wider community of neighborhood, school, and workplace that still excludes people with disabilities. Movement activists recognize the need for some private space where disabled people can get specialized training in adapting to impairment, and where an individual can forge a positive identity as a person with a disability. Save for these purposes, the movement seeks an end to most segregated education, employment, residential living, and recreational and social activities for disabled people.

Populism and Disability Rights

To return to the questions posed at the outset: Can disability rights become part of the populist agenda? If so, can that agenda empower people with disabilities? Problems in the contemporary disability rights movement and in populism itself make both unlikely. Although populists could incorporate disability objectives into their agenda, they are unlikely to be eager to do so. If they did, they might ameliorate local problems of the area's disabled citizens without removing the major, national blocks to equality and full participation for disabled people.

For its part, the weakness of the disability rights movement offers little in the way of short-run payoffs to populists seeking allies for non-disability-related struggles. Populism's pragmatism, its somewhat simplistic conception of community, its tendency to gloss over histories of oppressed groups within the community, its glorification of local control and undifferentiated aversion to national or "big" government, and its insistence upon letting political vision develop from a focus on discrete issues—all these problems suggest that it is of questionable value for either disability rights or substantial social change for the nation as a whole.

Regardless of its arena, populist organizing focuses on concrete, local, discrete issues. It is pragmatic, working with any group or individual ready to assist with the particular struggle of the moment. In those areas where disability organizations have made their presence felt, neighborhood or environmental activists may know of their strength and resources and seek them out as useful political allies. But in most cities and towns disability rights groups are small and have relatively little political clout and even less money to put into a campaign for general environmental or neighborhood improvements that will not resolve the disability-related problems of their constituency. In the short run, if neighborhood activists believe they will get little support from disability groups, they are unlikely to cultivate them and build the close relationships that might one day convince them to take up an issue particular to the disabled people in a community.

The lack of direct payoffs to populists speaks to a major weakness of today's grassroots disability movement: its small size and stretched-to-the-limit financial, staff, and volunteer resources. Although local independent living centers and national organizations of people with disabilities seek to represent the interests of all 36 million, with their diverse medical, mental, and psychological conditions and their diverse as well as common problems, they are actively backed by only a fraction of the constituency they claim. Like other oppressed groups, many people with disabilities are so worn down by the problems of getting medical and rehabilitation services, or earning a living, that they have neither time nor energy for political action. Others have so internalized society's negative attitudes toward disability that they cannot imagine that collective action would improve their lives.

Even more problematic for developing a fully representative movement, millions of people with less visible and thus less stigmatized conditions, who can avoid the day-to-day indignities and injustices of the more obviously disabled, never develop any consciousness of commonality with them. Some people with heart conditions, arthritis, or back or respiratory problems cannot manage today's inaccessible architecture and transit, but they have seen the problems as inherent in their medical conditions and have not been urged to join others to demand structural changes that would render the environment useful for them.

These same people, and others with histories of epilepsy, cancer, psychiatric treatment, diabetes, or hypertension, may be deprived of employment by non-job-related medical standards as discriminatory as those that exclude people who are paralyzed, deaf, or blind from jobs they can perform. Yet, although many individuals will fight their own cases of discrimination and sometimes win their right to work, such individual action often fails to foster group solidarity. These people may believe that joining with the more noticeably disabled and stigmatized might threaten their places in the mainstream. Unfortunately, they may be right. Still, their consequent avoidance of assuming a disabled identity pinpoints the superficial nature of populism's notion of community.

221

Disability rights activists have consciously adopted a minority-group perspective, comparing themselves with blacks, women, gays, and others who find themselves outside the white, straight, nondisabled, male-dominated power structure of American society. Populism eschews seeing "community" as made up of subgroups with different histories— including different histories of oppression within the same society. And by enshrining localism, local control, and local norms, populism runs the risk of enshrining local prejudice—prejudice that would keep black school children out of South Boston or seek a city ordinance to keep disabled people out of Cleburne, Texas, in the name of community control.

The challenge to populism is whether it can define "community" broadly enough to include people with disabilities. Without such a definition, it is no wonder that nondisabled people object to seeing resources that might go to ending pollution used to create curb cuts or to provide interpreters at public meetings. Some environmental modifications can benefit anyone whose broken leg, fatigue, or wheeling of a carriage or shopping cart makes stairs difficult. Other changes—interpreters, taped documents, open captioning—are of direct benefit only to those whose hearing or sight is impaired. When disabled people are routinely educated and employed alongside the nondisabled, it will be easier for the nondisabled majority to view the disabled minority as having general as well as "special" needs. They may realize that, once their needs are met, disabled people can make contributions as valuable as any other community members. Supporting disability objectives, then, affirms the potential of disabled people to contribute.

Frank Bowe justifies expending resources to create an inclusive society for people with disabilities by pointing to the costs of keeping them needlessly unemployed, uneducated, institutionalized, and immobile.[7] He contends that all levels of government now spend ten times as much to keep disabled people dependent as they do on programs to promote their independence and integration. If he is right, populists fed up with wasteful social programs, unresponsive government, and inefficient bureaucracy should be among the first to support shifting community resources to include disabled people as contributing community members.

Some disability activists believe they can change opposition to spending money for environmental modification, rehabilitation, and support services by reminding the nondisabled that the disability community itself is an open one, that at any time people can and will join by virtue of illness, accident, or age. You, they say, who have excluded us from employment and housing and chosen not to meet our needs may at any time need help yourself. Such appeals can backfire, however, and may serve only to heighten people's fears of facing disability issues.

Hopes for community inclusion rest better on an appeal to the spirit in populism that seeks to promote interdependence, to appreciate people as individuals, and to restore to the ordinary and powerless a sense of human dignity. Commenting on the aspirations of the disability rights movement, Nancy Crewe eloquently observes: "Beauty, health, youth, vigor, employability, communication, and even the ability to control one's own body are discarded as criteria for classifying some people as worthy of independence and others as unfit. Exterior characteristics are insignificant; only human dignity matters."[8] If populists can incorporate these aspirations into their own political vision, they could achieve a great deal —not just for people with disabilities but for the community at large. Properly viewed, disability could point the way to individualized educational plans for all schoolchildren, and to reasonable job accommodations for all employees.

If populists come to espouse an inclusive view of community and to believe that genuine neighborhood improvement requires access for people with disabilities, disabled people could achieve some worthwhile gains by working with them. If grassroots disability rights groups allied with community organizations on general issues, they could destroy the stereotype of the disabled as different, as having nothing in common with the nondisabled. For example, local groups could then monitor enforcement of architectural-barrier and antidiscrimination laws or could demand changes in local laws to guarantee access.

Other gains could be accomplished through collaboration with school and workplace organizations. Disabled adults and parents of disabled children could cooperate with other parents on school issues. Together they could ensure participation of disabled children in all public school activities. Neighborhood groups could work with independent living centers to press homebuilders to construct accessible housing and urge homeowners and landlords to construct ramps and other simple features to make existing facilities usable by disabled people. Workplace activism could include not only traditional health and safety concerns but also pressures on employers to carry out affirmative-action hiring and to make work locations accessible to people with disabilities.

223

When protesting the actions and policies of local merchants or local branches of national corporations, consumer groups could include disability issues of product availability and architectural access. When demanding increased citizen participation, the populists' agenda could include barrier-free meetings, interpreters at public meetings, and braille and tape handouts. When seeking to influence funding and service programs of social agencies, community groups could work with disability rights groups to ensure that all local agencies provide quality services to people with disabilities.

Progressive populists such as Harry Boyte, Tom Hayden, Jim Hightower, and Mark Kann ask us to distinguish "good," democratic, left-liberal, echoes-of-the-'60s populism from "bad," regressive, right-wing populism.[9] Just how are we to distinguish? How are we to know when those who want community control over utility companies will not also want a referendum on the exclusion of black or disabled children from the community's schools, or a referendum on excluding women and the disabled from nontraditional jobs? Only national action by courts and Congress has compelled local communities to rethink racism, sexism, and, in Bogdan's and Biklen's terminology, "handicapism"—discrimination against people with disabilities.[10]

Aversion to disabled people runs deep in our culture. It will not be easily or quickly eradicated. With the advent of mainstreaming (the integration of children with disabilities into previously segregated schools and classrooms), parents cried that their children would lose attention and resources and would be made uncomfortable by the presence of disabled children in their classes. Without federal law and the threat of losing federal dollars, we cannot know how many school boards would have caved in to such local opposition.

Local action will get all of us, disabled and nondisabled, only so far. Only through national action have we prevented or overcome the most flagrant forms of community exclusion for disabled people and other minorities, regulated minimum standards of service delivery and client rights in education and social services, and checked abuses of workers and consumers by the free enterprise system. People with disabilities are even more in need of such protection than the nondisabled. For the foreseeable future they will need some specialized service programs beyond general education and social welfare. Rehabilitation and supports for community living must be treated as a right to be protected by the federal government, not a privilege dependent upon local charity or whim.

In our frustration with bureaucratic and initiative-stifling federal programs, we forget that national government provides the bulk of the funding for rehabilitation effort for disabled people, sets out minimal standards for service, and assures a modicum of client rights not formerly found in state programs. Even now, rehabilitation and services to provide community living for the disabled differ substantially from state to state. The quadriplegic woman in Georgia needs the same opportunity for rehabilitation and the purchase of attendant services as her counterparts in California and Massachusetts. Decentralization and local control advance us only after we have won the minimal protections of self-determination and entitlement to service. Disabled people have only just begun to acquire such guarantees.

Furthermore, national action is essential to promoting employment for disabled people. Although many state civil rights laws have gone further than federal ones in prohibiting employment discrimination based on disability, not all have. Thus, the disabled must win coverage under Title VII of the Civil Rights Act of 1964. In addition, national action must restructure rehabilitation, income support, and medical benefit programs to eliminate their dependency-promoting, disincentives-to-employment components. Nondiscrimination laws and local support of employer initiatives will do little if disabled people risk losing attendant care, home services, and assistance with paying for costly drugs and medical supplies as soon as they obtain jobs that do not pay enough to cover the extra expenses some conditions impose. Large and small businesses, still far worse in their records of hiring disabled people than all levels of government, must be induced to do so through incentives such as tax credits for job restructuring and workplace accommodation. State treasuries and populist protest will never have the impact of federal support.

In sum, federal dollars and regulatory power are critical for promoting the community participation and economic well-being of people with disabilities. Obviously, the Reagan Administration does not sympathize with the suggestions advanced here. But to turn away from the federal government and embrace indiscriminate local control offers no real solution. This raises one last concern, applicable both to current populist formulations and current disability rights ideology: Social and economic problems are connected. No single-issue movement (disability rights) and no credo with a few slogans (populism) can improve our society. We need a clear vision of what morality, what social and political relationships, and what kind of economy and foreign policy we want for our nation.

Critics of populism from without and within must continue to challenge its adherents to make connections between what may seem like discrete issues. Environmental damage facing all of us, an unusable environment for some of us (the disabled), too few resources for educating all our children, and renewing our neighborhoods can all be traced to national policy—social, economic, foreign, and military—and corporate greed. No matter how many protests we engage in over utility rates, skyrocketing rents, plant shutdowns, unsafe offices and factories, unresponsive teachers, local leaders, and police, we will not make substantial change until we constantly make connections for ourselves and others about the roots of our problems.

Neither the populist focus on advocacy, self-help, and mutual aid nor the disability rights focus on equality and full participation lead us to a coherent agenda for solving national or global problems. Populists have not spelled out how advocacy, self-help skills, and local political reforms will lead people to discover the connections between their apparently separate problems. Disability rights activists have not yet begun to discuss whether unemployment of the disabled and cries of not enough resources for an accessible environment and quality education and rehabilitation are connected to how we, as a nation, choose to make and spend our money.

Like other civil rights and liberation movements, disability politics speaks to critical omissions in much left-liberal and socialist thought, which leans heavily on an economic analysis of social problems. Populism redresses other failings of progressive and socialist ideology by reminding us of the need for efficacy, control, competence, roots, and mutually supportive and empowering relationships. Both remind us that social change is about and for people and call upon us to enhance our appreciation of common humanity and individual differences. Without these, social change is arid.

But local control, disability rights, and personal empowerment are impossible in an economy or society unwilling to meet human needs. Populism may get neighborhoods more services and citizens a greater sense of personal control. Disability rights activists may change a few laws, reform certain service programs, and eventually bring their constituency nearer to the kind of life of the "average" citizen. Such reforms are valuable. Nonetheless, they leave basic social and economic arrangements untouched, because they are only intended to redistribute the national pie. If, in fact, all we do is get more of a rotten pie, what do we have to eat?

Notes

I wish to express my appreciation to Harry Boyte, Alan Gartner, and Patrick Peppe for discussions that clarified my ideas and provided useful insights; to Harlan Hahn and Richard Scotch for comments on an earlier draft; and to John Fousek for substantial comments and editorial contributions.

1. H. Hahn, "Paternalism and Public Policy," *Society*, March–April 1983, pp. 36–46.

2. J. Gliedman and W. Roth, *The Unexpected Minority: Handicapped Children in America* (New York: Harcourt, Brace, Jovanovich, 1980).

3. L. Haber and J. McNeil, *Methodological Questions in the Estimation of Disability Prevalence* (Washington, D.C.: Population Division, Bureau of the Census, 1983).

4. U.S. Bureau of the Census, *Labor Force Status and Other Characteristics of Persons with a Work Disability: 1982*, in Current Population Reports, Series P-23, no. 127 (Washington, D.C.: U.S. Government Printing Office, 1983).

5. F. Bowe, *Rehabilitating America* (New York: Harper and Row, 1980); J. Gliedman and W. Roth, *The Unexpected Minority*.

6. R. K. Scotch, *From Good Will to Civil Rights: Transforming Federal Disability Policy* (Philadelphia: Temple University Press, 1984).

7. Bowe, *Rehabilitating America*.

8. N. Crewe, "Freedom for Disabled People: The Right to Choose," in N. M. Crewe and I. Zola, eds., *Independent Living for Physically Disabled People* (San Francisco: Jossey-Bass, 1983), p. 361.

9. H. Boyte, *The Backyard Revolution: Understanding the New Citizen Movement* (Philadelphia: Temple University Press, 1980); H. Boyte, *Community is Possible: Repairing America's Roots* (New York: Harper & Row, 1984); T. Hayden, *The American Future: New Visions Beyond Old Frontiers* (Boston: South End Press, 1980); J. Hightower, *Eat Your Heart Out: How Food Profiteers Victimize the Consumer* (New York: Random House, 1976); J. Hightower, *Hard Tomatoes, Hard Times: The Hightower Report* (Cambridge, Mass.: Schenkman Books, 1978); M. Kann, *The American Left* (New York: Praeger, 1982).

10. R. Bogdan and D. Biklen, "Handicapism," *Social Policy* 7, no. 4 (March–April 1977), pp. 14–19.

Resources on the Disability Rights Movement

Representative National Organizations

American Coalition of Citizens with Disabilities, 1012 Fourteenth St. NW, Washington, DC 20005. (202) 628–3470.

Disability Rights Education and Defense Fund, 2212 Sixth Street, Berkeley, CA 94702. (415) 644-2555.

National Council on Independent Living, 1295 University Avenue, San Diego, CA 92103. (619) 296-8012.

National Federation of the Blind, 1800 Johnson Street, Baltimore, MD 21230. (301) 659-9314.

Selected Literature

Asch, A. "Understanding and Working with Disability Rights Groups." In H. McCarthy, ed. *Complete Guide to Employing Persons with Disabilities*. Albertson, N.Y.: Human Resources Center, 1985.

Brightman, A. *Ordinary Moments: The Disabled Experience*. Baltimore: University Park Press, 1983.

Gartner, A., and T. Joe, eds. *Images of the Disabled, Disabling Images*. New York: Praeger, 1986.

The Disability Rag (a journal of organizing and comment by disability rights activists, published monthly in print, large print, and on tape). P.O. Box 145, Louisville, KY 40201.

228

Seven
THE POLITICS
OF POPULISM

Nineteen
Tom Harkin

THE MAKING OF A
DEMOCRATIC POPULIST:
A PROFILE

An Interview by Harry C. Boyte

At moments in the spring of 1985 Tom Harkin, freshman senator from the state of Iowa, seemed almost to eclipse the media wizardry of Ronald Reagan with the politics of what he calls "democratic populism." Evening news shows featured Harkin night after night challenging administration farm policies; scenes of Harkin leading a group of farmers flashed across U.S. television screens. Together they solemnly planted 250 crosses opposite the White House, an act symbolizing the number of family farms going out of existence each day.

The Populist Caucus

Harkin had founded a new group called the Populist Caucus in the Ninety-eighth Congress with several other members of the House, including Lane

Evans, Byron Dorgan, Albert Gore, Jr., and James Weaver. After the 1984 election—when all caucus members had won, often running well ahead of Reagan even in conservative districts like North Dakota—the caucus grew to twenty-five. It included three of the four freshmen Democrats in the Senate, and urban populists like Marcy Kaptur, Barbara Mikulski, Charles Hayes, and Al Wheat.

Through the spring and summer Harkin argued in a wide range of Democratic Party forums for populism as the alternative to the conventional wisdom that decreed a "shift to the right": History shows that military battles were won when a decision was made to attack, not defend. We don't have to move to the right—nor abandon our ideals—to capture the American people's votes. And we will never win the hearts and minds of the people by telling them we have lost ours and could they please point in the right direction. We need to expose the Reagan economic policies for their true effect—and explain them in populist human terms that people can relate to.

I interviewed Harkin during the Midwest Academy/Citizen Action Retreat, an annual event that draws together more than a thousand activists, politicians, and others to talk about progressive organizing. This particular summer, the theme was "Building Democratic Populism." Harkin's face is weathered, like a farmer's, and tough. My mother died when I was ten, he *recounts.* We lived out in the country road by a railroad track, and sort of took care of ourselves. We were a pretty rough and tumble group. *But he speaks with folksy eloquence, mingled often with erudition. I asked why he calls himself a populist.*

In 1981 and '82, I'd been in Congress several years. I was thinking even then about running for the Senate, after we had lost both our Democratic senators from Iowa, both of whom were good. I had an advisory group, young people around Washington, that I met with once a month. We called it the Wednesday group. We'd bring in speakers like Paul Warnke, Lester Thurow, Gar Alperovitz.

One time we were having a discussion about economics and agriculture. This one guy there from Texas worked for the Department of Energy. How he came to be in this group I still don't know. He always wore cowboy boots and had a butch haircut. One day he said, "you know, you sound just like a populist."

I said, "What?"

He said, "You sound just like a populist."

I said, "Bullshit. Don't confuse me with those redneck know-nothings. Populists were racist, rednecks, know-nothings. They didn't know what was going on. They were anti-everything."

He said, "No, you got it all wrong. I'm going to get you a book if you'll read it." So he got me this book by Lawrence Goodwyn, *The Populist Moment.* I read it and it was like the scales had fallen off of my eyes. Then I read Hicks's book, *The Populist Revolt,* Fred Harris's *The New Populism,* the one by the two Kennedy guys, Jeff Greenfield and Jack Newfield, *The Populist Manifesto.* Then I went back and I read the Populist Party platform of 1892 and 1896. It was about this time that I started the Populist Caucus.

When the Populist Caucus formed, a reporter asked him about Richard Viguerie, the right-wing fundraiser and strategist who has taken to calling himself a populist. I asked him to see if Viguerie would agree to run on the Populist Party platform of 1892, *remembers Harkin.* I know I certainly would. It had a lot of good ideas.

Harkin claimed the populist tradition in the early 1980s, but his distinctive political vision grows from experience that long predated his self-description as a populist. His father was a coal miner in Iowa, a strong advocate of unions during the Depression, but also a fan of the demagogic and anti-Semitic "populist" Father Coughlin.

In the 1960s Harkin served in the Navy, and what he saw turned him strongly against the Vietnam war. As a young law school student and congressional aide, he went back to Vietnam in the summer of 1970 as part of a fact-finding mission in the wake of the U.S. invasion of Cambodia. Tom Harkin was determined to pursue the investigation thoroughly. But he discovered that most of the congressional delegation had no interest in learning anything more than what they gained from military briefings. Harkin followed up leads on his own. One catapulted him to national prominence.

Rumors had long circulated about the South Vietnamese confinement and torture of dissident student activists and Buddhist leaders on Con Son Island. Harkin found a former prisoner on Con Son who described a thirteen-month period of brutalizing imprisonment in "tiger cages," hidden behind the walls of a vegetable garden on the island. Despite vigorous denials from South Vietnamese officials, Harkin found the cages. He took a series of remarkable photographs that both South Vietnamese and the American congressman who headed the fact-finding mission tried to suppress. And that summer, he broke the national story in the pages of Life *magazine and* The Progressive. *Harkin's pictures added to the uproar about the war. They cost him his congressional job. Even two years later, Democratic leaders blocked his appointment to a position on congressional staff on the grounds he had acted "traitorously." But ultimately the experience powerfully shaped his views about politics.*

Whether an elected official tries to avoid or meet moral decisions head-on is a test of his political courage, *wrote Harkin of his experience.* What he does when confronted with a moral decision is a test of not only his political but his moral courage. . . . I was shocked to find how few members of Congress measure up and pass both tests. [But] I learned that you don't have to go along. One man can stand up and make a difference.

Barred from work on congressional staff, he decided to run himself. In 1972 I graduated from law school. I decided I was going to go back to Iowa and run for Congress against the Vietnam war. I'd been involved in the marches. I had friends killed over there, flying missions. I knew a lot guys who quit flying because they didn't want to bomb innocent people any more.

Talk about grassroots. I didn't have any money to do a poll, but figured I could ask questions as well as anybody else. So in January, I went to Iowa, borrowed a car, and drove throughout the whole fifth district, all over southern Iowa, small towns, farms. I had a yellow pad, a clipboard. I'd go to a house and say, "I'm with American Surveys; we're taking a poll. I'd like to ask you some questions." Sometimes I'd stop groups in elevators, or sit and listen to what people were saying. Then I'd dictate into a tape recorder on the front seat. You get a different feeling, you know. When I started going over this stuff, I found that what this right-wing congressman was doing and saying was not really what the people in the district thought. At least the ones I talked to. They were interested in other things. He was pro-war. And they weren't. And they weren't pro-military. Another thing I found was they didn't know who he was. He never came to their towns. He'd been in so long he took it for granted.

Then I went back about February for the county conventions. I was a senior in law school, never ran for office. They must have thought I was the craziest son of a bitch they'd ever seen. No political credentials. Said I was going to run for Congress. The issue I was going to run on was ending the war, at a time when the Vietnam war was still quite popular. I was going to nationalize the railroads, the health care system. I felt the little guy was getting screwed.

But a couple of people said they'd like to support me. And nobody else wanted to run against this guy. They were glad to have a sacrificial lamb. I went back to finish law school, but didn't even go to graduation. On graduation day I was out in Iowa.

We got a car and a van. The car dealer turned out to be a Democrat. We painted Harkin for Congress on the van. To get publicity, I said I'm going to knock on 10,000 doors. Ruth, my wife, decided she would too. We got these counters that click and go to 9,999. In June we started knocking on doors. We'd go to these little towns, take our camera with us, and get a picture in the local press, with the headline: "Harkin knocks on 939th door." Went from town to town all over southern Iowa. All through June, July, August. I swore after that I'd never knock on another door again.

We moved to Ames. Someone told the Democratic chairperson of the county that Ruth was an attorney, so she asked her to run for county attorney. I responded, you know, with the usual male stuff. "That's ridiculous. You can't do that to me! My life, my career down the tubes. You can't run for county attorney while I'm running for Congress."

Ruth said, "I told the county chair, 'Yes, I'll run.'"

Ruth Harkin won—the first woman ever elected to that position in the state of Iowa, and, with the exception of one Democrat elected for two years in the landslide of 1964, the first Democrat ever elected to a courthouse position in the county. Tom Harkin lost. But his 45 percent of the vote stunned political observers across the state. He got a job with the Legal Services Office; he also immediately began planning for the next election.

We started brainstorming in the winter. Sitting around drinking beer late one night, this friend who taught at high school said, "You know, the trouble with you is you've been away too long. You don't have the lingo. You don't know how to relate to farmers enough. My cousin's got a farm. You ought to go out this spring while he's putting in the crop and work with them a couple of days. Go to the local grain elevator, the local feed store, hang around, see how they talk."

The experience generated one of Harkin's most distinctive campaign features: "work days" in which he worked different jobs across the district. It proved effective.

I'd do a work day in a drugstore. We'd get the local paper to come in and take a picture. It was good advertising from the druggist's point of view. We'd have the story, with some quotes about what I had learned.

Then we'd clip it out and make copies, send it to every drugstore in the district. We did that with drug stores, grain elevators, hardware stores, farmers more than once. I even did a work day with a minister, sent it around to every minister in the district. It really paid off.

Harkin won an upset victory in the general election of 1974. Watergate undoubtedly aided his campaign—but, on the other hand, farm income was the highest in years, and he did well among farm voters. Once in the House he quickly established a reputation as a hard-working, effective, and outspoken progressive on issues that ranged from farm policy to science and technology.

Most people looked upon me as a liberal because I ran against this really conservative guy. But I used to take some stands that liberals didn't like. I've never been comfortable with big government—I've always feared big government. What I believe in is strong government that is by your side.

Populism, Jobs, Welfare

I've always felt that there's something about work and doing work that in itself is good. I can still remember my dad taking me out and showing me things he built when he worked for WPA in the Great Depression. He wasn't ashamed of it. It was a source of pride. He showed me a dam that they built. He showed me a high school, a park. They still stand today. So from those earliest times I was always against welfare. I understand the liberal argument. But I thought it's demeaning. I do accept the idea it's the government's responsibility to give them a job. People want to do things. I've always had trouble with the liberals. I would say, somehow we've got to give people jobs.

I've always felt very patriotic. I spent four years in ROTC, I spent five years in the Navy, active duty risking my life every day. Then I spent three years in the reserves. But it's like kids. Can you imagine saying, "I love my kids, but I don't care how they grow up, I don't care how they behave, whether they wash their faces or not, whether they study?" What kind of love is that?

Clyde Brown, who worked for me, knew from history that there were a lot of people from Iowa who refused to fight in World War I. He found news clippings from some of the most conservative counties. A local

236

druggist had refused to enlist in the war in 1918 and went to jail, by God. We used his quotes.

Harkin believes the new populism today is a response to a long-term economic crisis that erodes the basic aspirations of the middle class, as well as the poor. The populist movement is built on the premise that freedom and democratic institutions depend on the widest possible dissemination of wealth and power, *he argues.* But we've come to the point where too few people have too much money and too much power—we haven't seen this kind of imbalance since the late 1800s. *He often quotes the late Supreme Court Justice Louis Brandeis, who warned that "we can either have democracy in this country or we can have great wealth concentrated in the hands of a few, but we can't have both."*

The New Populism

Unlike earlier populist movements, Harkin's new populism has a strong internationalist dimension. Populists believe that if we want to ensure democratic institutions in Central America or Southeast Asia or wherever, we first have to fight for economic justice. Political rights like freedom of the press and freedom of speech depend on economic justice; otherwise, democracy is just a passing moment. *His leading role in recent fights against the Reagan administration's intervention in Third World nations lends weight to his argument.*

There is nothing sentimentalized nor simplistic about Harkin's faith in ordinary people. He readily acknowledges the parochialisms, fears, and superficial knowledge that can generate a demagogic or shallow "populism," and views the right-wing version as a danger and a reality. It's a very fearful society today, *Harkin points out.* What security is there? There's no job security, no health security, no safety security. People are really at risk. That's what the Jesse Helmses and the Richard Vigueries appeal to, that insecurity, that fear.

But the real populists, the kind Lawrence Goodwyn talks about, appeal to the good side. We're elected to office not to represent the public opinion, but to represent the public will. There's a difference. *Harkin tells the following story to illustrate this point.*

237

I was on the House Science and Technology Committee, chairman of the National Science Foundation subcommittee. We started looking into these studies that seemed crazy. And I explained what we found, in town meetings in my district.

I would say, "How many people here would be willing to spend $250,000 to study why people have red hair?" Nobody would raise a hand. Another study was on the kidney cells in rhesus monkeys. Then I'd say, "Out of the red hair study they discovered how to trace sickle cell anemia. Out of the monkey study came the Salk polio vaccine. Now, knowing that, how many would be willing to spend $250,000?" Every hand would go up.

That's the difference between public opinion and public will. Public opinion is a knee-jerk reaction, an instant reaction to something that doesn't sound right. Public will is something deeper, it has to do with people's understanding, their deepest motivations, their value system, what their goals are, what they feel is important for their family and their community and their society. You have to discern that, dig that out.

That to me is what populism is. It's going after that public will, digging, finding out what's under that skin. I see populism, and the kinds of things we're doing on a grassroots level, as giving people the information and data they need to make an informed decision.

This is the sort of insight that is most impressive about the man: he believes in the potential wisdom of ordinary citizens and simultaneously sees the obstacles to its developing.

Do you think the electric utilities want to tell people about their phantom taxes? Hell, no, they don't. They want people to think they're collecting a dollar for the government, but it only amounts to about 30 cents by the time it gets to the government. Political power means giving people the information. That's what populism is all about. *According to Harkin, democratic populism changes the very definition of politics through grassroots organizing on a continuing basis.*

At the Citizen Action conference in August 1985, Harkin freely credited the Citizen Action Iowa affiliate (Iowa Citizen Action Network) with playing a crucial role in his election campaign. In the past, the party candidate always came first—and the issues fell into place afterward, if at all, *he told the audience. Groups like Citizen Action change that.* Now, long before the election, we're out in the field—talking about gut issues like jobs, fair taxes, energy, the environment, and arms control. We give people hope, a way to change things. That is how we build their support.

238

It is an old insight, voiced by the leaders of democratic and populist movements throughout American history, from Thomas Jefferson and nineteenth-century suffrage leader Frances Willard to Martin Luther King, Jr. All these people maintained that the most important acts of citizenship are those leading toward the casting of the ballot. Harkin is unmistakably in this tradition, a key spokesperson for the new and emerging social force that is direct heir to those earlier movements.

Twenty
Jim Hightower

KICK-ASS POPULISM:
A SPEECH TO THE NATIONAL
PRESS CLUB

I am a practicing populist, a democratic politician from the hinterland
—come here today to the cultured East to bring what might seem an
unconventional message from the frontier. For those of you who can't
stand the suspense of wondering what that message might be, I will gracefully give you the nub of that report right here at the top. There are four
points to it. Number one, the great masses of Middle America have not
become nearly as yuppized, as Republicanized, as happy-faced as many of
the pundits and the Republican pollsters and other trend spotters would
have us believe. Number two, the political party that seeks refuge in the
great yawning middle ground of American politics is destined to lose.
Number three, Democratic leadership, contrary to popular opinion, is
experiencing vigorous growth at the grassroots level among people who
are running for and winning state and local offices. And number four, the
Democratic Party can indeed be the majority party again if it will seize the

populist moment that is presented to us today. And it's on that populism that I want to share a few thousand well-chosen words with you.

No matter how hard the political seers and sages try to divide the world neatly between liberals and conservatives, the truth is that's just not where most Americans live. No more than 20 percent, I would venture to say, of Americans are ideologically right wing or left wing, period. Most of them don't take, what you would consider in the intellectual communities, a true ideological position. If you were to go and knock on the door of 1331 West Hall Street in Denison, Texas, you would be greeted by my old daddy. Now, you've got to beware of Texans bringing you "old daddy" stories, you know that, but I'm about to give you one here. If you were to ask him, Is he a liberal or is he a conservative? he's going to say, "I'm a conservative." But if you ask him what he thinks about the utility companies raising his rates on a pretty regular basis and squeezing the little tiny profit margin that he's got; if you ask him about the multistate bank holding companies removing the source of capital from his hometown to the corporate centers in Dallas and, in fact, all the way up to New York City; if you were to ask him about the lobby clout of big business to write tax policies, to write regulatory authority, to write legislation that squeezes little people like him out of business, you would have tapped as progressive a human being as you ever want to be face-to-face with.

My point is that the great center of American politics is not square dab in the middle of the spectrum, equal distance from conservatism and liberalism. Rather, the true center is in populism. Which is rooted in that realization that too few people control all the money and power, leaving very little for the rest of us. And they use that money and power to gain more for themselves. Populism is propelled politically by the simmering desire of the mass of people to upend that arrangement. Now, this is hardly a centrist position, if by centrist you mean moderate. But it is at the center of most people's political being, and it is a very hot center indeed.

You can find it for yourselves. Whether you go out there, as some of you do, and take a scientific poll of eight hundred randomly selected respondents, or if you just go down and greet and meet the morning bunch at the Chat and Chew Cafe, you will quickly tap a deep strain of populist resentment of the powers that be—the bankers and the bosses, the politicians and the press, the big boys, and what generally is referred to as "the bastards." Middle Americans are not meek centrists, which we are being told is the majority constituency the political parties are supposed to be pursuing. These people are not meek at all. In fact, what they

241

are, in my view, is anti-establishment malcontents. They are disgruntled mavericks, and they are mad. They are mad about what's happening in their own lives. These are folks who have a deep belief in old-time, little-*d* democratic ideals of fairness, of egalitarianism, of tolerance and pluralism. But their daily experience teaches them something else. Their daily experience teaches them that life is not so fair, it is not so egalitarian or any of the rest of this stuff. Life, in fact, is much closer to the reality expressed by another song writer. A guy named Bob Wills, out of the state of Texas, who wrote a lot of good ole-time Western swing music, had a tune called "Take Me Back to Tulsa," and in it was this verse: "Little bee sucks the blossom, but the big bee gets the honey. Little man picks the cotton, but the big man gets the money." People are aware of that; they know that in their daily experience, and they resent it. There is an ingrained populist spirit that is widespread and deeply held in the body politic of this country today. These people are looking for political champions willing to kick ass to set that right again, to make that straight.

When I got elected, as always happens to politicians who are a little out of the norm, I suddenly had a bunch of lobbyists come to visit me. And one of them got a-hold of me and said, "Well you snuck into office, and I guess you're in for at least four years, but now what you need to do if you want to continue is to moderate your views. Go along to get along, generally take the cautious middle path." And then a farmer friend of mine came in and said, "Hell, Hightower, there's nothing in the middle of the road but yellow stripes and dead armadillos. We want you out there fighting for us—getting out there on our side of things." And that's not just a few people who feel like that, it is not just labor, it's not just poor folks, it's not just minority, environmentalists, Volvo-driving liberals; I contend it is the American majority, including the dirt farmer and the hard-scrabble rancher, including the Main Street business person, the entrepreneur, the nurses and the keypunchers, the waitresses and the clerks. Not just the beansprout-eaters but the snuff-dippers in this society as well, have this kind of feeling.

Now, like my old daddy, these people are neither right wing nor left wing, and, frankly, neither Republican nor Democrat. They'll vote for the candidate who appears most willing and who is most able to kick ass on their behalf. Now, this defies neat categorization and it confounds the political experts on a fairly regular basis. Remember back in 1968, after Bobby Kennedy was assassinated, that a bulk of his supporters bolted not to Hubert Humphrey, as everybody would have assumed, but to George

Wallace. Closer to my own heart—1980 in Texas—the good voters of
that wonderful state voted for Ronald Reagan, then they turned in 1982
and voted for Hightower, then they turned back in 1984 and voted for
Reagan. And I'm betting that they're going to come home to poppa again
in 1986, when I'm up.

My point is not that we must go sell all populism to the population.
The population already is populist, and they're not waiting on the Democratic Party to figure that out. Down on the Gulf Coast of south Texas,
there's a Spanish saying among the shrimpers: "Camaron que duerme se
lo lleva la corriente"—the shrimp that falls asleep is swept away by the
current. The Democratic Party has got to get back in the swim of things
again, and I think that means getting in the mainstream of Democratic
populism. We've got to go to the people of this country with a combination of old-time Democratic principle, with common-sense, problem-
solving solutions and with hard-core political passion. Principle is first,
and it is always foremost. And here, we as a Democratic Party go with our
strength. From Jefferson, Jackson, Roosevelt and Truman, Kennedy and
Johnson, ours has been the party not of the Rockefellers but of the little
fellers, of egalitarianism. We've got the principle working for us. Now,
unfortunately, we're hearing today voices inside as well as outside of the
Democratic Party, urging us to forsake all of that for a trendier tone in our
politics. They say that the Republicans have swept the heart of the country
away, winning with a more modern, up-beat, and most importantly, up-
scaled message and that we as Democrats should be following suit with
that. They say that we should give up all this tacky talk about farmers
going broke, about unemployment, about the increase in our poverty
statistics, about the need for equal rights in this country and around the
world. They say just surrender to the trend that is going throughout the
country—the Republican trend. They urge us to get happy, get with it
and, in fact, get Republican. I guess that's what they're really talking
about. Well, I tell you, if the meek ever inherit the earth, these timid
voices are going to be land barons, it seems like to me.

Where is the grit in this—the old-time Democratic grit? And more
importantly than that, where is there a Democratic future in that? We are
not going to build a Democratic majority by offering more cuisinarts and
L. L. Bean gift certificates to the people of this country. The yuppies are
not a base for any political party in my view, and certainly not the Democratic Party. If you lined up every yuppy that there is in America today,
they would stretch from here to the nearest gourmet stand. The well-off

already have a party working for them and doing very nicely for them. Even as we sit here partaking of this good meal, these folks are out there at the clubs right now enjoying a midday repast of cool melon mélange and asparagus and goat cheese and a delightfully fruity and frisky California white wine. But most of America doesn't live there. The majority of Americans are down at the 7-11 picking up a Budweiser and a Slim Jim and wondering if there's anybody in America who's going to stand up on their side. That is the populist constituency that's down there at the 7-11. And those are the people that the Democrats must begin to speak to.

Now, no one is advocating, least of all me, some sort of mule-stubborn dedication to the old, stale, tired policies and programs of the Democratic past, but neither can we abandon our base—the people who are the true Democratic Party, including the blacks and Mexican Americans in our culture, including the women. Mostly including the small business people and the entrepreneurs and the farmers. The mass of people who are in the middle class, the lower middle class, and the lower economic classes in our society—that's the vast majority. We cannot abandon that base, and we have a proud agenda of being able to seek a broad sharing of economic prosperity in this society that appeals to that base. It is an unfinished agenda—an agenda that needs new attention, fresh approaches, renewed dedication. American voters support this goal. They might not care to join hands and march off across the horizon together humming folk songs, but they are a whole lot more community minded, a whole lot less selfish than the prevailing yuppy Republican approach of "I've got mine. You get yours," "Caveat emptor," "Never give a sucker an even break," "Adios, chump." People are a little bit better than that if we reach out to them and appeal to them with a sensible program that puts substance to our old-time principles—a program that's got pocket-book appeal and that can deliver what it promises. At the center of this must be a consistent theme that the Democrats must begin to advocate again, of grassroots economic growth. Democrats have got to develop programs that make ours the party of genuine economic opportunity again, of upward mobility for all the people, not trickle-down mobility, but percolate up from the grassroots; an investment of our nation's economic future in the truly productive people of our society, by which I do mean those family farmers and the worker cooperatives and small and medium-sized businesses that are out there—entrepreneurs, minority businesses, the wildcatters, and the up-and-comers. Those are the people who create genuine wealth at the grass roots. That is a natural constituency for the Democratic Party. That is a constituency that no one is basically talking to right now, and it's a constituency that we can build a majority base on for our party well into the future. Pretty words. What in the world is he talking about in terms of specifics?

Well, let me just review in terms of agriculture, since that's what I'm involved in, some examples of what I am talking about. I'll review with you a little bit about what we're trying to do down at the Texas Department of Agriculture to put populism into practice. I don't have to tell most of you, there's a world of hurt in agriculture right now. People are going broke at a historic rate. Not only have we lost some 228,000 farmers in the last four years, we continue to lose them at a rate of 1,600 every single week. And we are faced, not with the loss of large numbers of farmers, but the total collapse of what we know of as the family farm and ranch system in this country. Those that are still in business today pretty much are on the brink of broke, as one old boy told me, because they're not getting a fair price for their commodities. They are getting a price that is beneath the cost of production. This affects us all, not just agriculture. The farmer's not buying supplies. That means the Main Street businesses are in trouble, too. If the farmer's not making money, can't pay off the note down at the bank, they're in trouble. The farmer's not making money, not buying tractors. I spoke to the United Auto Worker Division that represents some union members manufacturing farm machinery recently, out at Des Moines, Iowa. They have lost something like half of their membership in the last four years because of this farm collapse. I pointed out to them that the only difference between a farmer and a pigeon today is that a pigeon can still make a deposit on a John Deere. That is a reality that those union members do indeed understand, and they understand their direct link to agriculture.

Well, what do you do about this crisis? The classical liberal solution, of course, is well, let's give them some subsidy money in there. Well, we've been doing that, and that hasn't been producing very happy results for us. We've put in massive subsidies. We've had massive bankruptcies. The whole program's been a massive failure. Instead, it seems to me, we've got to find ways to give farmers a fair price structure in the marketplace, number one. And, second, give them an opportunity to sell their products at a better price. The first of those, the fair price structure, pretty much has to be done at a national level. Now, the Congress has an opportunity before it to do exactly that. Unfortunately, the House of Representatives have chosen just recently not to do it, to reject a populist solution in favor of a liberal solution. The populist solution that we proposed was the Farm Policy Reform Act introduced by Senator Harkin of Iowa and Representative Alexander of Arkansas—a program that was written by farmers themselves. We went to the countryside and said to farmers, "What if you were to write a farm policy. What would be in it?" This is the program that they came up with. The guts of it, without taxing your patience too long with arcane farm policy matters, is simply giving them a good business tool that other businesses enjoy. And that is the tool of supply management. McDonald's is not making more hamburgers today than they think they're going to sell. If they do, they adjust production tomorrow. Budweiser knew that I was in town today, so they increased allocation here in the nation's capital. But generally speaking, they're not going to produce more beer than they think they can sell. Only farmers in our society are in that position, because no individual farmer can cut back and have an impact on what's going to happen in the next county or the next state. That has to be a national program. So, what we did was to offer a supply-management program that would allow farmers to produce only the number of bushels and bales and gallons that there was an actual demand for in this country, in the world cash and credit markets, and in the world hunger market. That's how much we would produce. In return for which, farmers would get a high price-floor. That meant that what they produced would be sold in the marketplace, which meant it was zero crop-subsidy payment program to the farmers. There was no tax exposure under this.

Instead, as I say, the House of Representatives voted [in October 1985] to reject this, and it has voted out a piece of legislation that is going to cost somewhere between $33 billion and $100 billion over the next three years. Nobody seems exactly sure, and it's not going to save any farmers. Well, we're on to the Senate with that program. Senator Harkin is carrying the bulk of our water over there. We're going to be active. The problem isn't going away, and neither are we going to go away. But the point I want to make to you is that *that* was a populist-oriented solution to create a new mechanism, not to do anything negative to the Cargills and Continentals and the big cotton shippers and grain traders of the world that hold prices down on farmers, not to try to bust them up or reorganize the economy, but to create an additional marketing channel starting with the farmer—with the person who is the wealth creator in the society. And it did it without heavy infusions of tax dollars.

The second point I want to make to you is that although we could be doing that in Washington, we don't have to just wait on Washington for all of our solutions to come forward. Agriculture is suffering what are national and even global economic problems, but most farmers don't live in Washington. Most farmers live in Bugtussle and Tioga and Dimebox and towns like that. And that's where we've got to be working on modest but effective programs to serve some of them where they live. And that's what we've done at a state level in the Department of Agriculture—try to devise some new creative programs. Susan DeMarco headed our marketing and agriculture development programs. The Department of Agriculture assembled a staff from all over the country of people who had been thinking about these things, experimenting here and there with those things but who are unable, on a sizable scale, to implement them. And those programs are working, again, not using tax dollars, but using government as a catalyst to help the same old constituency that we've always been interested in.

A little example is the farmers' markets. You're not going to solve the global economic problem with farmers' markets, but over the last two and a half years we've established, with local authorities in the state of Texas, thirty-two farmers' markets. They will do about $5 million in business this year, and that would be about a 30 percent increase, on the average, in the income of the farmers who participate. It doesn't solve the global economic problem, but it does help those thousand farmers who participate out there. It helps them in a way they understand, which is cash money in their pocket and to take to the bank. We carried that same concept on into the direct wholesale market—helping to organize farmers so that they can sell directly in the retail stores.

We found this quick example. The first program we got under way was down in Hempstead, Texas—a little town outside of Houston. We found Kroger Corporation down there bringing watermelons from Florida to Texas, which of course, just outraged us. That was an act of defiance of the natural order of things, when one county over, right there in Waller County, right outside of Houston, were some of the best watermelon producers ever known in this great country. And these producers had no market for their crop. Sixty percent of their crop, the year before we started this program, rotted in the fields because they had no market, and what they did sell was sold out of pickup trucks on the side of the road, and they got a penny a pound for that. What we did was to go to Kroger and say, "Why don't you buy right here?" And they said, "Oh, we can't be running down the road now, buying watermelons." And we said, "We certainly understand that. So what we'll do is help them organize a co-op, and you'll deal with one supplier." And they said, "Well, we've got to have beaucoup melons, we sell a lot of them." "No problem, these guys are going to make you a lot of melons." And they said, "But, we've got to have a 27-pound melon." "All right, we're going to make you a 27-pound melon." And they ran out of excuses and so finally said, "We'll take a truckload of them." So we rolled a truckload in last year, rolled another one in, and sure enough, last year those farmers sold every melon that they produced—500,000 pounds of watermelon—to Kroger stores in Houston, Texas—not a penny a pound but 7¼ cents a pound and enjoyed a 165 percent average increase in their family income as a result. And the consumer got a good deal, too, because instead of paying $3.50 for an old, sour Florida watermelon, they were able to get a good sweet Texas Waller County melon for $1.98. A program that made sense for everybody involved, including Kroger, didn't cost the government anything to implement because we didn't put money into the co-op, we didn't manage the co-op. It is government playing the role of catalyst to plug these good productive enterprising people into a marketing system. Then we're out of it, and they go on.

We can do the same thing in the international market, which we're doing. We've hired staff through Latin America, in the Orient, in the Mid-East and up into Europe, to deal Texas products to buyers there, to buy directly from the Texas farmer and rancher, creating an additional marketing channel for those farmers and ranchers to be able to enjoy, and it's working. In 1983 when I came into office there were $6 million in livestock sales assisted through the Department of Agriculture. As of August of this year, we've done $50 million. We have the ability just to go out there and find sales. There are sales being made in the international export market. We find them and bring them back directly to our farmers. When you've got a state as big as Texas, with the agriculture diversity that it has, with as good-looking an agriculture commissioner as we have, you can go anywhere in the world and deal direct with those markets out there if you just put it together. And that's what I'm talking about. Again, government being a catalyst and working with local enterprising people to make money for them and for the local economy.

You can do the same thing in creating new industries. There are whole new markets out there that we can help people move into. In Texas it's the food-processing industry, for example. We process only 5 percent of the country's food even though we're the second-largest food producer in the country. So, it's just us old dumb Texans, we're producing that raw commodity, shipping it out of state, where they slice it and bread it and put it in a box and freeze it and sell it back to us at a hundred times the value we shipped out at. With food processing, it's a pretty simple technology. We may not be the brightest people on earth, but I think we can figure out onion-ring processing and beef slaughtering and sort of thing, and get that going in our local economy.

There are other new industries that are possible. The creation of a whole new industry is coming along throughout this country in the generation of electricity—people going into competition against the giant utility monopolies. Producers of electricity are using biomass sources—vegetable waste off the field, mesquite trees. We've found a couple of uses for mesquite trees in the state of Texas. We found one use by cutting the things into little blocks and putting them in a bag and curing them and selling them to Yankees for about $3 apiece to burn your fish with, and that's doing some good. But we need a bigger use of those mesquite trees out there and, you're not cooking enough fish to use up all that mesquite. So what we do have is the possibility of using that mesquite—a very good burning wood—to generate electricity. Same thing with manure. I've got an old friend in Texas who bought a feedlot out in west Texas. He had not been in the feedlot business; didn't fully understand what he was getting a-hold of. He went out to inspect the facilities and found a mountain of manure right in the middle of his feedlot. Startled, he went back home and pondered it. When he went back a week later, he had two mountains of manure. He began to look at the books and found that they were spending $250,000 a year just to move the manure from the pens over to the side of the lot. He figured there had to be a better way to do this and had this stuff scientifically analyzed. The good high-quality west Texas steer manure turns out to have the same BTU content as does the lignite coal that we're stripmining our state to get a-hold of. So he's building two 40-megawatt generators out there in west Texas using dried manure as the fuel source to generate electricity. We worked with the city of Austin, the capital of Texas, municipally owned utility, to buy the electricity—every kilowatt that he is going to produce. So for the first time ever, BS is going to flow from the countryside to the capital rather than vice versa, and the important thing is there's money going to be made out of that project at the original end of it.

249

My point is, again, that the role of government in all of these populist approaches to problem-solving is to serve as an activist—as an antiestablishment institution helping people help themselves by getting involved in free enterprise. I believe in free enterprise, but not like Exxon does. Exxon puts it up a sign at its annual meeting and says, "We are free enterprise," and then clubs anybody who dares to try to come out against them.

I believe in a thousand flowers blooming out there. And that means that government can form partnerships, be a catalyst to help free up the enterprise of people. And so you use the "free" in free enterprise, not as an adjective, but as a verb. And if we do that, then we have a program that we can go to the people with. That's my fourth and final point, which is that we've got to go to those people with passion. You hear all of these people saying we've got to tone it down, avoid loud noises and hot appeals. Don't upset the people. The Democrats keep getting that kind of advice. And these people point to the South and say, "Oh, the South's filled with all these conservative moderates. Now let's not wake them up; they'd be real upset if anybody said anything loud." The South is a culture that has invented better than two dozen pepper sauces to put on their breakfast eggs. That is not a moderate culture, it seems to me. And we like our politics just as spicy as that. You cannot beat pepper sauce with milk toast, and that's pretty much what these people would have us do. If you want to look at recent history, look at Mr. Reagan, who was the hot right-wing radical candidate against Mr. Carter, son of the South and a clear moderate, or against Mr. Mondale. The hot candidate beat the moderate candidate both times, and I think will every time. We have a saying in the South down in Texas about passion hotter than high-school love. I don't think that we're going to reach that intensity quite in politics, but people do want to know that you believe in your own program and believe in the constituencies that you claim to want to serve. So we want—need—to combine that populist principle, programs and passions, and if we do that we'll win. Not automatically, of course, but at least you're in the fight, and you're in the fight with integrity, and you're in the fight with the hope to win and a hope to make a difference in this country. This is no time for Democrats to be ducking their heads and hiding, hibernating and hoping this Republican wave is going to go away. It's a time to go to the countryside and to fight.

An old-time southern populist, Huey Long, once said, "If you want some ham, by God, go into the smokehouse." And that's what we've got to do, get out into the smokehouse of politics with our politics. Those who do are winning. Tom Harkin in Iowa last year, in the face of a Reagan onslaught—we had all kinds of victories like that. In North Dakota in the gubernatorial race up there; Ray Mabus down in Mississippi; Don Seigelman in Alabama; the whole ticket in Texas in 1982—who went to the people, didn't hide our light under a bushel, went out there and said what we are for and won a victory there. Larry King called me on election night and said, "Well, Hightower, you won, you slipped in." And I said, "Yeah, Larry, it was so good. They tried all that stuff, called us perverts and communists, and the people didn't buy it." Larry said, "It may be better than you think. Maybe they bought it and they liked." It's not quite that good, but it does work, and we're working on it now at a national level. We're organizing with—I'm involved with Senator Tom Harkin and with Representative Lane Evans out of Illinois in the formation of a new populist forum to give this viewpoint some focus and to give it some attention. We're fighting, in my view, not just for the hearts and minds of the Democratic Party but for its guts. Are we going to offer them milk toast or are we going to offer them hot sauce? I think that's the question that we really face right now.

I'll leave you with this thought because it sums up what it is, I think, we're really trying to do. There's a moving company in Austin, Texas, that has an advertising slogan that we have adapted. This moving company says, "If we can get it loose, we can move it." Well that's what we're talking about, getting the Democratic Party loose and moving it on behalf of all the people of this country for a change.

Twenty-One
Barbara Mikulski

A POPULIST, A FEMINIST, AND A PROGRESSIVE:

A SPEECH AT PLACID HARBOR, MARYLAND

On October 4 and 5, 1985, citizen leaders from community, labor, minority, women's, environmental, peace, and other groups met with political figures from the congressional Populist Caucus and elsewhere at the retreat center of the Machinists Union, in Placid Harbor, Maryland, to talk about the future of the progressive movement in America. Representative Mikulski gave the following speech to the group.

Today, I am very pleased to be here with my fellow populists and my sister progressives. I'm glad to be here with my friends from the House and from the Senate. I also wanted to be here with so many of you whom I respect from the trade union movement, from street organizing, from a variety of activities. You've been the fighters, the advocates, the organizers, and you're needed more than ever now. I'm delighted to find out at last who I am. I am a countertrend. Whether it's the factory or the farm or the new demography of America, when we put us all together we are the

252

mainstream. But somehow or another, this society makes us feel like we're the outsiders.

This conference is extremely important, not only for the chance to talk about techniques of organizing, but also to talk about the message and the framework we want to pursue.

I define myself as a populist. I define myself as a progressive. I define myself as a feminist. Many of you know me as Congresswoman Mikulski, a title that I'm really proud of and worked hard to get. Others of you here know me as the insider who helped move Geraldine Ferraro along a historical path. But I define myself not in terms of these institutional roles.

My identity is wrested in my way of living and operating. I am an organizer. I got into politics because of being an organizer. Like so many of the people in this room, I was shaped by the actions and the passions of the time.

I came in in the 1960s, through the social movements of the time. When I got started I didn't know I was a feminist. In 1962 and 1963 in downtown Baltimore the second wave of the American women's movement hadn't started. But I knew something deep in my heart from being a street organizer in the war on poverty: the way you get things done is by making the personal political.

I came into civil rights not because I read a book and thought it was the right thing to do. I got into civil rights because one day I walked out of juvenile court with one of my colleagues, a black woman with a master's degree in social work from Howard University who helped guide me on the path that I needed to follow. She and I could not have a beer or a sandwich together in downtown Baltimore. I could go to her places but she couldn't come to mine. So we began to organize the civil rights movement in Baltimore.

Then, when I was working as a social worker, the city planners, the Robert Moses types, decided that they wanted to split Baltimore with a sixteen-lane highway. It was going to come through the older ethnic communities and the first black home-ownership neighborhood in Baltimore.

Well, we were told we could not make a difference because the stack was against us. I said, "You know what? We can fight. The first thing we have to do is organize a 'Hell, No, We Won't Go' committee. In order to do that, we've got to be willing to say that we're willing to fight."

We formed a group called the Southeast Council Against the Road, SCAR. Then we did something that they said couldn't be done. We went over to black West Baltimore where a friend of mine named Parren

253

Mitchel was also thinking some political thoughts. We knew that that expressway was coming through the very first black home-ownership neighborhood in Baltimore. Our cousins over there had formed a group called RAM. So we put our heads together and formed a citywide coalition called MAD, Movement Against Destruction. As you can see from those early days, I was known for my linguistic moderation.

What was so important about that story is important now. We found that as we began to organize, they said the honkies and the blacks in Baltimore would never get it together. But we did. The people had been segregated in the military. They had been segregated in their hometown. But we were not going to be segregated in this fight. When we formed that coalition, we also reached out to other people whom we needed to have involved. We turned to the graduate students at Johns Hopkins Hospital to provide the technical assistance when we read those environmental impact statements. We said, "What does air mean? What does water mean? Give us the alternatives." So we could go strutting in with books as big and fat as their crowd had. Then we reached out to those wonderful blue-rinsed hair ladies of the Rowan Park Archeological Society and the Maryland Historic Trust because they wanted to save historic buildings. We figured we wanted to make history. We said there was room for everybody if we put our heads together. And I believe it's that kind of model that will work now as we work on issues, whether it's hazardous waste or toxic waste or whatever.

As we began to move, we formed a mass-based community organization, SECO, the Southeast Community Organization. There came a point when I found that the more doors we knocked on, they all led to city hall and the state house. If we were going to be successful, those doors had to be opened by somebody inside. I decided to run for the Baltimore City Council.

People have always told me my elections will be tough. But during that election we took the citizen group and turned them into citizen volunteers in a political campaign. But we had a deal with the people who were going to work on my campaign. We said, we're not going to form a political machine, like the very group we're going to fight. We're going to form an "ad hocracy." That electoral coalition will come together at that particular time to elect a particular person. You are putting lawn signs up for me today, but I know that you could very likely turn around and picket me tomorrow if I'm in the City Council. So we were able to keep that independence. We were able to keep that flexibility. People then knew they were in control and they were in charge.

So when I decided to strut out and run for Baltimore City Council, I went door to door, knocking on 15,000 doors. I was mugged by forty-seven chihuahuas. But I ended up beating two political machines. That was the kind of coalition we worked to put together.

I know many of you have been to Baltimore, and you now see something called Harbor Place and something called Renaissance. When we were doing our organizing, we were told we were part of the problem. We were standing in the way of economic progress. But it was the neighborhoods' forming the alliance that created Harbor Place and the Renaissance. This takes me to the concept of organizing.

We organized not because it was the right thing to do. We organized on the basis of a deeply felt need. We had to save our homes and save our neighborhoods. Then we put together our facts and we had fun. Brothers and sisters, sometimes our organizing is so Armageddon-ish, so dour, that even John Calvin wouldn't want to sign up. You've got to have fun. You've got to create energy, that "Big Mo," as they call it. And we did. One of the ways, a quick technique: When we wanted to draw attention to our neighborhoods, we held the Bells Point Festival to show who we were and what we were. That festival's still going on there. Then we organized our coalitions, based on mutual need and mutual respect. What we did then, you're doing now. Just remember: organize with a felt need, make the personal political, get your facts together, and have fun.

Those are the same principles that I took from the neighborhoods to the City Council to the Congress. This takes me to two other concepts, the idea of inside organizing and the idea of outside organizing. My colleagues here in the House and the Senate will tell you that those of us in the House and in the Senate and in the city councils and in the state houses, we're doing the inside organizing. We're working to put together coalitions—which are now stretched. We can see it from the Northeast, the Midwest. Sometimes we're in battle with our colleagues from the farm belt. But while we're organizing on the inside, there has to be outside organizing. Without outside organizing, there's not the impetus in the House to do the inside organizing.

So where do we find ourselves now? Well, it's been a long time since those early days when we organized the SECOs and the SCARs and so many other things. We've gone through social movements. The civil rights

movement, the peace movement, the women's movement, the environmental movement, the human potential movement. Now we're right
smack in the fundamentalism movement. We've gone through four presidents and, in my church, four popes. Think of it. Sixteen years, six
movements, four presidents and four popes. That's enough to tire anybody out.

But that doesn't mean we cannot face where we are. The exciting
thing is that we're only fifteen years from the year 2000. We are on the
threshold of a new millennium. We can organize in terms of a framework
for the future if we think about it. What is the best way to think about it?

You've talked a lot about the new-collar voters, which is essential and
critical. At the same time, we have to talk about the new poor. We have to
take a look at America and see the number of senior citizens growing. We
know the American family is changing: single parents, the baby boomers
are having babies of their own. All of this will have a tremendous impact
on what we organize and why we organize.

People are focused on paying bills and making it. The frustration that
I see in America is not only about equity and fairness. It's the frustration
of the good guys and the good gals who get screwed. There is a deeply felt
concern that there is something fundamental that is wrong. In Baltimore
in the Third Congressional District I have a police officer making twenty-
five grand a year. I have General Electric in my district, which made $6
billion. The cop on the beat has to risk his life taking on the dope pushers
and trying to survive the paper pushers. And he knows he pays more
income tax than General Electric a few blocks down the street. He paid
$6,000 in taxes. General Electric just laid off 635 workers and has a $235
million tax credit surplus. They tell me they cannot compete. That cop is
mad. The General Electric worker is mad. That is the issue. All the other
stuff is baloney.

Another frustration is those who save. People will say they are being
screwed. They aren't the high rollers or the junk bonders. They put their
money in Maryland in the savings and loan institutions. Right now, that
means that people's savings are at risk in my own state.

The other issue deals again with the way you qualify for Medicaid
nursing. People say there is a generational tension growing between the
young and the old because of all we give to the elderly. But we find in
Middle America today if you save your money and have to go into a
nursing home you have to go bankrupt and pauperize yourself in order to
survive. So these are the issues: day care, single parents, good schools,

256

safe streets. These are things people can picture. People they can see. We can no longer organize just on something called "fairness." We can no longer organize on something called "equity." It doesn't generate energy. It doesn't generate passion. People can't feel it. They can't touch it. If they win it, they don't know what the hell they've got when it's all over.

There is also another fundamental need that organizing should address. That's the need for affiliation. The need to belong. The need to be accepted. The need to have a sense of being both protected and protector. This creates a sense of identity and belonging. All of this will lead to political action. You can't deal with Medicaid and Medicare without having a revolution of all the generations on your hands. What we need to do when we organize is to focus on our values. We have to take them back from the Reagans. Self-help. Self-determination. Community. All of those important kinds of things. We need also to pursue what I call "habits of the heart."

We have all read the new book *Habits of the Heart* [see Bibliography at the end of this volume], looking at America on the 150th anniversary of the travels of Alexis de Tocqueville. Tocqueville was a Frenchman who traveled around America and took a look at our country. He was awed by its spirit of individualism. But he also saw another spirit, which he called the "habits of the heart." Those are communities that express our commitment to each other. They shape our character and our social order beyond laws. They are the groups we belong to, to have a sense of belonging and to accomplish a civic good.

We need to cultivate those habits of the heart as we are organizing. My job as we begin to organize is to do this. We need to take those deeply felt needs and turn them into public policy. What your job is, is to create public action, to create a critical mass so we can get the inside moving. I believe people are ready to cultivate those habits of the heart. To wake up. To connect to each other here and around the world. We need to link each other up in a way that has never been done before.

When we think of ourselves as organizing, we must also realize that organizers are not only technicians, but we also have to be leaders. What are we in this for except for the fact that we want to make it a better, bigger, wider world than what we found? In order to be leaders we have to be leaders not only in our neighborhood, but in the world. One of the ways we fulfill ourselves is global linkage here and around the world.

So when we organize trade unions in Detroit, let's link ourselves up with those trade unions struggling to survive in Poland. When we're organizing the mine workers in West Virginia, be sure to keep in mind the exploited farm workers in South Africa. As we struggle with the issues of immigration about who gets into our country, let's remember around the world another issue, the emigration of those who would like to be able to get out, like Soviet Jews. As we work for battered women here in America, let's remember the battered women everywhere. When we take on the bullies in this country, let's make sure we don't support the bullies in other countries. In the world with those new satellites, they said it all when they said, "We are the world. We are the children. We are the future." I look forward to working with you.

Eight
ROOTS

Twenty-Two
Mary G. Dietz

POPULISM, PATRIOTISM,
AND
THE NEED FOR ROOTS

In twentieth-century America patriotism is a political concept with
no clear political sense or reference. To say precisely what it means (besides a sentimental but unpolitical love of country) is exceedingly difficult,
though people are often eager to declare themselves for it or against it.
Most often, these declarations bear the mark of ideological sympathies.
Indeed, "patriotism" seems hopelessly caught within the rhetorical nets of
American electoral politics, its meaning determined not by a framework
of coherent conceptual notions but by the shifting winds of political
sophistry and party debate. And so "patriotism" inhabits our political
language and our political thought, shrouded in dense clouds of ambiguity.

Yet this was not always the case. The mid-nineteenth century found
Alexis de Tocqueville in America, observing the advantages of democratic
government. The public spirit of the citizens captured his attention and
puzzled him. "How is it," he asked,

261

that in the United States, where the inhabitants arrived just
yesterday in the land they occupy . . . where, to say in one word the
instinct of country can hardly exist—how does it come
about that each man is as interested in the affairs of his canton, and
of the whole state as he is in his own affairs?

Tocqueville provided his own answer: "It is because each man in his sphere takes an active part in the government of society."[1]

As was his habit, Tocqueville coined a new phrase to describe this civic spirit of active self-governance. He called it "reflective patriotism," and distinguished it from "instinctive patriotism," the undefinable, unpondered passion for *patria* that "does not reason, but believes, feels and acts."[2] By offering this distinction, Tocqueville intended to lodge a precise political judgment about America. His thesis was that, lacking the roots of instinctive patriotism, the United States developed a patriotism of another kind, one rooted in a set of particular *political* values—constitutional rights, republican liberty, and democratic self-governance. American civic spirit, as Tocqueville saw it, was not mediated by a primordial attachment to some mythical past, by reverence for glorious traditions, or even by the mere expression of constitutional rights and political liberties. Reflective patriotism was, rather, the actual practice of liberty, the exercise of rights, and the active citizenship of Americans in town meetings, on local boards, and municipal institutions, as well as in the higher levels of government. It was, in its essence, a patriotism "less generous, perhaps less ardent" than instinctive patriotism, but "more creative and more lasting," a civic spirit that would endure as part of American national identity.

Sadly, Tocqueville's formidable predictive powers were not borne out in the case of reflective patriotism; it proved to be neither more creative nor more lasting than the instinctive variety that America came to acquire soon enough. Almost as Tocqueville was articulating it, reflective patriotism was swallowed up in a series of material and intellectual developments that diminished the practice of self-governance and rendered civic republicanism little more than a dim memory. In place of reflective patriotism a different sort of attachment to country emerged, a vainglorious nationalism that reinforced chauvinism and imperialism abroad and promoted exclusionary politics at home. If the prevailing mentality of reflective patriotism was an open public-spiritedness that joined self-interest and community, then the dominant outlook of nationalism was a narrow selfishness and superiority, a privatized and often violent vision that manifested itself in statist language. When Tocqueville later said that patriotism was "most often nothing but an extension of individual egoism," I think it was nationalism he had in mind and perhaps perceived on the horizon of American politics.[3]

As its title indicates, this volume addresses the rise of a new populist movement in America. Many of its contributors are quite rightly concerned to render populism, in the words of one, "indigenous to our time."[4] Important as this task is, I would suggest another equally vital one. Populists should look not only to the creation of new programs and policies, but also undertake an act of political and conceptual recovery that will itself give direction and coherence to a program of political change. The recovery involves, among other things, the revitalization (or more appropriately, the rescue) of patriotism from its current trappings. This act of recovery is not a mere matter of linguistic legislation or rhetorical sleight-of-hand, for to give coherence to patriotism is to rethink the meaning of "country," and to embark upon a restoration of national identity.

As a beginning, I suggest we turn to another French political theorist, one who wrote a century after Tocqueville in response to a crisis of national identity in her own country. But insofar as she attempts a general reconstruction of patriotism, Simone Weil speaks not only to France but also to the concerns of a revitalized populist politics. Her thought offers one possible starting point for the regeneration of civic spirit in America.[5]

If Simone Weil were alive today, she would, I think, be an outspoken critic of technological civilization and a powerful witness to the uprootedness of our contemporary condition. The barren character of human relations and institutions in the modern age troubled her deeply; so did the loss of community: "The village, district, province, or region—all the geographical units smaller than the nation—have almost ceased to count," she wrote. "The actual significance of these collectivities has well nigh disappeared, except in one case only—that of the nation" (p. 100). Weil was no romantic harboring utopian visions of bucolic societies or dreaming of the end of technology and the state. Her view of the nation as the key unit of political organization in the twentieth century was a decidedly realistic one, but it was also a critique. The nature of her critique hinged upon what the nation—and particularly, the enlargement of state power, the centralization of government, and the bureaucratization of daily life—imperiled, something Weil called "roots." "To be rooted," she argued, "is perhaps the most important and least recognized need of the human soul." Further, "a human being has roots by virtue of his real, active, and natural

263

participation in the life of the community, which preserves in living shape certain particular treasures of the past and particular expectations of the future."(p. 43). The natural sources of an individual's identity—family, home, vocation, religion, tradition, and the country that protects these selfsame "roots"—are what Weil thought were the most valuable aspects of human communities. Her idea of community was not the contractual, liberal one of social life as an "artifice" wherein individuals live together but essentially go their own way, careful only to avoid (unnecessarily) harming others. Rather, a community is a rich network of interrelationships within which we are born and to which we are inextricably bound. Its influences mold our habits, our values, our ways of thinking, just as our "active participation" shapes and creates the dimensions that distinguish our community from others'. Rootedness in community is spatial, territorial, and multitudinous. In the deepest, most intimate sense, our roots tie us to home and neighborhood; more widely, they connect us to village or city, metropolis, or countryside, and more sweeping still, our roots, at least since modern times, are in the nation.

Rootedness is also historical. Roots connect us to what Weil called our "most valuable possession in the world of temporal affairs": our sense of continuity in time (p. 100). The community anchors us in the past and bears upon our future. As a part of it, we know familial as well as political ancestors and founders, the "treasure" as Weil put it, of what has come before us. If we pay attention to our roots we know our "selves" more fully too—as social and historical beings who share a territory, a set of richly woven traditions, cultural inheritances, and a past in need of remembrance, retelling, and respect. For Weil, then, roots are both earthly ties to a place and they are "spiritual nourishment," a source of sustenance and meaning, identity, and purpose extended over time. Loss of the past, both collectively and individually she said, is the "supreme human tragedy" (p. 119).

The problem is that roots—both spatial and temporal—have nearly ceased to exist in the modern world. Weil saw uprootedness everywhere; people are severed from their connections to family, homeplace, vocation, religion, and their own traditions by the manifold horrors of the age: war, genocide, political oppression, religious persecution, colonialism, deportation, terrorism. But these ugly realities are not the only causes of rootlessness. Behind them is another related set of conditions, less apparent and more gradual perhaps, but no less a force in the uprooting of entire countries. Put simply, the rise of the nation-state and the efforts of its rulers to establish the state itself as the locus of authority severely undermined the connection between the individual and his or her locality, and distorted the meaning of historical continuity as well. Weil dated this moment in France in the seventeenth century, when Cardinal Richelieu "adopted the principle that whoever exercises a public function owes his entire loyalty . . . not to the public or to the king, but to the state and nothing else" (p. 115). Thus began the erosion of the sphere of local life and the fashioning of the dangerous myth of state omnipotence. In place of roots came allegiance to government or regime; in place of a living historical past came the "manufactured" past of history texts, the bastions of official culture. In place of community life came administration. Weil noted, "The development of the State exhausts a country."

The effects of expanding central power, new potent "statist" symbols, and mass education were not fully realized, however, until the late nineteenth and early twentieth centuries when, in the face of war ("the mainspring of all this business," Weil wrote) and in the name of *patria*, the state demanded and received the absolute loyalty of its members. Weil sometimes called this absolute loyalty "national egoism," sometimes "the illusions of *ersatz* greatness," sometimes "loveless idolatry"; but whatever her terms for this national spirit (we might call it "nationalism"), she clearly thought it dangerous and unnatural. To use Weil's own metaphor, nationalism is the creation of the "ironbound machine of State," a force that feeds upon uprootedness and in turn uproots the spatial and temporal connections between a people and their country by putting in their place an abstract "absolute value." It is a surface-level but resilient allegiance whose characteristic attribute is pride, and the object of pride—the nation itself—is beyond criticism. "It is what is expressed in the English saying, 'right or wrong, my country,'" Weil noted. "But people often go further. They refuse to admit that their country can ever be wrong" (p. 150).

Roots are in peril, then, but not because of the sheer fact of nationhood or the geopolitical reality of the contemporary world, not even solely because "the state" has eroded them. Clearly, Weil thought the problem was not just it but *us*. Roots are in peril because the meaning of belonging to country has been warped by nationalistic impulses that masquerade as "love of country" and by shallow sentiments that bear no resemblance to vital civic consciousness. Unlike many defenders of community, however, Weil thought that roots could be recovered and nurtured within the context of the nation-state, but only if we reorient our sense of national identity and undertake a rescue of our spatial connections and our sense of continuity in time. Nationalism will not do—it is a killing ground. Though France was her primary concern, Weil's point was a global one—the task for all citizens is to reconstitute themselves as patriots. Her suggestions for patriotism were general; citizens should apply them in ways unique to their own history and geography, and constitutive of their own traditions, customs, and political inheritances.

To begin with, Weil argued, we need an alternative to the self-aggrandizing exhortations of nationalism. Primary bonds to spaces and homeplace, that "instinctive patriotism," as Tocqueville called it, must be revived in place of the nation as "absolute value." Weil would have us re-imagine what a country is—not a world giant or an eternal verity (one distorts space, the other time)—but something "beautiful and precious . . . very frail and liable to suffer misfortune" (p. 177). Expanding on this, she wrote:

> Just as there are certain culture beds for certain microscopic animals, certain types of soil for certain plants, so there is a certain
> part of the soul in everyone and certain ways of thought and action communicated from one person to another which can only
> exist in a national setting and disappear when a country is destroyed. (p. 159)

For Weil, the protective cover for these multitudinous roots and diverse communities, the "national setting," was deserving of preservation and care at all costs. To keep the "culture-bed" flourishing and distinctive manners and mores alive, Weil suggested that a people adopt an attitude of compassion toward their nation, in contrast to nationalistic pride. The care-taking concern for something precious and shared is fixed on the specific, concrete attributes of a nation's geography, culture, and traditions, not on self-augmenting images of collective might. The point is to treasure and preserve "ways of thought and action" that make us who we are, not to impose them upon others, or to view them as inexorably "right." As Weil eloquently put it, compassionate patriotism is "the watchful and tender concern to keep country out of harm's way, which can give to peace . . . something shining, touching, poetic, sacred" (p. 179).

There is much that is "conservative," in Edmund Burke's sense, about Weil's understanding of patriotism as compassion and country as root-fixing ground. She shared with him a vision of the nation as a fragile web of traditions, institutions, customs, and inherited characteristics that could be destroyed and, once destroyed, not readily reconstituted. She believed that the patriot's task was to keep intact—in Burke's famous phrase— that "partnership between those who are living, those who are dead and those who are to be born."[6] Yet, despite these Burkean intimations, Weil's understanding of patriotism also has radical implications wholly compatible with her concern for roots. Her radicalism emerges, for example, in her critique of the political institutions and economic structures she thought destroyed roots, the centralized state that overwhelms local associations, and capitalist economies where labor is dehumanized, working life divorced from family, and family life itself undermined. Her patriotism was radical in another, more programmatic way, however, for she also associated rootedness with "real, active, and natural participation in the life of the community," with a vital civic life.

When Weil spoke of participation in the community, she had many activities in mind—a "culture-bed" both nourishes and thrives upon countless forms of collective association. In particular, however, she was concerned about what might be called the political expression of rootedness in country, about patriotism as citizenship. For Weil, as for Tocqueville, patriotism had much to do with the practice of popular sovereignty, democratically conceived and pursued in all dimensions of public life. But, unlike Tocqueville, Weil wrote in a time when citizen politics was in jeopardy. The political spaces that Tocqueville admired, those that made "reflective patriotism" possible, had nearly ceased to exist. In the contemporary world, as Weil put it, the "people's expression for concern for the problems of public life" is barely audible; the "simple organs" that allowed for the political expression of popular sentiment have been submerged by "irresponsible collectivities"—interest groups, national political parties, and the state itself. "If one disclosed to the devil the organization of public life," Weil wrote, "even he would not be able to imagine anything more ingenious."[7] The task, then, is to seek a new organization of public life, to foster popular movements and the growth of those simple organs that would bring the village, province, and region to life and make the exercise, not merely the exhortation, of citizenship an integral part of a nation's identity.

Weil knew, however, that the recovery of patriotism as citizenship could not be achieved in a vacuum. If it was not to succumb to idle romanticism or empty abstractions, it too had to be rooted, made real in terms of a nation's unique culture and history, and thereby rendered

267

accessible to popular memory and imagination. So, for example, she thought 1789 a vibrant source for the French political imagination, not because the revolution had established democratic institutions or planted roots deep enough to sustain a public spirit of political participation into the twentieth century, but because it served nevertheless as an "inspiration." The inspiration alone could revive awareness of what Weil called the "underground" part of French history—its republican spirit, its liberating currents, its wellsprings of popular sovereignty—concrete examples of human striving for the sort of patriotism she recommended. In short, Weil thought a peoples' recovery of certain historical examples, those that are democratic, participatory, and egalitarian, was a crucial part of the revitalization of citizenship. Without historical examples, as "guideposts for future remembrance," the concepts and principles that betoken citizenship would lose their significance and fail to endure as anything but empty slogans, open for manipulative and propagandistic ends.[8] Thus, for Weil, the recovery of patriotism required not only the re-imagining of country but also an attention to the political roots of participatory citizenship, local self-government, and popular sovereignty that are part of a nation's past. She thought these popular "grass roots" as vital to a country's living presence as its cultural and territorial ones, and that patriots must revitalize them, or stand in danger of forfeiting power in public affairs to impersonal institutions and the centralized state.

I began this essay by suggesting that the new populism in America make the recovery of patriotism, as Weil understood it, one of its primary political tasks. I will conclude by indicating, briefly, how I think a revitalized populist politics can both benefit from and is particularly well suited to "refashioning the soul of a country" in the manner she prescribed.

Both in the late nineteenth century and in its more recent incarnations, populism has at least two distinctive features. Its distinctive social feature has been its appreciation of the need for roots, for bonds of association that are immediate, local, self-sustaining, and deserving preservation. Its distinctive political feature, the one from which it draws its name, has been a commitment to popular sovereignty. In the literal sense, populism champions the idea of the people's empowerment over and against the formal, impersonal institutions of society and the state. For both of these reasons, the populist movement is particularly well suited to the sort of patriotism Weil conceived of as an alternative to the bleak and dangerous prospects of nationalism and statist politics. To put this another way, by virtue of its own social and political predispositions, populism carries within it the potential for reconstituting national identity along the lines Weil suggested in *The Need for Roots*.

I say "potential" because we must not ignore the fact that populism has more than one face in the flux of contemporary American politics, and not all of these faces are compatible with Simone Weil's prescriptions. The "patriotic" exhortations of the new right or certain party politicians, offered under a "populist" rubric, are often more akin to the loveless idolatry Weil repudiated than to the sort of spirit citizens should cultivate. And, all too often, self-proclaimed populists and "patriots" exhibit the dark side of collective bonds of association when they exclude, exploit, or harass those deemed unworthy of or unsuitable for inclusion in the community. These are serious political problems for a populist movement, and they cannot be ignored.

Nevertheless, there is much in what we might call "genuine" populism —in the political movement that fixes its principles not in the ideology of the new right or in mean-spirited social conservatism, but rather in a commitment to democratic, egalitarian politics, social justice, decentralization, and community power—that *is* compatible with Weil's prescriptions. We might expect, for instance, that a political movement that has in its tradition a concern for the nation's "common wealth," for its natural bounty and resources (as the populists of the 1930s did), and an expressed identity with the land, crafts, and smallholdings (as the agrarian movement of the 1890s did), would be open to re-imagining "country" in the manner Weil suggested, as a "vital medium" that sustains and nourishes its inhabitants. Indeed, Weil herself thought that the notion of country as a "culture-bed" in need of care-taking was particularly accessible to ordinary people, those who, "have a monopoly of a certain sort of knowledge . . . the reality of misfortune; and for that very reason . . . feel all the more keenly the preciousness of those things which deserve to be protected from it" (p. 171). "Ordinary people" are precisely those to whom populism speaks; thus, if Weil's intuitions are right, we might hope that a populist movement is exactly the right sort of seedbed in which "compassionate patriotism" might flourish and serve to challenge the dominant "war patriotism" of pride, pomp, and "USA number one!" I would think that feminists with populist sensibilities would also find the conception of compassionate patriotism particularly appealing, insofar as it draws upon an ethic of care and nurturance rather than upon one of power, might, and military supremacy.

269

Populism seems quite suited to Weil's alternative patriotism in another way as well. The spiritual force of her conception, the idea that "roots" in locality, region, family, and custom are vital sources of a people's identity and self-understanding, is also deep in populist tradition. Part of the task of a populist patriotism, following the intimations of Weil, would be to present an alternative, in theory and practice, to the restless, rootless mentality (and lives) of contemporary Americans. In a fast-paced, techno-logical culture where the lure of mobility (both geographical and socio-logical) is a given, populist patriotism and politics could provide a dif-ferent vision or at least remind us of (in Weil's words) those "national souvenirs," both human and organic, deserving our attention and respect. This need not (nor indeed should it) mean that populists will undertake nostalgic forays into times past, but rather that they will seek to conserve and promote the life of the community and its roots wherever possible in times present. This populist conservatism can take many forms, among others, the support of urban renewal and the reclamation of neighbor-hoods, the fostering of community self-help projects, public service pro-grams and cooperatives, the preservation of historical sites and ethnic communities, arts, and folkways, the decentralization and democratization of the workplace, and the fight against impersonal, impenetrable institu-tions far removed from the realities of everyday life. The latter is a long-standing part of populist practice; the others are welcome ingredients of a revitalized populist spirit in America.

Finally, the radical aspects of Weil's patriotism, those fixed in the idea that active citizenship is the political expression of rootedness in country, are deeply imbedded in populist practice and need to be revitalized by the contemporary populist movement. If populism is to remain true to its name, it must, pace Weil, place "the people's expression of concern for the problems of public life" at the forefront of its political ideals. It can do this, in part, by calling for and creating institutions and "free social spaces," or what Hannah Arendt once called "organs of action," that allow for the popular exercise of liberty and self-government.[9] Populists can also embark on a course of democratic political action by appealing, as Weil suggested, to the "underground past" of American history and isolating historical examples as guides for recollecting the democratic movements and practices that are a part of our historical legacy. Along these same lines, Lawrence Goodwyn has suggested the Massachusetts "Regulation" during the American Revolution, the populists' rural mobilization of the 1880s and 1890s, and the sit-down strikes of the 1930s as examples of democratic movements, and there are others.[10] Populists need to recover these historical examples and use them to counter "official" history, and as inspirations for a different sort of civic identity in America.

Reconstructing patriotism, as Simone Weil knew, is a formidable and delicate political task. But in America, in an age of alternately barren and bellicose attachment to country, populists would do well to consider it, and to make a democratic "re-imagination" of country one of their vital concerns. Perhaps our last best hopes for a creative and lasting patriotism, of the sort Tocqueville admired and Weil advanced, lie with them.

Notes

1. Alexis de Tocqueville, *Democracy in America*, ed. J. P. Mayer (New York: Anchor Press, 1969), pp. 236–37.

2. Ibid., p. 235.

3. Ibid., p. 367.

4. See S. M. Miller in Chapter 11 of this volume.

5. Unless otherwise noted, all references in parentheses in the text are to Simone Weil, *The Need for Roots* (Boston: Beacon Press, 1952).

6. Edmund Burke, *Reflections on the Revolution in France*, ed. T. Mahoney (New York: Bobbs-Merrill, 1955), p. 110.

7. Simone Weil, "Note sur la suppression generale des Partis Politiques," *La Table Ronde* 216 (Feb. 1950): 12.

8. The phrase in quotations is Hannah Arendt's. See *On Revolution* (New York: Viking Press, 1963), p. 222.

9. The idea of "free social spaces" comes from Sara Evans and Harry Boyte, "Schools for Action," *democracy* 2, no. 4 (Fall 1982): 55–65.

10. Lawrence Goodwyn, "Organizing Democracy," *democracy* 1, no. 1 (Jan. 1981): 41–60.

Twenty-Three
Joe Holland

POPULISM AND AMERICA'S SPIRITUAL CRISIS

Introduction: A Cultural-Spiritual Crisis

For some time, America has been in a transitional crisis. In liberal left
networks public debate over the nature of this crisis focuses on politics
and economics. These remain important dimensions, but in my judgment
the crisis runs deeper. At its foundation, I believe, the crisis is cultural,
and ultimately spiritual.[1]

America's inherited cultural-spiritual foundation—the source of our
national psychic identity—no longer corresponds to our social experience
as a nation. *The country's cultural meaning system is breaking down.* This is
the heart of the contemporary American anguish.

If the new populism is truly to empower people, it will not be sufficient to speak to people's economic "interests," nor to their political
"control." Rather, the new populism will need to set the political economy

272

within the deeper structure of the nation's meaning system, especially its spiritual meaning. It is this deeper level of the nation's cultural meaning system that, for example, opposed yet powerful figures like Ronald Reagan and Bruce Springsteen both tap into.

The uprooted liberal left elite has largely abandoned the cultural-spiritual terrain of this deeper meaning system—on behalf of a dangerous privatization of religious energies. This has lead to a profound secularization of America's public life. In an extraordinarily religious nation like America, such elite-imposed secularization inevitably precipitates a populist religious backlash. We have seen this backlash organized politically by Ronald Reagan and the new right.

Because the liberal left largely abandoned this symbolic terrain, the conservative right had a free field to construct a destructive populist religious vision. Such a religious vision is based on fear, resentment, control, and pride. Ultimately, I propose, it is the worship of a national idol.

Religious energies are ever present in human culture. They may be idolatrous or worshipful, demonic or divine, creative or destructive, life bearing or death dealing. To deny public meaning to spiritual energies through privatization and secularization is gradually to choose cultural death. The same choice is embodied in the public celebration of idolatrous religion.

Hence, a fundamental task for the new populism is to speak an alternative populist religious vision, drawing on the spiritual energies that give life, that overcome fear and resentment, that risk loosing control, that seek a new healing beyond wounded pride, that are not idolatrous but prophetic. But the new populism will be able to do this only if it roots itself in the creative side of America's religious traditions.

In exploring an alternative populist religious vision, I would like first to offer a sketch of the journey of human culture; second, to describe the special dynamics of the present crisis within American culture; and third, to point to some creative and prophetic resources from America's spiritual traditions, from which an alternative populism might drink.

The Journey of Human Culture

The present cultural crisis is due to the micro-electronic revolution, which created computers, television, satellite hook-ups, and jet travel. The micro-electronic revolution in turn marks the end of one age of

273

human culture, the modern era, and the beginning of a new age of human culture. For lack of a settled name, I will simply call this new age the postmodern era.

The West has thus far passed through three cultural ages and is now entering a fourth. As Marshall McLuhan has taught us, each of these ages was based on a distinct information technology.[2] The theologian Thomas Berry has done a brilliant analysis of these three ages—critically in relation to our present ecological crisis, and creatively in relation to the deepest spiritual meaning of the human journey.[3] We may call these three ages the primal, classical, and modern periods.

In the primal era culture was based on the unmediated oral tradition, especially on storytellers narrating the community's spiritual identity. This was what Berry calls "the tribal-shamanic age." In this age, humanity lived in intimate communion with the rest of nature, within itself, and with the Creator. But humanity had not yet awakened to the psychic depth of its inner subjectivity nor to the technological power of its outer creativity.

In the classical era human culture dualistically fragmented into high and low spheres, with low culture still rooted in the unmediated holistic oral folkways of the primal stage, but with high culture increasingly based on the mediated fragmenting instrument of handwritten texts. In turn, a profound dualism spread across classical culture. As the literate high culture of the aristocracy "transcended" the oral low culture of the peasantry, so too came the hierarchical divisions of racism, classism, sexism, the separation of the sacred from the profane, of priest from people, and of humanity from the rest of nature.

This was the hierarchical-priestly age. It created the classical cities and empires, based economically on the extraction of agricultural surpluses from a politically dominated peasantry. It was also the age that produced the great world religions, based on handwritten books. Its cultural foundation was the spiritual vision of transcendence, borne by a literate elite. In spite of its oppressions and alienations, this age laid the cultural foundation for all subsequent development of the human mind and of human technologies. Its strengths and weaknesses are an inescapable ground on which we still stand.

The third cultural age is our own modern era, progressively revealing itself as the technocratic-secular age. In this age humanity powerfully expands its inner psychic depth and its outer technological power. The result staggers the imagination and witnesses to the incredible creativity imbedded in the human species. Such creativity became possible in the modern age only because of the new information technology of printing, a technology that enabled scientific knowledge to break beyond its classical aristocratic boundaries.

But in the process, modernity began to lose touch with the communitarian bonding of its primal roots. It lost touch with the rest of the natural world—imprisoning itself in an anti-ecological fabrication incapable of renewing life. It lost touch with the spiritual energy of life's Creator—collapsing instead into sterile secularism and religious privatization. Finally, it lost touch with its own communitarian fabric—leading to the erosion of family life, the disintegration of neighborhoods, the promotion of an atomized loneliness. The ecological-social-spiritual holism of the primal age was finally undermined.

This happened across the modern ideological spectrum, from capitalism to communism and throughout the various points in between. One extreme worships through the market, the other through the state, but both worship the same modern idol of autonomous technology. We can now blow the world up rapidly by nuclear war or poison it slowly by ecological contamination. We have progressed so far that we can destroy our species and millions of other species with us. Hence, the task is not to replace one modern ideology with another, but to move to a postmodern cultural consciousness—deepening humanity's psychic and technological creativity, yet healing its modern distortions.

The postmodern era might be described as the ecological-holistic age. The root paradigm is ecological, and all of reality is integrated into a creative ecological-social-spiritual whole. The new information technology making possible this creative holism is micro-electronics.

The anti-ecological journey of human consciousness away from the earth began with classical transcendence and triumphed with modern autonomous technology. The healing of modern destructiveness needs to be fundamentally a return to the earth, to a new form of ecological technology and to a new form of ecological spirituality.

The major spiritual prophet of this ecological vision was perhaps the Jesuit priest Pierre Teilhard de Chardin.[4] Through his notion of the "noosphere," Teilhard came to understand that humanity is not master or steward of creation—placed like some extrinsic object on this planet to control it from the outside. Rather, humanity is a specific mode of being of the earth itself, indeed of the universe, in its developmental process.

Humanity is the earth beginning to think. Humanity is the flowering re-flective consciousness of earth's own creative energies.

The major technological prophet of this new age was perhaps the economist E. F. Schumacher.[5] He came to realize that economics needed to be reshaped in communion with the earth, and with all the species that dwell in it. So, too, he realized that technology needed to be shaped in service of the social ecology of human community.

The return to communitarian bonding with the earth means also a return to social bonding. The tribal holism of our primal roots now emerges on a global scale. The modern era was nationalistic, but the post-modern era is simultaneously global and local. We discover that we are but one family—across all racial, sexual, class, national, or cultural lines.

Perhaps the greatest testimony to the birth of this new culture was the 1985 Africa Live Aid rock concert. Millions and millions of young people all over the earth—across racial, sexual, and class boundaries—entered into a global yet tribal celebration. Their common song, "We Are the World," could be sung in unison across the world only because the post-modern micro-electronics laid the technological foundation for a global culture. But the spiritual power of the music came from the primal life-beat and ecstatic immersion of the African musical tradition. Reputedly giving material aid to a physically starved African continent, the concert was simultaneously drawing spiritual energy from Africa for a religiously starved technocratic world.

This postmodern recovery of social bonding has profound economic and political implications.

Competition can no longer be the primary motive of our economic interaction, for it makes us isolated enemies of each other. Nor can government administration, for then we become passive objects to be manipulated. Rather, economic life needs to grow cooperatively out of our rooted community life, and to bond with communities across the earth. Politics becomes in turn the defense or recovery of community at every level from the local to the global. Such community is the creative communitarianism of an ecological-social-spiritual whole.

In the social sphere, politics grants primacy to community organizing and global networking. It is not based on modern adversary conscious-ness, but rather on the consciousness of concentric circles of community. These concentric circles span every level from bioregions, to nations, to georegions, and finally to the global. New forms of political institutions also need to arise in service of this concentric communitarian bonding.

276

Finally, the postmodern recovery of our ecological and social roots is intimately tied to recovery of our spiritual roots. Here we discover that the artistic energies of the earth, brought to reflective consciousness in the human species, flow from the artistic energy of the Creator. The Creator is present across creation as it continues to unfold its flower, in all we can see from the galactic formations of astrophysics to the quantum particles of subatomic physics; in the ecological processes of water, earth, and air; in the lush vegetation and the splendid panorama of animals, indeed in all the species; and finally in the every aspect of our own lives—in our bodily functions of digestion, excretion, respiration, blood circulation, brain activity, reproduction; in our roles in family, work, play, friends; in everything.

The Creator is present wherever creativity is present. When we consciously probe the creativity of our inner depth and our outer power, we touch more profoundly the divine energy. Conversely, the Creator is shut out whenever we block creativity, be it in nature, in society, in our work, in our families, in our friendships, in our inner selves, or even in our understanding of religion.

This is the vision that bears the energy of postmodern culture. In this age of transition, cultural vision comes first as the source of energy. From it follows politics, but politics becomes creative only to the degree that it draws on the energy-bearing vision of holistic communitarian creativity embracing the ecological, the social, and the spiritual. From a holistic creative communitarian politics comes, then, a holistic creative communitarian economics, artistically rebonding humanity with the earth, with itself, and with the Creator.

The political community exploring this postmodern vision is that group we call "the Greens."[6] The new populism has already begun a dialogue with the American Green movement. We hope that this will continue. But let us turn now to the uniquely American side of the modern cultural crisis.

The Central Role of the American Crisis

There are two dimensions to America's participation in the cultural-spiritual crisis of modernity. One dimension is that America represents the heart of the modern technocratic world. So if modernity is in cultural trouble, then America is in the midst of that trouble. The other dimension flows from the distinct religious self-understanding of American culture. These two dimensions—the scientific and the religious—are grounded in the twin roots of American culture, Enlightenment rationalism and Protestant theology, both given free and complementary reign in America without the restraint of the European classical tradition.

Since the scientific or Enlightenment dimension is the general crisis of modern technocracy, which I have already spoken to, I will address here the more specifically religious side of America's participation in the modern cultural-spiritual crisis.

America was founded on a Protestant vision of the relationship of nature and grace. Modern Protestantism brought many gifts to the journey of human culture, but its understanding of nature and grace now becomes problematic. In the Protestant vision, nature and grace were seen as antagonistic, with nature totally corrupted by original sin, and grace triumphing over it from outside. By contrast, classical Catholicism had understood nature and grace as complementary though hierarchical, with nature only wounded by sin and still bearing a residual natural goodness. But what did this Protestant theological subtlety mean when translated into American politics?

America understood itself as the new creation of grace. It defined in biblical terms as a new Israel, a new Jerusalem, a clearing in the wilderness, a new Eden, a new Adam. This meant that America saw itself born in a grace-filled innocence, freed from the total corruption of the rest of humanity. By contrast, Europe was the "old world" of corrupt nature, from which God had supposedly delivered this new nation. Similarly, the rest of the "new world" was seen as buried in ignorance and superstition, hence also subject to corruption.

Of the new nations, only America had this special consciousness of innocence. To our south in Latin America, the independence movement arose within a Catholic culture. To our north in Canada, where independence was not so highly prized, the European tradition remained stronger.

This special consciousness of a redeemed, divinely chosen, and gracefully innocent America rendered the nation open to marvelous energies of technological development. Here internal innocence became external messianism. Americans felt specially called to change the world. They approached massive technological problems with buoyant optimism. They went to "save" Europe in two world wars. They reached out to

278

"modernize" the whole Third World. Understandably, they felt themselves number one.

But there was a negative side to this consciousness. Internally, innocence meant blindness to harsh sins of racism, sexism, classism, and ecological assault. Externally, messianism meant blindness to the growing neocolonial military and economic power of American hegemony, as well as to what American development was doing to global ecology.

In the 1960s the micro-electronic revolution's instrument of television revealed America's sins to the nation. Night after night in what once was the hidden refuge of the home, people watched on television a brutal American neocolonial war in Southeast Asia. During the same years they watched the struggle of black Americans and white allies to challenge American racism. So, too, they saw the "other America" of America's poor, which Michael Harrington had so compassionately written about in a book that inspired the "War Against Poverty."[7]

Thus television revealed to America, or at least to the then rising generation of youth, the contradictions of American culture—a nation officially innocent and messianic, yet now revealing a harsh imperialism, a long-standing racism, and a broad-scale poverty. The result of this revelation was the cultural upheaval of the 1960s. That cultural upheaval can now be seen in the wider context as one of the three decades of shifting cultural politics.

The first decade was the 1950s, against which the 1960s reacted. The 1950s was dominated by a politics of cultural naïveté—the inherited view from the nation's foundation. Again, this was based on America's representing redemption and the rest of the world, corruption. America was number one, without any doubt.

The second decade was the 1960s, marked by the politics of cultural cynicism—the new left's shattering of the contradiction. But while the 1960s rejected the American mythology of innocence and messianism, it nonetheless continued the underlying theology of an antagonistic relationship between nature and grace. So, if America was not totally innocent and messianic, then it must be totally corrupt and imperialistic. The theology stayed the same; it only changed sides.

As a result, the new left of the 1960s confronted the nation with its sins but offered no resources for creative healing. The new left found nothing in the American tradition on which a transformative politics could build, only condemnation. In the process, this negative approach to

279

politics was often extended to other highly symbolic institutions beyond the nation, for example, the family, and sometimes religion. "Flag, family, and faith" became three powerful cultural symbols that the new left abandoned in the 1960s, only to have the new right take them up in cultural triumph in the following decade.[8]

The new left was of course correct to confront the nation with its sins. But in failing to find alternative sources of creativity in the roots of American culture, the new left was gradually marginalized in American political culture.

The third decade was the new right backlash in the 1970s against the new left of the 1960s. This was the politics of cultural nostalgia. It created the presidency of Ronald Reagan.

The Reagan triumph, I believe, was primarily due to his cultural reassurance. In the midst of an external and internal assault on America's spiritual identity, Ronald Reagan reassured the American public that things were okay, that we still were number one, the Americans really are "a different species," that America really is "the last best hope of man [sic] on earth." Ronald Reagan held the old American identity together against all odds, a feat of no small triumph, perhaps personally symbolized by his youthful appearance within an aging body.

In addition, the Republican coalition took seriously several important themes neglected by the Democratic coalition. It raised high the theme of family as a fundamental social institution. It embraced religious energies as public, not private. It proposed a decentralized vision of society. By contrast, the Democratic coalition stressed the adversarialism of individual rights, a privatized definition of religion, and a politically centralized nation.

Of course, the Reagan presidency can be accused of proposing a patriarchal vision of family, of embracing an idolatrous religious vision, and of only rhetorically speaking of decentralization. But at least the Republicans knew where the postmodern populist cultural energy was flowing, even if they chose only to manipulate it. By contrast, the Democrats seemed to be running in an opposite direction to postmodern populist culture.

A creative new populism lies, I believe, with a politics that can confront America's sins, but still tap American roots, especially recessive sources of cultural-spiritual energy, and flow with the direction of postmodern culture. Let us now turn, in conclusion, to some suggestions about where some of those religious roots and energies might be found.

280

Traditional Spiritual Resources
for a Creative Future

The point of this essay has been to show the importance of culture for politics. It was not really to sketch an alternative political culture. Nonetheless, I will offer a list of some resources we need to explore in the future. I ask the reader's indulgence for not developing more fully these resources and also for not including all that might be listed. Consider this section an unfinished list for future work:

1. *The Spiritual Hunger of Ordinary People.* One often had the suspicion that for the new left it was the ordinary people, the majority of whom consider themselves middle class, who were the real enemy. By contrast, a creative populism would try to learn from the spiritual struggles of Middle America, from its hunger for meaning in work, family, and community. Especially for less "sophisticated" groups, including the poor, this spiritual hunger often takes evangelical form. Without some sharing of these evangelical energies, there is little hope for any alternative populist movement.

2. *The Spirituality of the Earth and the Native American Peoples.* The native peoples of this land are the bearers of our country's deepest spiritual traditions. They refused to break with the primal vision. Culturally and spiritually they resisted classical dualisms and modern secularization. Since the spiritual energy of the earth is the cultural foundation of the postmodern period, the spirituality of the native peoples becomes our first guide.

3. *The Spirituality of Woman and the Feminine Face of God.* The turn from the earth was also a turn from the feminine face of God, revealed in the primal Earth Mother. As a result, spirituality became more alienated from the earth, more phallic and warlike. The spiritual healing of culture needs to draw deeply on the religious experience of women, on the new probings of feminist theology, and on this repressed feminine side of the divine.

4. *The Life-Giving Spirituality of Black America.* Where white Christianity saw America as a new Israel, black Christianity experienced it as a new Egypt. Yet out of oppression comes new promise for America. This historical suffering of African-Americans is a rich treasure of spiritual renewal—often expressed through black music and preaching. Black America also bears the healing spiritual symbol of darkness, one of the

281

most mystical images of God. Our white-oriented "en-light-ened" spirituality sorely needs the healing of the mystery of darkness.

5. *The Familial Spirituality of Hispanic America.* In a nation of atomized individualism, the Hispanic traditions have kept alive their communal sense, rooted especially in family and its religious mystery. Hispanic religious energy teaches us the importance of rituals of celebration to sustain and renew family and its extension in community. These are also lessons our alienated culture sorely needs. The fiesta spirit of Hispanic culture is a great gift to America.

6. *The Global Sacramental Spirituality of Catholicism.* American Catholicism is presently releasing strong cultural energy in the nation. Bishops' pastoral letters on peace and the economy, along with a strong grassroots Catholic pro-life movement, are evidence of this new energy. This Catholic energy retrieves a complementary sense of grace and nature, an awareness of the sacramentality of all life. Also because of Catholicism's transnational character, in contrast to the often greater nationalism of other religious traditions, it also brings a sacramental awareness of the unity of the whole human family.

These then are some, but hardly all, of the spiritual resources for our own American tradition. *Whether a new populism can become a real alternative to the reigning right-wing populism may depend on whether it can drink deeply of such spiritual energies.*

Notes

1. I have written more about this cultural-spiritual crisis in a series of working papers published in recent years by the Center of Concern (3700 13th Street, Washington, D.C.). These essays are titled "The Post-Modern Shift Implicit in the Church's Shift to the Left" (1983), "The Spiritual Crisis of Modern Culture" (1984), and "The Post-Modern Cultural Earthquake" (1985).

2. Marshall McLuhan, *Understanding Media: The Extensions of Man* (New York: McGraw Hill, 1964).

3. See Thomas Berry's collected essays in *The Riverdale Papers*, covering several years of his work and available from The Riverdale Center for Religious Research, 5801 Palisades Avenue, Riverdale, N.Y. 10471.

4. Pierre Teilhard de Chardin, *The Future of Man*, trans. Norman Denny (New York: Harper & Row, Harper Torchbooks, 1959), esp. chap. 10.

5. E. F. Schumacher's best-known work is *Small is Beautiful: Economics as if People Mattered* (New York: Harper & Row, Perennial Library, 1973).

6. For more on the Greens, see Charlene Spretnak and Frijof Capra, *Green Politics: The Global Promise* (New York: E. P. Dutton, 1985).

7. See Michael Harrington, *The Other America: Poverty in the United States* (Baltimore: Penguin, 1963).

8. See my pamphlet "Flag, Faith, and Family" (Chicago: New Patriot Alliance, 1979).

Twenty-Four
Sheldon S. Wolin

CONTRACT AND
BIRTHRIGHT

This essay is meant as a contribution to the revitalization of democratic theory. Democracy has become a bland, all-purpose formula easily mouthed by its enemies. Political reactionaries appeal to it by direct mail as they promote the cause of the free market and the censorship of textbooks. Neoconservative theologians, frocked and unfrocked, found institutes to celebrate the democracy of corporate power. The president welcomes the remnants of a discredited dictatorship as freedom-fighters in the cause of democracy.

Usually when an effort is made to give meaning to the term "democracy," it is identified with free elections. Thus democracy is said to be

This chapter appears with slight revisions in *Political Theory* 14, no. 2 (1986), p. 179–93. ©1986 by Sage Publications, Inc. Reprinted by permission.

both a system of government in which the ruling elites are periodically held accountable to the voters and a political process that allows for political opposition, including the opposition of a free press. The criteria associating democracy with a form of government and with a process of legitimation have been invoked to stigmatize a Marcos and the Sandinistas or to champion a Duarte. Form and process represent, however, a narrow vision of democracy; they serve to blur the powerful presence of an anti-democratic politics. A political structure has evolved of corporate power, mass media, consultants and political merchandisers, big money owners, academic entrepreneurs, and foundations. Its representatives have learned how to cooperate among themselves and to concert their power to the end of managing democratic forms so as to render public opinion a work of art rather than an expression of public deliberation.

Through their efforts a distinctive political culture has been created. For the present purpose a political culture may be defined as a union of beliefs and practices that conditions the way collective power is used in and upon the beings and things that populate the social and natural world. The dominant political culture emphasizes opportunity, success, status, wealth, manic energy, endless innovation, and competitiveness. The un-stated values are implicit in the stated ones. They translate as: power, domination, and imperial grandeur so expansive as to make those who have bought into it sufficiently credulous as to believe that the same ethic that generates the drive to power also conduces to a social conscience. Democratic institutions have been all but overwhelmed by an antidemo-cratic culture with the result that while the form of democratic institutions may remain relatively unchanged, the institutional practices serve non-democratic ends.

In order to avoid being duped by formalities and the mere rhetoric of democracy it is important to distinguish between institutions and prac-tices. An institution stands for a set of rules and procedures or formal steps, such as the procedures by which a legislature operates. Practices, however, are a combination of formal rules and folkways: they are for-malities that have been shaped by a culture. A practice is cultivated, that is, it results from being cared for rather than merely being observed. A democratic institution becomes a democratic practice when power is used carefully for deliberated ends by those who value their common humanity and their common world.

Populism is the culture of democracy. Historically it has stood for the efforts of ordinary citizens and would-be citizens to survive in a society

285

dominated by those whose control over the main concentrations of wealth and power has enabled them to command the forms of technical knowledge and skilled labor that have steadily become the hallmark of so-called modernizing societies. A culture rooted in survival is very different from a culture dedicated to consumption and set to seasonal rhythms designed by fashion. The latter is a market-culture littered by the disposable remains of yesterday and shaped by manipulation of attitudes and desires. It is a culture of temporary use and abandonment.

A culture of survival is conditioned by the experience of hard times in a changing world. Its practice issued from taking care of living beings and mundane artifacts, from keeping them in the world by use and memory. To sustain the institutions of family, community, church, school, and local economy demanded innovation as well as conservation. These arts were proof that culture is essential to survival, not ornamental. Populist political culture is a reflection of the historical experience of hard times: of drought, depressed markets, high railroad and grain storage rates, and manipulated currencies. Although the American populist tradition has been importantly agrarian, the survival of hard times is not a uniquely agrarian experience. Blacks and other ethnic groups have endured it and continue to struggle. The working classes and the urban poor have also had to cultivate the arts of survival.

The reason why democracy should be grounded in a populist culture is not because those who live it are pure, unprejudiced, and unfailingly altruistic. Rather, it is because it is a culture that has not been defined by the urge to dominate and that has learned that existence is a cooperative venture over time.

In what follows I shall try to delineate the nature of these two antithetical political cultures. The populist and democratic culture is symbolized by the notion of "birthright," the antidemocratic culture by that of "contract."

Once when Jacob was boiling pottage, Esau came in from the field, and he was famished. And Esau said to Jacob, "Let me eat some of that red pottage, for I am famished!" . . . Jacob said, "First sell me your birthright." Esau said, "I am about to die; of what use is a birthright to me?" Jacob said, "Swear to me first." So he swore to him, and sold his birthright to Jacob. . . . Thus Esau despised his birthright. (Genesis 25:29–34)

286

The story of Esau recounts how a man sold his birthright. In ancient times a birthright usually fell to the eldest son. He succeeded his father and received the major portion of his father's legacy. A birthright was thus an inherited identity and implicitly an inherited obligation to use it, take care of it, pass it on, and, it was hoped, improve it. An inherited identity is, by definition, unique: Esau was the inheritor of Isaac, and hence a descendant of Abraham, the founder of Israel. Esau was also the inheritor of the profound experiences of his father Isaac whom Abraham had been prepared to sacrifice for his God and Esau was also the inheritor of his father's father and so on, according to the genealogies so beloved in the Old Testament, back in time to Adam and Eve. Esau's was thus a collective identity, bound up with a people and extending over time.

This unique identity Esau had bartered to fill a need that could be satisfied by any number of different foods. The Old Testament nowhere suggests that Esau was even remotely in danger of starvation. He had bartered what was unique and irreplaceable for a material good for which there were a number of available substitutes.

Although Esau is depicted as a crude man, the Old Testament leaves no doubt that his decision was free and uncoerced, even though there had clearly been an element of cunning on Jacob's part. The power of the biblical narrative depends upon the juxtaposition between the free nature of the choice and the unfree nature of a birthright. One does not choose to be the eldest son of a particular father: that is a matter of one's special history. Contrary to the claim of Jean-Paul Sartre, the idea of a birthright denies that we are "thrown into the world."

Birthright has its own distinctive mode of discourse. As its name suggests, birth/right relies strongly on the language of natality. It is a way of "conceiving" the person; and we shall see shortly how the fate of Esau and his brother Jacob is prefigured in the womb of their mother. Birthright language conceives the person as preformed, as an incorporation of elements of family, cult, and community. It asserts that we come into the world preceded by an inheritance. This is why if Esau is to disencumber himself of his inheritance he has to enter into a mode of discourse contrary to the mode of discourse surrounding a birthright.

In contractualist discourse the self is performed rather than preformed. It awaits constitution. So it makes itself by a series of bargains. It is a negotiated and negotiable self. Accordingly, the biblical narrator says that Esau "swore" and "sold," that is, Esau entered into a contract of exchange.

287

But the contractual mode presumes precisely what the birthright mode rejects, that the exchanged objects are equal in value. It is not that it is impossible to reduce a birthright and a bowl of pottage to a common measure of value, but rather that the nature of one is more deeply violated than the other by that operation. In other words, there is an intuitive sense that protests that a birthright is not the kind of thing that should be the object of a contract—in much the same way, perhaps, that we feel that Faust committed an act of self-mutilation when he contracted with Mephistopheles to make over his soul in exchange for power.

The idea of a contract is familiar to us not only as a legal instrument by which most business transactions are negotiated, but it is one of the archetypal metaphors of political theory. It is associated with such masters of political thought as Hobbes, Locke, Rousseau, Paine, and Kant. It has represented a distinctive vision of society and nowhere has it been more influential, both in theory and practice, than in the United States. It is a core notion in two of the most widely discussed political theories of recent years, those of John Rawls and Robert Nozick.

Briefly put, contract theory conceives of political society as the creation of individuals who freely consent to accept the authority and rules of political society on the basis of certain stipulated conditions, such as each shall be free to do as he or she pleases as long as their actions do not interfere with the rights of others; or that an individual shall not be deprived of property except by laws that have been passed by duly elected representatives; and so on. Now the contractual element is needed, according to the theory, because all persons being free and equal by nature and society being by nature in need of coercive power to protect rights, preserve peace, and defend against external invasion, the freedom of individuals will have to be limited and regulated. Individuals will contract, therefore, to surrender some part of their rights in exchange for the protection of the law and the defense of society from foreign or domestic enemies.

For more than three centuries the contract way of understanding political life has been criticized for being unhistorical, but the criticism has usually taken the form of arguing that contractualism gives a false account of how societies have actually come into existence. To which the contract theorist has quite properly replied that he has not been engaged in historical description but in prescribing the principles of a rights-oriented society. Yet that reply does expose an assumption, namely, that it is possible to talk intelligibly about the most fundamental principles of a political society as though neither the society nor the individuals in it had a history. It stands, therefore, in sharp contrast to the conception of a birthright that, although not strictly historical in its approach to collective identity, might be said to have a quality of historicality.

I want to suggest that the conception of a birthright provides a more powerful way of understanding our present political condition than does contract theory, and that contract theory is less a solution to the political problem of our times than an exacerbation of it. I began with the story of Esau because it bears on the birthright that each of us has. Like Esau's, our birthright is an inheritance. Like Esau's, it is inherited from our fathers. Like Esau's, it is a birthright that concerns a unique collective identity. Like Esau's, our birthright is not being extracted from us by force; it is being negotiated or contracted away. Finally, like Esau we have made it possible to contract away our birthright by forgetting its true nature and thereby preparing the way for its being reduced to a negotiable commodity, with the result that its disappearance is not experienced as loss but as relief.

The birthright that we have made over to our Jacobs is our political-ness. By "politicalness" I mean our capacity for developing into beings who know and value what it means to participate in and be responsible for the care and improvement of our common and collective life. To be political is not identical with being "in" government or being associated with a political party. These are structured roles and typically they are highly bureaucratized. For these reasons they are opposed to the authen-tically political.

A political inheritance or birthright is not something we acquire like a sum of money or our father's house; nor is it something we grow into naturally without effort or forethought, like reaching the age of eighteen and automatically being entitled to vote. It is something to which we are entitled, as Esau had been, but we have to make it consciously our own, mix it with our mental and physical labor, undertake risks on its behalf, and even make sacrifices. What the "it" is was suggested more than 2,500 years ago when Heraclitus implored his fellow-citizens to "cling to the common," that is, search out the concerns that represent what our collec-tivity identity is about and seek to use them, take care of them, improve and pass them on.

Politicalness comes to us as a birthright, as an inheritance, and hence it has an historical quality without being merely historical. A birthright is defined by the historical moments when collective identity is collectively established or reconstituted. For Americans these moments include the seventeenth-century beginnings in New England; the revolutionary founding and the redefinition of it symbolized by the ratification of the constitution; the Civil War with its vision of a nation-alized society and its inconclusive attempt to radicalize republicanism; and two world wars that have affixed collective identity to the dream of world hegemony and have reconstituted the moments represented by the New Deal and the civil rights movement so as to make them functional elements.

Historical moments "are"; they have spatial and temporal attributes that can be described. But, as elements of a birthright, they have to be interpreted. Interpretation is not historical description, but a theoretical activity concerned with reflection upon the meaning of past experience and of possible experiences. Because birthrights need interpretation, they are contestable and, because contestable, there is no finality to the interpretation. Birthrights are transmitted, and because of that their meaning will have to be reconsidered amidst different circumstances. We inherit from our fathers, but we are not our fathers. Thus the Constitution is part of our inheritance. Its formation and contents can be described historically, but the interpretation of its origins and its contents have been highly contestable subjects and remain so. No interpretation enjoys undisputed hegemony.

Now, one reason for the contestability of historical things, whether located in the more remote past or the more immediate present, is their ambiguousness. Human actors intervene to enact a law or promote a policy, but they are never able to circumscribe its consequences, many of which prove to be unwanted. Or the intervention itself embodies contradictory motives, such as when a law reflects the aims of those who hope to prevent the law from achieving the ends of its proponents and so attach a "rider" to it. Most, if not all, defining historical moments are full of ambiguities. Our Constitution, for example, proclaims liberties and inhibits democracy. Every war since the Mexican War has had its ambiguities, although this is not to say that some wars are not less ambiguous than others: World War II, for example, was less ambiguous than World War I—and World War III may be totally unambiguous.

Our birthright is composed of these ambiguous historical moments and so its political meaning is rarely obvious. If we are to deal with the ambiguities of our birthright, we need an interpretative mode of understanding that is able to reconnect past and present experience and we need to think in different terms about what it means to be political. We

290

cannot, for example, experience the past directly. We can, however, share in the symbols that embody the experience of the past. This calls for a citizen who can become an interpreting being, one who can interpret the present experience of the collectivity, reconnect it to past symbols, and carry it forward.

This conception of the citizen differs from the conception made familiar by contemporary liberal and conservative thinkers and their neo-variants. The latter conception tends to be two-dimensional. The individual is usually pictured as responding to the world as if in a situation of choice in which decisions will be made according to whether a choice will advance or reduce, protect or threaten the interests of the chooser. The temporal dimensions of choice are typically reduced to two, the present and the future. In this context recall President Reagan's famous query to the voters, "Ask yourself, are you better off now than four years ago?" Thus the citizen was asked to think about the past as a thin slice of time, four years, and to reduce its political meaning to economic terms, and then to assess it in personal rather than communal or collective terms. It was not a request for an interpretation of the meaning of four years of the Reagan regime, but a calculation of personal gains. It was a question that tacitly rejected as nonsensical the possibility that "I" could be better off but that "we" were not. It was Esau-talk.

The reason that the president could successfully address this appeal to the voters is that social contract thinking has become so engrained as to seem to be a natural part of the social world. There are two crucial assumptions made by social contract theory that present a particularly sharp contrast to the notion of a birthright. One is that the contracting individuals are equal because they have no prior history, the other that the contract represents a "beginning" in which society starts afresh like the beginning of a new footrace.

Each of these assumptions is deeply antihistorical. Individuals could be considered equal, that is, uniform in some important respects only if they had no autobiographies with different backgrounds and experiences, that is, if they had no personal histories. Obvious as this may seem, the contract theorist had to deny it, at least for the moment prior to the act of consent; otherwise no one would agree even to equal terms if they knew that others would be carrying forward previous advantages and hence could perpetuate or even increase their advantages. So the contract theorist has to posit a memoryless person, without a birthright, and so equal to all the others.

291

In the seventeenth and eighteenth centuries the memoryless person was said to exist in a state of nature where no social, political, or economic distinctions existed. In our own day the notion has been perpetuated most ingeniously by John Rawls in his conception of a "veil of ignorance." Rawls asks us to imagine an apolitical condition in which individuals who know nothing specific about their personal identities choose certain conditions that they would accept precisely because they do not know who they are or what advantages or disadvantages they enjoy. They are forced by the logic of this situation to choose conditions that will be fairest for all. The same lack of historicality surrounds the society that results from the Rawlsian contract. It begins with no past, no legacy of deeds or misdeeds, nothing to remember. The contract depends upon collective amnesia.

But in suggesting that, I do not mean to devalue the idea of equality but to claim that its present chimerical status, where it seems impossible to achieve yet impossible to abandon, is due in no small measure to the spell cast by contract thinking. We tend to assume that equality represents a condition that we are trying to recapture; that once, we were equal, as in the moment before the contract; and so the task is to eliminate barriers, such as segregation or sex discrimination. When this is done, equality is restored because equality has come to be identified with equal opportunity. But equal opportunity merely restarts the cycle of competition in the race, and races are designed to produce a single winner. Then it becomes obvious that social competition cannot be compared to a footrace between trained athletes; that the race for education, jobs, income, and status is rarely between equals, but between those with greater advantages and those with greater disadvantages. The end result is that the quest for equality becomes an exercise in guilt, which is typified in Rawls's solution. Rawls argues that inequalities can be advantageous if they spur economic activity that improves everyone's situation, which, by definition, would include that of "the least advantaged." But this is an argument for improving the lot of those who are unequal. It does not follow that in doing so we reduce inequality, much less eliminate it.

In reality the issue may be a different one: what kind of a collectivity is it that approaches its central value of justice by making the lot of the disadvantaged the test? The answer is that necessarily such a society will have to commit itself mainly to developing the economy because only in that way will the lot of the disadvantaged be improved. As a consequence the elites will be formed in response to that need and the structure of society will be shaped toward economic ends. The answer presupposes a polity that is, in reality, a political economy rather than a democracy. I shall return to this point.

I want now to set over against the social contract conceptions of membership and collectivity the notion of inheritance as suggested by the Esau story. One reason why Esau may have bargained away his history or inheritance was because in addition to the material benefits—his father's flocks and land—a birthright brought with it some accumulated burdens. He would inherit his father's "name," that is, a family history that would likely have included its share of debts and obligations, responsibilities, quarrels, feuds, and so on. To live in the world for any length of time is to know shame, guilt, dishonor, and compromise.

It is not irrelevant to the notion of inheritance as a burden that the Old Testament describes Esau as a hunter. The designation signified someone who prefers to travel unencumbered and who is disinclined to settle down. His brother Jacob, in contrast, is characterized as "a quiet man, dwelling in tents" (25:27). The Old Testament clearly aims to depict opposing types. It notes that before their birth "the children struggled together within" their mother's womb (25:22). Their mother, Rebekah, was told:

> Two nations in your womb,
> and two peoples, born of you shall be divided;
> the one shall be stronger than the other,
> the elder shall serve the younger. (25:23)

Even when they were being born, Jacob was said to have grabbed hold of Esau's heel (25:26). In their encounters it was Jacob who always won by virtue of some strategem. Thus, as their father Isaac lay dying, Jacob and his mother Rebekah conspired to deceive Isaac into believing that Jacob was Esau. As a result the dying father gave his precious "blessing" to the wrong son.

Our natural response is to say, "Foolish father!" But the truth is that all fathers are foolish and all birthrights are a mixture of good and evil, justice and injustice. When Esau learned that Jacob had also tricked him of his blessing, he demanded that Isaac give him another. Isaac complied but, under the rules, he could not retract the first and superior blessing given to Jacob. So he gave Esau another but inferior blessing, with the predictable result that Esau was resentful and threatened to kill Jacob, who then fled. Thus the birthright sows seeds of conflict and the effort to mitigate the effects creates further conflicts.

An inheritance, then, is a mixed blessing from foolish fathers. And, lest we forget the scheming Rebekah, from foolish mothers as well. The same is true of our birthright. The Founding Fathers left us a mixed blessing, a constitution that showed how power might be organized without leading to arbitrary authority, but also a document that was silent about women and accepted the institution of slavery. What is true of the Constitution is also true of the legacy of later centuries of American history. There was unparalleled economic opportunity and social mobility but there were numerous blots and stains: the treatment of the Indians, the aggression against Mexico, the cruel war between the states, and, beginning in 1898, the imperialist expansion of American power abroad, and, not least, the use of the atomic bomb.

When set over against this ambiguous legacy, the function of social contract thinking becomes clear: to relieve individuals and society of the burden of the past by erasing the ambiguities. This function assumes practical importance because contractualism is not solely an academic philosophy. It is part of American political mythology, of the collective beliefs that define our identity and help to shape our political attitudes and opinions.

Parenthetically, although myth is a feature of so-called advanced societies—which might for the present purposes be defined as societies in which science and rationality become identified and their promotion becomes an object of public policies—there is a difference between the status of myth in such societies and its status in premodern and primitive societies. In an advanced society the study of history tends to be demythologizing as a matter of principle; as a consequence, myth and historical consciousness coexist uneasily. In premodern societies, especially primitive ones, the historical consciousness can be critical without being instinctively debunking.[1]

This point has a practical bearing. President Reagan is rightly described as a president who appeals to "traditional values" and to the "nation's past." However, if those appeals are governed by the dehistoricizing tendencies of contract theory, as I believe they are, his appeals are not to history even when they appear to make reference to it. Rather, history returns as myth because the critical relation between myth and history has dropped out.

Returning now to the main theme, anthropologists tell us that myth is kept alive by rituals. Accordingly, we should expect our political rituals to perpetuate the myth of contractualism.

One of our firmest rituals is the inauguration of a president. In his second inaugural address President Reagan gave expression to the myth and so preserved it:

> Four years ago I spoke to you of a new beginning, and we have
> accomplished that. But in another sense, our new beginning
> is a continuation of that created two centuries ago, when, for the first
> time in history, government, the people said, was not our
> master. It is our servant; its only power that which we, the people,
> allow it to have.

The president's formulation repeats the mythic formula of contract that there is not only a political beginning but, in principle, there can be any number of new beginnings. The basic myth that ties the beginnings together is that "the people" was the dominant actor in the mythic drama: like an Old Testament god the people spoke and said, "Let government be servant and its powers limited." Note, however, that the myth is also being utilized to delegitimate as well as legitimate. The president also spoke disparagingly of recent efforts to employ governmental power to correct perceived social ills and wrongs:

> That system [presumably the original Constitution] has never failed
> us. But for a time we failed the system. We asked things of
> government that government was not equipped to give. We yielded
> authority to the national government that properly belonged
> to states or to local governments or to the people themselves.

Thus a new beginning can, like a form of ritual, absolve us of past wrongs and put us in a saving relationship to "the system," which like some patient father-god will welcome back the prodigals. By restoring the original contract we are washed clean and made innocent once more. Moreover, we are all, potentially, made equal again: blacks, Chicanos, Puerto Ricans, Jews, northern WASPS, and southern gentle-folk can each and all accept the sacrament: "Let us resolve that we, the people, will build an American opportunity society in which all of us—white and black, rich and poor, young and old—will go forward together, arm in arm."

The sacrament of innocence is absolution from the foolishness of our fathers and mothers. It soothes us with the knowledge that we were not there when blacks were treated as a species of property; when Native Americans were massacred and deprived of their ancestral lands; when suffragettes were attacked and humiliated; when the early strikes of workers were broken by the combined force of government and business corporations; when the liberal government of FDR refused to admit refugees from Hitler's Germany; or when the bomb was dropped, not once but twice. As the president remarked in the inaugural address, "We, the present-day Americans, are not given to looking backward. In this blessed land, there is always a better tomorrow."

Bitburg was the symbolic occasion when contract/amnesia was celebrated at the expense of birthright/memory, as an American president and a German chancellor confused themselves and the world about the distinction between forgiveness and forgetfulness, victims and victimizers.

Against this "sweet Oblivious Antidote," in Shakespeare's phrase, we might set the words of Richard Hooker, an English theologian of four centuries ago:

> Wherefore as any man's deed past is good as long as he himself
> continueth; so the act of a public society of men done five
> hundred years sithence standeth as theirs who presently are of the
> same societies, because corporations are immortal; we were
> then alive in our predecessors, they in their successors do live still.[2]

Clearly, by Hooker's understanding, and that of the birthright idea, we can never renounce our past without rendering the idea of a political community incoherent. The reason why we cannot has to do with the power that is aggregated by a political community. A political community exercises power in the world and against it. When we accept our birthright, we accept what has been done in our name.

Interestingly, the president also made allusion to the idea of a birthright: "We will not rest until every American enjoys the fullness of freedom, dignity and opportunity as our birthright. It is our birthright as citizens of this great republic." At the center of the president's conception of birthright was the fundamental notion of contract theory, the idea of freedom:

By 1980 we knew it was time to renew our faith, to strive
with all our strength toward the ultimate in individual freedom
consistent with an orderly society.

We believed then and now there are no limits to growth and
human progress when men and women are free to follow
their dreams. . . . The heart of our efforts is one idea vindicated by
25 straight months of economic growth: freedom and
incentives unleash the drive and entrepreneurial genius that are the
core of human progress.

Freedom is thus conceived in essentially economic and material terms: it is not Esau's birthright that is at stake for the president, but Esau's contract with Jacob for disposal of his birthright. For the president nowhere in his speech suggested that our birthright includes our right to participate, our right to be free from political surveillance, our concern to protect urban habitats and natural environments—in short, what was omitted was our birthright as political beings. Perhaps the most striking example of the reduction of our birthright to a bowl of pottage occurred in the use that the president made of Lincoln's Emancipation Proclamation for freeing the slaves: "The time has come for a new American Emancipation, a great national drive to tear down economic barriers and liberate the spirit in the most depressed areas of the country."

The president's image of "the opportunity society" symbolizes a profound transformation in collectivity identity that has been accelerated during the years since World War II. Americans have virtually ceased to think of themselves as a political people. The memory of politicalness is reserved for the moments when its associations can be pressed into the service of Cold War propaganda. For purposes of contrast with the Soviet Union the United States suddenly emerges as a "democracy." Democracy is not invoked when the discussion is about enforcing desegregation statutes; intruding religion into the schools; or preventing discrimination excepting reverse discrimination. On most occasions the present administration identifies democracy with a threat to orderly and efficient decision-making or to rational cost-benefit analysis.

The silence about politicalness and the cynicism about democracy are related. Politicalness is at odds with the conditions required by the form of polity that has come into being, but that form lacks legitimation, and so the democratic principle of "we the people" is shamelessly exploited to provide it. The new polity can be christened "the political economy." The

297

name stands for an order in which the limits of politics are set by the needs of a corporate-dominated economy and of a state organization that works in intimate collaboration with corporate leadership.

In the theory of the political economy, society is absorbed into "the economy" and instead of economic relationships being viewed as imbedded in a complex of social and political relationships, they are treated as though they constituted a distinct system that is at once autonomous (or nearly so) as well as constitutive or defining of all other types of relationships. The primacy of economic relationships does not operate solely as an explanatory device but as a first principle of a comprehensive scheme of social hermeneutics. Economic relationships constitute an interpretative category of virtually universal applicability. It is used to understand personal life and public life, to make judgments about them, and to define the nature of their problems. It supplies the categories of analysis and decision by which public policies are formulated, and it is applied to cultural domains such as education, the arts, and scientific research. It is, we might say, a conception striving for totalization.

To the political economy a genuinely democratic politics appears as destabilizing. This is because those who govern fear that democratic institutions, such as elections, free press, popular culture, and public education can become the means to mobilize the poor, the less well-educated, the working classes, and the aggrieved ethnic groups and to use them to bring demands for a revision of social priorities and a redistribution of values. This would kindle inflationary pressures and divert social resources to nonproductive uses, such as health care, low-cost housing, and toxic-waste disposal. Accordingly, the ruling elites, whose legitimating ideology is furnished by neoliberalism and neoconservatism, have to discourage the mobilization of poorer groups by asserting that a rational investment policy requires different priorities. So, for example, the Pentagon's spokesman refuses to trim the defense budget and openly asserts the priority of defense over so-called social spending.

The depoliticalization of the poor and the working classes was most clearly demonstrated in the anti-inflation strategy adopted by the state. Virtually every commentator agrees that the rate of inflation was successfully lowered at the expense of employment, which is to say, at the expense primarily, although not solely, of the working classes and minorities. The significance of this choice goes beyond the important matters of jobs and standards of living to the vital question of whether an unemployed person has not been deprived in some crucial sense of membership. For if the

298

economy is the crucial sector of a political economy, it means that employment is, so to speak, the mark of citizenship in the important sense of being involved in productive activity that is widely believed to be the most important activity in society and, ultimately, the foundation of American power and security. Economic production, we might say, is to the political economy as the laws of political citizenship were to Aristotle's polis, namely, the mark of whether one was "in" or "outside" the polity.

It is clear that in today's high-tech society there are a substantial number of persons, mostly minorities, who are superfluous: they are unemployed and have practically no foreseeable prospect of becoming employed, except perhaps temporarily, and many are trapped in a cycle of unemployment that comprehends two and sometimes three generations. In a rapidly changing economy that replaces the skills of human operatives by machines in accordance with the relentless pace of technological innovation, superfluous members are being created constantly. If by chance some are returned to the work force in a period of economic upturn, this does little to reduce their anxieties about the future. Everyone knows that business cycles return. The consequence is to produce noncitizens who will be most reluctant to take political risks of the kind required by politicalness.

Similarly, when in the name of "the economy" public spending on social programs is cut, this means more than the loss of substantial economic benefits. It reduces the power of individuals. Health care, education, aid for dependent children, job training—each of these holds out hope to an individual that he or she can increase personal power to cope with the world. When social programs are reduced, then restored somewhat, only to be reduced again, tremendous power is lodged in the hands of the state, or of those who operate it. The economy becomes a means of denying power to some and denaturalizing them, as it were, rendering them wary of political involvements.

Underlying these programs that combine pacification with demoralization and depoliticization of the lower classes is a fear of Esau. We should recall the "blessing" Isaac finally gave to the frustrated and enraged Esau, who had been doubly cheated:

> By your sword you shall live,
>   and you shall serve your brother;
> but when you break loose
>   you shall break his yoke from your neck. (Genesis 27:40)

299

The advent of the political economy does not signal the disappearance of the state, despite the frequent and well-subsidized rhetoric extolling the free market and attacking government regulation. Under the regime of political economy the state is actually strengthened. Lest we forget, the military has for over 3,000 years been a key element in political power and a crucial one in the apparatus of the modern state. The astronomical rise in defense budgets, and the revival of an interventionist foreign policy, all signify an increase in the power of the state. The same can be said of the increasing control over information being exercised by the state.

The basic reason why the present administration is concerned to mystify the presence of the state and to denigrate its value is obvious: it wants to discredit the state as an instrument of popular needs without substantially weakening it. It should never be forgotten that the state is not necessarily weakened by reducing social welfare programs but that it is often strengthened under the guise of introducing more efficient management practices.

For those who care about creating a democratic political life, a strong state must be rejected because the idea of a "democratic" state is a contradiction in terms. By its very nature the state must proceed mainly by bureaucratic means; it must concentrate power at the center; it must promote elitism or government by the few; it must elevate the esoteric knowledge of experts over the experience of ordinary citizens; and it must prefer order and stability to experiment and spontaneity. The result of state-centeredness is a politics in which at one extreme are the experts struggling to be scientific and rational while at the other is a politics of mass irrationality, of manipulated images, controlled information, single-issue fanaticism, and pervasive fear.

A democratic vision means a genuine alternative. It means the development of a politics that cannot be coopted, which is precisely what has happened to the original democratic dream of basing democracy upon voting, elections, and popular political parties. These forms, as we know from the experience of this century, can be taken over by corporate money and manipulated by the mass media. Democracy needs a noncooptable politics, that is, a politics that renders useless the forms of power developed by the modern state and business corporation. This means different actors, different scales of power, and different criteria of success.

First, democracy means participation but participation is not primarily about "taking part," as in elections or office-holding. It means originating or initiating cooperative action with others. This form of ac-

300

tion is taking place throughout the society in response to felt needs, from health care to schools, from utility rates to housing for the poor, from nuclear energy to nuclear weapons, from toxic waste disposal to homesteading in urban areas. One of the most important aspects to these developments is that political experience is being made accessible, experience that compels individuals to deal with the complexity of interests and the conflicting claims that have hitherto been reserved to politicians and bureaucrats. In this way the political has become incorporated in the everyday lives of countless people.

Second, democracy means diffusing power rather than centering it. Power can be diffused only if problems are defined in smaller terms. Not all problems can be, and it is not necessary to abolish the state. Yet the more that is taken on by smaller groupings, the less justification for central regulation and control. But power has also to be generated differently. Hitherto it has been primarily conceived in terms of federal dollars derived from taxation. While it would be very important to increase local control over fiscal resources, money is not the only form of power. Each person is potential power. He or she has skill, energy, intelligence, and a capacity for shared effort. This is not to foolishly deny the importance of material resources; it is to suggest that democracy can evoke forms of power not available to bureaucratic and centralized organizations.

A democratic political life would, I believe, set terms that would make it difficult for the corporate bureaucratic system to coopt its activities. It would generate a politics that could not be handled by the categories that are essential to state-centered, bureaucratic, and mass-electorate politics. It would nurture a political life that would be decentered rather than centralized, pluralistic rather than hierarchical, participatory rather than managerial, egalitarian rather than efficient.

It offers, I believe, the best hope for deconstructing the political economy and reconstituting our birthright.

Notes

1. See Sheldon Wolin, "Postmodern Politics and the Absence of Myth," *Social Research* 52, no. 2 (Summer 1985), pp. 217–39.

2. *Of the Laws of Ecclesiastical Polity*, Bk. I. x. 8.

CONCLUSION

Harry C. Boyte

POPULISM
AND FREE SPACES

Populism is not a text or a body of dogma. It has no written codes, no finished works, no canons of orthodoxy. Populism suggests a different way of thinking about politics and power than the normal terms of "left" and "right." It is a participatory discussion that, if it is a democratic populism, reflects the complexities and differences inherent in "the people."

Tensions come alive in a book like this one. There are many voices and disagreements among the authors, and vantage points that differ immensely as well. But in a broad way, the book has what might be called a populist style, evolving, dynamic, and open, rooted in themes of inheritance and human community.

For all its diversity, populism thus points toward a different approach to political conflict and change than conventional politics does. It moves beyond the framework of static choices within which most debate occurs —government versus the capitalist marketplace; tradition versus freedom;

305

community versus the liberated individual; attentiveness to the concerns of those excluded from conventional definitions of "the people" versus an appreciation for historical and communal ties. A democratic populism changes the context. It looks at society from the bottom up. As Mary Dietz points out, populism has conservative overtones, valuing the continuities across generations and time. But populism also entails participatory perspectives that are radical in their implications. To develop more fully the possibilities within populism, these ideas of participation need to be expanded and elaborated by the concept of free space that emerges from a recent generation of social histories.

Adrienne Asch asks, "Will populism empower the disabled?" The question is raised in other terms by Cornel West about black Americans and Elizabeth Minnich about women. It is a worrisome issue for many others who have felt historically excluded or marginalized by conventional definitions of "the people" in American history, from Indians, Chinese, Mexicans, to contemporary gay or lesbian communities. There is nothing certain about empowerment of communities that have not fit the norm. It takes constant struggle and challenge to transform and widen notions of peoplehood and community in inclusive, democratic ways. What populism does, however, is change the places and language in which such challenge and struggle occurs. Populist language and places reflect in turn the democratic history of just those who have been excluded.

How are democratic changes in cultural life possible? Where do ordinary people, steeped in lifelong experiences of humiliation, develop the skills, confidence, and spirit needed to move from being victims of oppression to acting in their own behalf? How do people develop the capacity to challenge the ways things are and imagine a different world? To the extent the conventional left has addressed such issues—and they have normally not been well addressed by most approaches to social change— it has held that people revolt out of a deep sense of alienation, rage, and estrangement. The left calls for an alliance of all those who see themselves as dispossessed and victimized. It champions those "who are naught," as the famous song puts it, who have lost "all but their chains." But the fact is that those broad, democratic movements that have challenged and changed American society are not movements of victims or people who see themselves mainly as estranged. Such movements have grown from a populist rereading of American history, that simultaneously draws upon and transforms core themes and ideas in the culture.

Cornel West argues that populism rests upon "the two major ideological pillars of this country's self-definition," conservative cultural values like racism, sexism, and nativism, on the one hand, and Lockean, individualistic liberalism, on the other. But the black freedom struggle itself has demonstrated again and again in American history how much more complex, rich, and multidimensional is the country's cultural heritage than this argument would suggest. Following the War of 1812, black slaves off the South Carolina coast planned a rebellion to take advantage of the political uncertainty and composed a song to express their vision:

> Let Independence be your aim,
> Ever mindful what 'tis woth.
> Pedge your bodies for the prize,
> Pile them even to the skies!
> Firm, united let us be,
> Resolved on death or liberty
> As a band of Patriots joined
> Peace and Plenty we shall find.

The song's radicalism and militancy are unmistakable. The slaves planned another revolution, if necessary, to win their freedom. But the ideological themes that fuse together here are the main currents of early nineteenth-century American political philosophy, especially the republican and natural rights beliefs of the American Revolution itself, reworked by the slave community in ways that would have appalled the white male founders of the nation. Similarly, Christian religion was originally taught to slaves in an effort to "root out all living connection with the [African] homeland," as Vincent Harding has put it. But, as Harding observed, black slaves found within that very religion a transformative source of self-affirmation. "The religion of white America was insistently, continually wrested from the white mediators by black hands and minds and transformed into an instrument of struggle." Centuries later, Martin Luther King, Jr., stirred millions of blacks and whites alike by portraying the civil rights movement as representative of the "best of the American Dream and the most sacred values in the Judeo-Christian heritage," bringing the entire nation "back to the great wells of democracy" of its origins.[1]

Elizabeth Minnich suggests that populist appeals may reflect "a yearning for some old, sorely missed experience of union, of cause, of community," and holds that "the old values of community and church or synagogue, like the old values of political movements and causes, . . . *also left out women*." Dominant interpretations, formal descriptions, conventional languages of community, religious group, public life—all these did, indeed, often marginalize women's central roles and presence in sustaining just these relationships. But feminist movements throughout American history again and again emerged precisely out of religious and communal spaces—where women simultaneously drew upon and honored the traditions of domesticity, faith, and heritage they had largely kept alive and also found there and developed subversive, hidden dimensions of such traditions. Thus, Sara Grimké replied to a group of ministers in the 1830s who questioned her right as a woman to speak publicly by saying, "How monstrous, how anti-Christian is the doctrine that woman is to be dependent upon man! Where in all the sacred Scriptures is this taught? This doctrine of dependence upon man is utterly at variance with the doctrine of the Bible."

When the new feminism emerged in the 1960s and 1970s, it was not a movement of alienated and atomized individuals but of communities. Feminism represented the repoliticization of women's relationships that had been seen as simply "social," from the networks of the new left to lesbian bars, from church women's clubs to the Girl Scouts and Catholic orders of nuns, that generated the assertion that "sisterhood is powerful." Minnich's question—"Can there be populism *without* feminism?"—is critically important in the world of the 1980s and beyond. But, I would argue, its reverse is equally important to consider: can there be a feminism with any prospect for democratically, fundamentally changing American society that does not have, as well, a deeply populist character?[2]

Despite the relative lack of attention to the ways in which democratic transformation of communal and traditional values occurs, there is little mysterious or unknowable about the features that generate and sustain democratic movements. A new generation of social history especially suggests crucial insights that need to be incorporated by a new progressive populism. Such history draws attention in particular to the vital role of voluntary associations with a relatively open, participatory cast, what Sara Evans and I have called "free spaces." Such free spaces, complex and imperfect as they necessarily are in the real world, nonetheless have specific features that make them unique sources of democratic energy, experiment, and vision.

Voluntary groups, ranging from churches and synagogues to reform organizations, service and self-help groups, union locals, consumer cooperatives to PTAs, form a vast middle ground between private identities and large-scale institutions. They are places that ordinary people can often "own" in important ways, spaces grounded in the fabric of daily life with a public dimension that allows mingling with others beyond one's immediate family and friends. They are institutions that people can shape and reshape, use as alternative sources of information about the world, employ as media for connecting with others in ways more substantive than transitory encounters. When such voluntary associations are free spaces, relatively open, flexible, and controlled by a group themselves, they can furnish critical experiences in democratic sociability and become the foundation for broad, social movements.

Thus, under slavery, the very possibility of thinking and speaking in ways that opposed the dominant culture depended upon the creation of community institutions that slaves "owned" themselves, about which slaveowning whites had little knowledge. The black church especially played this crucial role as a free space. From the beginning, slaves recast what they learned from whites, drawing on the African past and discovering subversive themes within Christian teachings and scripture. Within their places of worship—often on the margins of plantations, in secret, well-hidden areas called "hush harbors," sometimes in independent black churches in cities—slaves could dream of freedom and even plot insurrections. For the black community the preacher was the mediating figure with the white world. He fought for control over spaces, finances, and the life of the service. He hid its subversive dimensions from view, nurturing hope and spirit among his congregation while he bided his time and looked for signs.

The civil rights movement grew directly from this ancient tradition of independent black churches. Many factors came together after World War II to produce the historic stage—the experience of the war itself, fought in part against brutal racism; the Supreme Court decision outlawing segregated schools; economic changes that led to growing black populations in the cities; the example of African independence movements and other developments. But the movement across the region drew its language and themes from black religion. Even where ministers proved hesitant, the churches became drawn into the struggle through the activities of church members. In Birmingham the Reverend Fred Shuttlesworth summed up the entire heritage when he replied to a local sheriff's attempt to prohibit ministers' encouraging congregations to participate in a boy-cott: "Only God can tell me what to say in the pulpit." Out of such religious traditions, in turn, came the conviction of the democratic possi-bilities of nonviolence, and the Dream of an America where all races and peoples would be "bound together by a single garment of destiny."[3]

Similarly, the history of feminist movements in America highlights the importance of public arenas in the fabric of community life. For women to claim democratic rights and principles of equality, they required environments in which they could develop public identities and skills, simultaneously drawing upon and changing traditions that defined women in terms of family and personal worlds. In the nineteenth century, home missionary societies, moral reform clubs, movements like the Women's Christian Temperance Union, women's schools and prayer groups fur-nished the free spaces in which women gained a sense of their own strength and independence. As WCTU leader Frances Willard noted about the temperance crusade, for instance:

> Perhaps the most significant outcome of this movement was the
> knowledge of their own power gained by the conservative
> women of the Churches. They had never even seen a "women's rights
> convention," and had been held aloof from the "suffragists"
> by fears as to their orthodoxy; but now there were women prominent
> in all Church cares and duties eager to clasp hands for a
> more aggressive work than such women had ever before dreamed of
> undertaking.

In the student and civil rights movements of the 1960s, women found specifically female social spaces within the contexts of struggle and politi-cal action that gave them a new sense of their own abilities, skills, and a language of "participatory democracy."[4]

Finally, the farmers' cooperatives of the first Populist movement were created to escape crushing debt loads and domination by banks and mer-chants. Drawing on older traditions of rural churches and the Grange, they also proved for a time a remarkable independent cultural space as well. Through alliance with blacks, organized in parallel cooperatives, and the relatively open, participatory structure of the cooperatives, farmers began to rethink the history that had tied together whites (men) regardless of class. And they even raised tentative questions about the bedrock racist

310

assumptions of southern culture. The first Populists were certainly not without prejudices. But they advocated measures like education for blacks and voting rights that made the movement seem like a revolutionary threat to the white supremacist racial order. In North Carolina in 1898 the white business leadership called for "redemption of North Carolina" from the black and white, Republican-Populist fusion ticket that had controlled the state legislature and had begun to pass far-ranging reforms. One leader gloried in "The vibrations of our coming redemption from all wicked rule and the supremacy of that race destined not only to rule this country but to carry the Gospel to all nations." Tensions and violence flared across the state. And the forces of "progress" and white supremacy shattered the coalition. "Not before in years have the bank men, the mill men and the businessmen in generation—the backbone of the property interests of the State—taken such sincere interest in affairs," boasted the Charlotte *Observer*.[5]

In sum, free spaces, voluntary groups grounded in the fabric of community life, are the places where democracy has acquired deepened meanings again and again in American history. The problem is that conventional approaches to change marginalize their role.

Progressive strategies that stress, most centrally, the role and importance of the federal government, as several authors in this collection do, understate the core principle that government is never seen as the "solution" to problems by broad, active democratic movements. Out of people's experience in free spaces comes the confidence and perception that *the people*, themselves, are the active force of change—and government once again becomes the public's servant. Thus, for instance, the nineteenth-century Knights of Labor, a populist-style movement of laboring men and women protesting the rise of giant trusts and cartels, "looked to self-organized society—not to the individual and not to the state—as the redeemer of their American dream," as historian Leon Fink has observed. "Neither ultimate antagonist nor source of salvation, the state represented a mediator in the conflict between the civil forces of democracy and its enemies."[6]

More recent theories of social change found in many parts of the peace movement, among radical ecologists, cultural feminists, and others have sought to reconnect political and social action with deeper wellsprings of human motivation. Out of all these diverse forms of activism comes the stance known as Green politics in Europe, with identifiable counterparts in the United States, as Charlene Spretnak points out. Seen

311

as alternative models of community or prophetic perspectives on critical social problems like the degradation of nature and the arms race, Green politics, like prophetic movements in the past, can help catalyze and encourage cultural and social options and possibilities far beyond their own immediate participants. But taken as *the* model for movement building and politics, Green politics has severe limitations. If the left, most characteristically, seeks to render every human relation political in ways that resemble large-scale, impersonal institutions, the approach that emerges characteristically from the Greens is the personalization of politics, the effort to translate one's heartfelt opinions directly into organizational forms, political expressions, and policies. The result is an array of experimental groups, ranging from moral witnesses to spiritualism with an Eastern influence, alternative communities, simplified lifestyles, groups run by consensus decision making, and the like.

But Green political action displays a striking preference for the new, the alternative, and the morally unambiguous. Throughout the recent literature in this vein one finds virtually no mention of mainstream voluntary networks as critical arenas of democratic change and action. Yet such settings, from churches and synagogues to PTAs, the neighborhood group or the Camp Fire Girls, are in fact the places in which most Americans—of diverse races, ethnic groups, and backgrounds—are invested, through which most people struggle to build communities or by means of which most people gain what voice they have in the larger society. In its focus on the "New Age," new values, institutions, and relations, Green politics ironically shares much of conventional liberal-left ideas about social progress.[7]

Populism still has no developed theory of free spaces. But, as Robert Bellah points out, it is closely associated with voluntary life and traditions in America. Indeed, in many ways it repoliticizes those communal forms of association and participation, from self-help groups or the local block club to churches, synagogues, and the Boy Scouts and Girl Scouts, whose civic dimensions have been obscured, often savagely, by modern languages of politics based on contractual models of human relationship. In the context of the origins and dynamics of a broad social movement, such free spaces can become activated in new ways. Free spaces are places between private life, on the one hand, and larger institutions, on the other, that people own themselves, through which they can act with dignity, power, and vision on an ongoing basis. In such places people are able to draw upon personal experiences, values, and sentiments in a context that also teaches them broader public skills and ways of democratic discourse —a view of the broader community beyond their immediate circle of relations.

To say populism is socially conservative, a common depiction, is much too simple and one-dimensional precisely because of the dynamic and democratic public life that takes hold in such voluntary civic organizations, or free spaces. Today, a focus on such voluntary civic commitments suggests not only resources for struggle against centers of unresponsive power and wealth. It also suggests new ways of thinking about the broader efforts to democratize modern society. Such places are invariably complex and ambiguous—there are no perfectly democratic environments in the real world. But nonetheless, American voluntary institutions and networks still offer innumerable and untapped opportunities for people to develop more self-confidence and sense of their power and dignity, find out new facts about the world, come to know other groups—including those that may be seen as "outsiders" or "culturally deviant," like gays, develop a hope that raw competition between different groups may not be the only way forward, and so forth. In free spaces, populist themes can be integrated with those of other groups and movements in a substantive way.

An understanding of the role of free spaces in a democratic populism suggests strategy different from the statism of the liberal left, on the one hand, or the personalism of the Greens, on the other. Moral witnesses, alternative institution building, and prophetic criticisms are important elements in the process of social change. So, too, are election campaigns, large coalitions, massive public actions, effective work in the public media and in the court system, and so forth. But the heart of democratic movement involves ongoing education and action through those locally based voluntary networks with which most citizens identify and through which they seek to make a difference.

A focus on free spaces, moreover, not only highlights different *means* of social change but also indicates different *ends* as well. A vocabulary of democratic action that draws from free spaces in America is, necessarily,

313

far richer in cultural and historical resonances than conventional progressive politics, which often sounds today like a planner's manual. It is a language of inheritance and birthright that celebrates the marvelous cultural particularities of America. Populism also finds the overarching themes and symbols to express our common aspirations for freedom. Finally, the meaning of that freedom is different than our inherited notions of "progress" lead us to imagine. No longer can the socialist ideal of men and women joined in new communities amputated from their histories be seen as the appropriate vision for the future. A democratic and egalitarian society will rest, necessarily, upon a rich pluralism of free, nongovernmental associations. Through such free spaces we can take initiatives on our own terms. And we can reflect, together, what it means to be "a people," and many different peoples, dedicated to liberty and justice for all.

Notes

1. The origins and base of the new populism are described in some length in Harry C. Boyte, Heather Booth, and Steve Max, *Citizen Action and the New American Populism* (Philadelphia: Temple University Press, 1986); song in Vincent Harding, *There Is a River: The Black Struggle for Freedom in America* (New York: Harcourt, 1981), pp. 62, 71; Martin Luther King, Jr., *Why We Can't Wait* (New York: Harper & Row, 1963), p. 99.

2. Grimké, in Alice Rossi, ed., *The Feminist Papers: From Adams to de Beauvoir* (New York: Columbia University Press, 1973), p. 308.

3. The concept of free space is described at length in Sara M. Evans and Harry C. Boyte, *Free Spaces: The Sources of Democratic Change in America* (New York: Harper & Row, 1986), and more briefly, along these lines, in Harry C. Boyte and Sara M. Evans, "The Sources of Democratic Change," *Tikkun*, May 1986; on the black church as free space, see Evans and Boyte, *Free Spaces*, chap. 2; Shuttlesworth, quoted from Aldon Morris, *Origins of the Civil Rights Movement* (New York: Free Press, 1984), pp. 79–80.

4. Frances Willard, quoted from Barbara Leslie Epstein, *The Politics of Domesticity: Women, Evangelism and Temperance in Nineteenth Century America* (Middletown, Conn.: Wesleyan University Press, 1981), p. 100.

5. See Evans and Boyte, *Free Spaces*, chap. 5; Methodist electoral leader, quoted from Frederick A. Bode, *Protestantism and the New South: North Carolina Baptists and Methodists in Political Crisis, 1894–1903* (Charlottesville, Va.: University of Virginia, 1975), p. 131; Charlotte *Observer*, p. 138, as quoted in Evans and Boyte, *Free Spaces*, p. 180.

6. Leon Fink, *Workingmen's Democracy: The Knights of Labor and American Politics* (Urbana: University of Illinois Press, 1983), p. 34.

7. For a sampling of Green literature see, for instance, Fran Peavey, *Heart Politics* (Philadelphia: New Society Publishers, 1986); Kirkpatrick Sale, *Dwellers in the Land: The Bioregional Vision* (San Francisco: Sierra Club Books, 1985); Arthur Stein, *Seeds of the Seventies: Values, Work and Commitment in Post-Vietnam America* (Hanover, N.H.: University Press of New England, 1985); Fritjof Capra and Charlene Spretnak, *Green Politics: The Global Promise* (New York: Dutton, 1984); Joan Bodner, ed., *Taking Charge of Our Lives: Living Responsibly in the World* (San Francisco: Harper & Row, 1984).

BIBLIOGRAPHY

BIBLIOGRAPHY

Key Historical Works

Mari Jo Buhle, *Women and American Socialism: 1870–1920* (Urbana: University of Illinois Press, 1981), an exploration of women's involvements in populist and socialist movements.

Lawrence Goodwyn, *Democratic Promise: The Populist Movement in America* (New York: Oxford University Press, 1976); and (in paperback) *The Populist Moment: A Short History of the Agrarian Revolt in America* (Oxford, 1978). Goodwyn's two books are the major, standard works.

Steven Hahn, *The Roots of Southern Populism* (New Haven: Yale University Press, 1982), a fine work on the movement in Georgia.

Julie Roy Jeffrey, "Women in the Southern Farmers Alliance: A Reconsideration of the Role and Status of Women in the Late 19th Century South," *Feminist Studies* 3 (Fall 1975), the classic discussion of the ways in which the first Populist movement opened a remarkable new public space for women.

Bruce Palmer, *Man Over Money: The Southern Populist Critique of American Capitalism* (Chapel Hill: University of North Carolina Press, 1980), a description of populist ideas.

C. Vann Woodward, *Tom Watson: Agrarian Rebel* (New York: Oxford University Press, 1963), a remarkable biography of the key southern Populist leader.

Manifestos and Statements of the New Populism

Gar Alperovitz and Jeff Faux, *Rebuilding America* (New York: Pantheon, 1984), an excellent recent argument about populist economics that challenges reigning wisdom, liberal and conservative.

Bishops' Pastoral, letter on "Catholic Social Teaching and the U.S. Economy," especially eloquent on themes of the dignity of work and the importance of viewing economic activity as embedded in human community (Washington, D.C.: National Conference of Catholic Bishops, 1985).

Harry C. Boyte, Heather Booth, and Steve Max, *Citizen Action and the New American Populism* (Philadelphia: Temple University Press, 1986), a detailed account of populist organizing campaigns today around issues like energy, farms, and toxic waste, coupled with a broader statement of democratic populist vision and its differences with demagogic "populism" from the right wing.

Robert Collier, "Democratizing the Private Sector: Populism, Capitalism and Capital Strike," *Socialist Review*, March 1985, an articulate argument for a populist economics that focuses on the rampant speculation and greed seizing the economy.

319

Mark Green and Robert Massie, Jr., eds., *Big Business Reader: Essays on Corporate America* (New York: Pilgrim, 1980), the book associated with Big Business Day.

Jeff Greenfield and Jack Newfield, *A Populist Manifesto: The Making of a New Majority* (New York: Warner, 1972).

Fred Harris, *Now Is the Time: A New Populist Call to Action* (New York: McGraw-Hill, 1971). Both Harris and the Greenfield/Newfield books are now classic statements, reflecting the early reemergence of a new populism.

Tom Hayden, "Which Way, Democrats?" *Economic Democrat*, Jan./Feb. 1985, a statement by the leader of Campaign for Economic Democracy (C.E.D.) and one of the leaders in Citizen Action.

Jim Hightower, *Eat Your Heart Out: How Food Profiteers Victimize the Consumer* (New York: Random House, 1976), and *Hard Tomatoes, Hard Times: The Hightower Report* (Cambridge, Mass.: Schenkman Books, 1978 ed.), eloquent and impassioned statements on family farming and populism by the key architect of much rural populist political strategy.

———, "I Didn't Lose, I Just Ran Out of Time," *Washington Monthly*, Oct. 1980.

Flora Lewis, "The New Populism," New York *Times*, July 22, 1985.

Ralph Nader and Mark Green, eds., *Corporate Power in America* (New York: Penguin, 1977).

Progressive, June 1984, special issue on "The New Populism," with articles by Lane Evans, Heather Booth, Derek Shearer, Harry Boyte, Larry Goodwyn, and others.

William Schneider, "What the Democrats Must Do," *New Republic*, March 11, 1985.

Derek Shearer and Martin Carnoy, *Economic Democracy* (White Plains, N.Y.: Sharpe, 1980), the book which revived the concept of "economic democracy" from 1930s populist movements and elaborated the notion with many examples.

Social Policy, Summer 1985, special issue on "The New Populism," with pieces by S. M. Miller, Frank Riessman.

Right-Wing Populist Statements and Manifestos

William Carb, ed., *Profiles in Populism* (1982), a far-right document, combining overt racism with attacks on capitalism, that formed the basis for the "Populist Party" in 1984, whose candidate was Bob Richards.

John McClaughry, "Populism for the '80s Gaining Momentum," *Human Events*, April 16, 1983.

William Schambra, "The Quest for Community, and the Quest for a New Public Philosophy," American Enterprise Institute Public Policy paper, Dec. 5, 1983, an influential and important argument about little-understood sources of Reagan's rhetorical appeal through his use of populist themes of empowerment, community, and the like.

Richard Viguerie, *The People Versus the Establishment* (Lake Bluff, Ill.: Regnery-Gateway, 1984).

———, "Populism, Yes," *National Review*, Oct. 19, 1984.

New Populism, Descriptive and Journalistic Treatments

Heather Ball and Leland Beatty, "Where Have All The Farmers Gone?" *Texas Humanist*, May–June 1985, on the rural revolt and possible ties to urban populism.

Harry C. Boyte, *Community Is Possible: Repairing America's Roots* (New York: Harper & Row, 1984), descriptions of local organizing.

Ronald Brownstein, "A New Popular Populism," *Esquire*, July 1984.

Alan Crawford, "Right Wing Populism," *Social Policy*, May–June 1980.

Robert Fisher, *Let the People Decide: A History of Neighborhood Organizing in America* (Boston: Hall, 1984), a very fine, historically grounded discussion of the community organizing tradition and the emergence of an urban populism in the 1970s and 1980s.

Rob Gurwitt, "The Revival of Populism," *Congressional Quarterly*, April 21, 1984, a look at populism's growing electoral appeal.

John Herbers, "Grass Roots Groups Go National," *New York Times Magazine*, Sept. 4, 1983.

Robert Kuttner, "Ass Backward," *New Republic*, April 22, 1985, an important piece on the ways Democratic Party fundraising patterns (deemphasizing small donors for fat-cat appeals) has weakened the party's connection to its traditional populist base.

Richard Margolis, "The Two Faces of Populism," *New Leader*, April 18, 1983.

David Moberg, "Evans Runs Again on Populist Agenda," *In These Times*, Oct. 17, 1984.

_____, "Not All the News Was Bad News," *In These Times*, Nov. 14, 1984, on populism in the election.

David Osborne, "Joe Kennedy Makes a Name for Himself," *Mother Jones*, April 1985, an argument that Kennedy is the first "neoliberal populist."

Brad Pigott, "Populist Revival in Mississippi?" *Southern Changes*, Jan.–Feb. 1984, on prospects for populist coalition between blacks and poor and working whites.

Richard Reeves, "The Ideological Election," *New York Times Magazine*, Feb. 19, 1984.

James Ridgeway, "Jim Hightower and the Populist Revolt in Texas," *Village Voice*, May 8, 1984.

Frank Riessman's Newsletter, July 1985, an overview.

William Schneider, "The Perils of Populism: A Political Fashion Is Revived," *New Republic*, July 15, 1985.

Joan Walsh, "The First Hurrah," *In These Times*, Feb. 27, 1985, on the Flynn administration.

Theoretical Treatments of Modern Populism

Robert Bellah et al., *Habits of the Heart* (Berkeley: University of California, 1985), an influential study of the erosion of themes of community, citizenship, and commitment from most political language—and the power of "populism."

321

Carl Boggs, "The New Populism and the Limits of Structural Reforms," *Theory and Society*, Summer 1983, a "Gramscian" critique of the new populism, organizations like Citizen Action, and the like.

Harry C. Boyte, *The Backyard Revolution: Understanding the New Citizen Movement* (Philadelphia: Temple University Press, 1980), an extended argument that distinguishes the new populism from conventional liberal and left politics.

———, "Populism and the Left," *democracy*, April 1981, a comparison of Marxist and populist languages and understandings of social change.

Craig Calhoun, "The Radicalism of Tradition," *American Journal of Sociology*, March 1983, an important essay on sources of change that challenges many aspects of conventional approaches (both left wing and mainstream).

———, *The Question of Class Struggle* (Chicago: University of Chicago Press, 1982), a populist argument about the sources of working-class radicalism in late eighteenth-century and early nineteenth-century England.

Sara Evans and Harry C. Boyte, *Free Spaces: The Sources of Democratic Change in America* (New York: Harper & Row, 1986), an analysis of the sources and sustaining bases of democratic social movements, including populism.

James Green, "Populism, Socialism and the Promise of Democracy," *Radical History Review*, Fall 1980.

———, "Culture, Politics and Workers' Response to Industrialization in the U.S.," *Radical America*, Jan.–April 1982, a long, thoughtful Marxist criticism of the populist challenge to conventional left theory, which concedes many points.

Mark Kann, *The American Left* (New York: Praeger, 1982), an examination of strategic approaches of American radicals at different periods that argues that a populist connectedness with core cultural themes has proven a precondition for successes.

———, "The Costs of Winning City Hall: New Populists and Municipal Power," *Urban Resources*, Fall 1984.

———, *Middle Class Radicalism in Santa Monica* (Philadelphia: Temple University Press, 1986), a look at new populism with middle class overtones.

———, "The New Populism and the New Marxism," *Theory and Society*, Summer 1983, a reply to Boggs.

Vladimir Khoros, *Populism: Its Past, Present and Future* (Chicago: Imported Publications; Moscow: Progress Pbns., 1984), a remarkably sympathetic treatment from a Soviet social scientist, distinguishing populism in the Third World from advanced industrial society variants and showing its differences with Marxism.

Ernesto Laclau, *Politics and Ideology in Marxist Theory: Capitalism, Fascism, Populism* (London: Verso, 1977).

Fred Matthews, " 'Hobbesian Populism': Interpretive Paradigms and Moral Vision in American Historiography," *Journal of American History*, June 1985, an interesting argument that populism has become the dominant—if implicit—theme in mainstream history.

Social Policy, special issues: Sept. 1979, "Organizing Neighborhoods," and Winter 1982, "Cities and the Politics of Local Control," an examination, descriptively and theoretically, of community organizing and local populist politics in recent years.

Simone Weil, *The Need for Roots* (Boston: Beacon Press, 1955), the first major modern theoretical statement of a populist vision in the aftermath of the triumph of Stalinism in the Soviet Union.

Sheldon Wolin, "The People's Two Bodies," *democracy*, Dec. 1980, an examination of the two contrasting visions of American destiny (one democratic, the other militarist and imperial) that have always coexisted in American culture.